Focus on the Language Classroom

An introduction to classroom
research for language teachers

ANGUAGE TEACHING
and Peter Strevens

s for language teachers and others who:
ed about the key issues facing the language teaching
ay;
derstand the theoretical issues underlying current debates;
elate theory to classroom practice.

his series:

Focus on the Language Classroom:
An Introduction to Classroom Research for Language Teachers

Dick Allwright
Lancaster University

Kathleen M. Bailey
Monterey Institute of International Studies

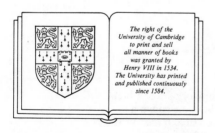

The right of the
University of Cambridge
to print and sell
all manner of books
was granted by
Henry VIII in 1534.
The University has printed
and published continuously
since 1584.

Cambridge University Press
Cambridge
New York   Port Chester

Published by the Press Syndicate of the University of Cambridge
The Pitt Building, Trumpington Street, Cambridge CB2 1RP
40 West 20th Street, New York, NY 10011, USA
10 Stamford Road, Oakleigh, Melbourne 3166, Australia

© Cambridge University Press 1991

First published 1991

Printed in Great Britain
by Bell & Bain Ltd, Glasgow

Library of Congress Cataloguing-in-Publication Data

Allwright, Dick
    Focus on the language classroom: an introduction to classroom research for
    language teachers / Dick Allwright, Kathleen M. Bailey.
    p.   cm. – (New directions in language teaching)
    Include bibliographical references.
    ISBN 0 521 26279 8
    ISBN 0 521 26909 1 (pbk.)
    1. Language and language – Study and teaching.
    2. Classroom environment.
    I. Bailey, Kathleen M. II. Title. III. Series.
    P53.A475   1991
    418'.007—dc20   91-4395 CIP

British Library Cataloguing in Publication Data

Allwright, Dick
    Focus on the language classroom: an introduction to classroom research
    for language teachers.
    1. Schools. Curriculum Subjects. Language Skills. Teaching
    I. Title
    407.1

ISBN 0 521 26279 8 hard covers
ISBN 0 521 26909 1 paperback

CE

To Peter Strevens

Contents

Contents

Contents

Acknowledgements

Many people have helped with the development of this book during the years that it has been in preparation. We are especially grateful to Peter Donovan of Cambridge University Press for his valuable feedback and incredible patience; to Leo van Lier for his wide-ranging bibliographic suggestions and his insightful criticisms on the manuscript; to our series editors, Howard Altman, and the very greatly missed Peter Strevens, and a knowledgeable anonymous reader, who all reacted in helpful detail to an early version of the volume; to Steve Gaies for his thoughts about the structure of the manuscript and his work on the early chapters; to David Tsugawa for his careful artwork, given our sketchy first thoughts about figures; to Mary Davis for her infallible good humour and efficiency in the face of endless photocopying requests, express mail orders, and the transmission of lengthy transatlantic fax messages.

We are also mindful of the great contributions made over the years by our students, our colleagues, and the teachers who have come to our workshops and allowed us to visit their classes. In particular, we are grateful to those teachers and students whose lives we have observed and recorded, and in some cases used as data in this book. The work of Mike Long and Craig Chaudron has been especially influential in our thinking about its contents, even though we have not always seen eye-to-eye with them in terms of methodology or practical emphases.

Kathi Bailey's participation in this venture was supported in part by the Allen Griffin Award from the Community Foundation for Monterey County. Since Monterey is known as a multi-cultural community, the members of the Foundation were glad to support the development of an introductory book about classroom research, for language teachers working in a variety of settings.

As the project neared completion, it was used in manuscript form with students of classroom research at San Francisco State University and the Monterey Institute of International Studies. We appreciate their feedback, and the careful proof-reading of Susie Scott and Tracey Derwing.

On the home front, in California, Ted Dale word-processed, read drafts, and deleted every fifth line of our prose. In the process of the book's evolution, Mark went off to first grade, where he learned to read and to understand what books are. We are both humbled and encouraged by Mark's comment upon seeing that the final manuscript had no colourful illustrations: 'Well, it is sort of a boring book, but maybe teachers will like it.'

Dick Allwright
Lancaster University

Kathi Bailey
Monterey Institute of International Studies

The authors and publishers would like to thank the following for permission to reproduce copyright material:

Foreign Language Annals and G. Moskowitz for *The effects of training foreign language teachers in interaction analysis*, 1968: 1 (3) pp. 219–22, reprinted as Appendix A on pp. 202–3, and for *Interaction analysis: a new modern language for supervisors*, 1971: 5 p. 213, reprinted as Appendix B on pp. 204–5; Excerpt from *Classroom Oriented Research in Second Language Acquisition* by H. W. Seliger and M. H. Long. Copyright © 1983 by Newbury House Publishers, Inc. Reprinted by permission of HarperCollins Publishers, as Transcript 6 on pp. 109–10; *Language Learning* and C. Chaudron for *A descriptive model of discourse in the corrective treatment of learners' errors*, 1977: 27 pp. 37–9, reprinted as Appendix G on pp. 220–1; Longman Group UK Limited and L. van Lier for *Examples of qualitative and quantitative procedures in data collection and analysis*, 1988 p. 57, reprinted as Figure 2 on p. 43; Newbury House Publishers, Inc. and R. L. Allwright for *Turns, topics and tasks: patterns of participation in language learning and teaching*, 1980 pp. 180–1 of D. E. Larsen Freeman (ed.) *Discourse analysis in second language research*, reprinted as Transcript 7 on pp. 125–6; Newbury House Publishers, Inc. and K. M. Bailey for *A model of competitiveness and anxiety and the second language learner*, 1983 p. 97 of H. W. Seliger and M. H. Long (eds.) *Classroom oriented research in second language acquisition*, reprinted as Figure 9 on p. 177; Newbury House Publishers, Inc. and N. J. Nystrom for *Teacher–student interaction in bilingual classrooms: four approaches to error feedback*, 1983 pp. 171–2 of H. W. Seliger and M. H. Long (eds.) *Classroom oriented research in second language acquisition*, reprinted as Transcript 3 on p. 85; Oxford University Press for extracts from *Towards an analysis of Discourse*, 1975 pp. 25–7, by J. M. Sinclair and M. Coulthard, reprinted by permission as Appendix F on pp. 214–15; TESOL and J. F. Fanselow for Appendix C taken from 'Beyond Rashomon – conceptualizing and describing the teaching act' by J. F. Fanselow (1977), *TESOL Quarterly* vol. 11 pp. 35–9. Copyright 1977 by TESOL. Reprinted by permission on pp. 206–12; TESOL and M. Fröhlich, N. Spada and P. Allen for

Appendix F taken from 'Differences in the communicative orientation of L2 classrooms' by M. Fröhlich, N. Spada and P. Allen (1985), *TESOL Quarterly* vol. 19 pp. 53–6. Copyright 1985 by TESOL. Reprinted by permission on pp. 216–19; TESOL and M. H. Long for Figure 4 taken from 'Teacher feedback on learner error: mapping conditions' by M. H. Long (1977), *On TESOL '77* p. 289. Copyright 1977 by TESOL. Reprinted by permission on p. 101 and for Figure 6 taken from 'Native speaker/non-native speaker conversation in the second language classroom' by M. H. Long (1982), *On TESOL '82* p. 214. Copyright 1983 by TESOL. Reprinted by permission on p. 122; TESOL and M. H. Long, L. Adams, M. McLean and F. Castaños for Appendix D taken from 'Doing things with words – a verbal interaction in lockstep and small classroom situations' by M. H. Long, L. Adams, M. McLean and F. Castaños (1976), *On TESOL '76* pp. 144–5. Copyright 1976 by TESOL. Reprinted by permission on p. 213; TESOL and P. Allen, M. Fröhlich and N. Spada for Appendix F taken from 'Communicative orientation of language teaching: An observation scheme' by P. Allen, M. Fröhlich and N. Spada (1984), *On TESOL '83*. Copyright 1984 by TESOL. Reprinted by permission on pp. 216–19.

While every effort has been made it has not been possible to identify the sources of all the material used and in such cases the publishers would welcome information from copyright holders.

Preface

Classroom research investigates the processes of teaching and learning as they occur in language classrooms. Its findings are important to classroom teachers, researchers, and theorists. Methodologically speaking, classroom research is very diverse – ranging from relatively simple observations to tightly controlled experiments. The field has grown greatly in the past ten years across the whole spectrum of education, across levels and across disciplines, with new findings leading to new research methods, and vice versa. Classroom research is a dynamic area of investigation and one bearing fruitful results of major relevance to many facets of teaching, syllabus design, materials development, testing, and teacher education. For all these reasons, we feel there is a need for a basic text introducing language professionals to classroom research.

This book was therefore written specifically for language teachers, to document many of the recent developments in language classroom research, and to summarise them in non-technical terms. It is not a book written for experienced researchers. Rather, it is a book written by two researcher/teachers specifically for teachers who may have little or no background in research practices or statistical reasoning. The intended audience, then, includes both teachers new to the field, who may be in the midst of their pre-service training courses, and experienced teachers, who would like to be updated on relevant research findings. Since these findings pertain both to foreign language learning and to second language learning, research in both contexts will be discussed.

The book has three main aims: 1) to bring language classroom research to the attention of teachers of English to speakers of other languages, as well as to teachers of other foreign languages; 2) to explore the implications of classroom research findings and procedures for the actual practice of language teaching; and 3) to encourage and help teachers to become explorers themselves, in their own classrooms, partly for the sake of increasing the overall understanding of classroom language learning, but mostly for the sake of improving *their* learners' chances of making good progress.

The overall goal, then, is to help bridge the gap between research and teaching, and more particularly between researchers and teachers. It is understandable that teachers are suspicious of researchers, since the results of research projects rarely seem to have much direct practical relevance, and the process of research – of actually having a researcher, usually a complete stranger, come into your classroom to investigate your particular teaching situation – must sometimes seem an unwelcome extra burden. And yet teachers and researchers (at least the sort of researchers this book is concerned with) are necessarily interested in the same two fundamental questions: what works in the classroom, and why? It seems likely that many professional researchers have given research a bad name precisely because they have failed to demonstrate that they really are concerned with such basic questions.

Perhaps some researchers *are* purely parasitic. We hope in this book, though, to show that language classroom research can be directly relevant to teachers, and not only the results of such research, but also the actual practice of it as well. We hope to show that teachers, whatever they think of professional researchers, might actually enjoy and profit from looking upon their classroom teaching as an excellent opportunity for conducting their own investigations – not so that they can, in their turn, become 'parasitic researchers', but so that they can become more effective language teachers, better able to help the learners with whom they work. Perhaps the learners themselves could also begin to investigate their own second language learning. Given their vantage points, teachers and learners may well come up with insights from which we could all benefit.

There are signs that a reconciliation between teachers and researchers is already taking place. Slowly the profession as a whole is realising that, no matter how much intellectual energy is put into the invention of new methods (or of new approaches to syllabus design, and so on), what really matters is what happens when teachers and learners get together in the classroom. We all know that some teachers seem to succeed however out-of-date or out-of-fashion their methods are, but only recently have researchers begun to treat this as a central fact about teaching and learning, instead of as an inconvenient bit of untidiness best swept under the carpet. This shift of emphasis, from concentrating on planning decisions (what method to use, what sort of syllabus to adopt, and so on) to concentrating on looking at what actually happens in the classroom, has led researchers to have much greater respect for classroom teaching. The more we look the more we find, and the more we realise how complex the teacher's job is. And teachers, in their turn, faced at last with researchers who have at least some idea of the enormous complexity of everyday classroom life, are beginning to be more receptive to the whole research enterprise. There seems, in fact, to be a growing reconciliation between such researchers and language teachers, a growing feeling of common purpose and concern.

We hope to make a convincing case, in this book, for the unity of purpose behind classroom research and language teaching, to promote this reconciliation process, and ultimately to blur altogether the damagingly sharp distinction between research and teaching from which our profession has suffered too long. Being a good classroom teacher means being alive to what goes on in the clasroom, alive to the problems of sorting out what matters, moment by moment, from what does not. And that is what classroom research is all about: gaining a better understanding of what good teachers (and learners) do instinctively as a matter of course, so that ultimately all can benefit.

Introduction

Books about language teaching, however 'practical' they may be, are almost always about 'planning' rather than about 'doing'. They aim to help us decide what *would* be the best way to teach a class, or what *would* be the best sort of syllabus to use. The purpose of this book is different, and importantly so. This book is about what *actually happens* – not just what happens to the plans we make, but what happens anyway, independently of our designs. This focus on the classroom is important because teachers and researchers alike want to know which classroom events, planned or not, make our learners' task easier or more difficult.

As authors, we two would be wasting our time, of course, if the connection between the planning, the teaching, and the learning were a simple and direct one; if everything we teachers planned (and only what we planned) got taught, and if everything that got taught was learned. We all know though that in human learning nothing is so simple. Teachers know this and so do researchers. We also know that 'the best laid plans' do not guarantee perfect results. And we all know that lessons we have not properly planned are sometimes spectacularly successful. It is worth focusing on the classroom, then, on the doing rather than the planning, just because it is surely whatever actually happens in the classroom that really matters, that makes a difference to our learners' progress.

For a long time we thought that the teaching method was the most important thing – that all we had to do was find the 'right' method. But enough research has now been done for us to be quite sure that we were wrong. Method does matter, of course, but only to the extent that it makes a real difference to what actually happens in the classroom.

In the 1960s and early 1970s there were some important research projects that tried to compare the major methods of the time. The most famous of these was the Pennsylvania Project (Smith 1970), which compared the 'audiolingual' method and the 'traditional' method. The study's inconclusive results were, in the words of the Project Director, 'personally traumatic to the project staff'. From the outset the researchers had expected a clear superiority for audiolingualism, but instead they found no significant differences on several measures, and superiority of the traditional method on traditional measures of reading skill.

There was a great deal of discussion at that time about why the results should have been so inconclusive, and one of the main reasons seems to have been precisely that there was this gap between the planning, the teaching, and the learning. It was one thing to 'plan' that a certain number of teachers should teach for a certain period of time, several years, following this or that method, and quite another thing to be sure that all the teaching had gone as planned, and yet another to believe that the learning would in any case directly mirror the teaching. We are a bit wiser now. Focusing more on the classroom could have helped the Pennsylvania Project by providing a clear picture of the sorts of teaching the learners actually got during the experiment.

Researchers who do focus on the classroom, who really begin to study what goes on there, find very much more happening than just the more or less messy implementation of some particular method. Looking in classrooms we see so much going on that it becomes easy to understand why the choice of a global teaching method cannot be what really makes some classrooms better places for learners to be in than others. Unfortunately, we see so much going on in the classroom we soon realise that understanding this mysterious chemistry is becoming more complicated rather than easier. Researchers and teachers alike want to know what *really* matters, what *really* helps learners, but of course there are no straightforward answers. This book, then, is *not* a book of answers to the question 'what matters?'. It *is* a book of explorations, a book about what researchers have learned so far from attempts to study what happens in language classrooms. It is a book about how we, as teachers, might go about continuing the explorations in our own classrooms.

One major claim underlies the whole book: in order to help our learners learn, it is not 'the latest method' that we need, but rather a fuller understanding of the language classroom and what goes on there. Part I will set the scene historically and then introduce the reasoning behind our position. In Part II we will explore some of the major methodological issues which have dominated language classroom research to date.

In Parts III, IV, and V, the core of the volume, we will be looking at the findings – the sorts of things researchers have discovered since language classroom research began in the late 1960s (just as the method experiments began reporting their inconclusive results). We will look first in Part III at 'oral errors' and how teachers deal with them – one of the prominent topics in early classroom-centred research. Next we will consider some of the complexities of 'classroom interaction' (Part IV): how language learners and teachers take speaking turns and what functions classroom talk fulfils in the language learning process. Part V, on 'receptivity', will summarise the research on learners in terms of such personal matters as anxiety, competitiveness, motivation, and self-esteem, to see if there is evidence that these issues matter or that they make much of a difference in language learning. Finally, in Part VI, we will close with our ideas about 'exploratory teaching' – an attitude, a stance that teachers can take to utilise these ideas about classroom research in their own settings.

Throughout the book, after each chapter, there will be *Discussion starters*, and *Suggestions for further reading*. There are also ideas for practical activities that teacher training groups or individual teachers might like to undertake to explore each topic in more depth.

The *Discussion starters* are intended to be helpful in at least three different ways. First we hope they will encourage readers to relate the main points of the content to their personal experience, both as teachers and as learners. Second, these questions and tasks should prompt discussion that will lead to a better understanding of the points themselves, and third, such discussions should often prove useful in assisting readers to decide which of the practical activities they wish to undertake, and to clarify for themselves the issues involved.

The first aim of the practical activities (both the Mini-projects and the Major projects) is to give you, as a reader, some experience in analysing data. In some instances, these projects will provide opportunities for you to collect your own data to think about and to talk about, instead of depending solely on whatever we, as authors, have already supplied within the chapters themselves. But collecting your own data also means becoming a classroom researcher yourself, and our second aim is precisely to give you practical experience in small-scale classroom investigations so that if you wish to do such things in the future, you will not only know the thinking behind them but also have some practical understanding of what tasks are involved.

Some sorts of data collection can be done very quickly, perhaps in less than one class hour, and without any elaborate preparation. Such activities are easy to use for beginning your explorations, either in isolation or in conjunction with the *Discussion starters*. Other sorts of data collection take much longer and demand not only much more preparation but also a great deal of work on the interpretation of the data you have collected. Such activities should be given enough time and enough thought so that you can properly take into account all the methodological considerations introduced in Part II. We have aimed at providing a balance between activities that can be done by a person working alone and activities that call for teamwork. Some of the individual activities will in fact be more fruitful if several different people do them at the same time, in different settings, and this we have also indicated where appropriate.

Finally, and particularly since this is an introductory text, we have included *Suggestions for further reading* at the end of each chapter. Citations are also given throughout the text, but since this book is intended for teachers rather than experienced researchers, we have tried to make the prose less cumbersome by listing additional references in the

Introduction

Suggestions for further reading rather than only using the normal academic style of within-text referencing. These *Suggestions* provide ideas about articles and books you might read if you become intrigued by some aspects of the topics under discussion. These readings were chosen because they are 1) classic treatments of the issues, 2) clear, readable discussions, or 3) widely available in language teaching circles around the world, or ideally all three. We have not attempted an exhaustive review of *all* the pertinent studies, but we do believe the background information given in this volume will prepare teachers to read the classroom research literature with confidence and critical wisdom, and to become exploratory teachers in their own classrooms.

Part I Classroom research: what it is and why it is important

The two chapters in this first section of the book will provide the framework for interpreting what follows. Chapter 1 explains what we mean by classroom research and traces its history in the language field, in order for the reader to gain a backdrop on the issues which have emerged as lasting concerns. We will then turn, in Chapter 2, to the question which underlies this book: why focus on the classroom? These two chapters, taken together, constitute a general framework for looking at what happens in the language classroom.

A note of caution is in order here regarding the relationship of language classroom research to other fields of science. Classroom research differs from other types of research with which you may be more familiar. Compared with psychology or with medicine, for example, it seldom approaches the relative simplicity and rigorous control of formal experiments. Compared with general educational research, on the other hand, language classroom research adds the extra but necessary complexity of dealing with situations where language is both what is being taught and the means by which it is being taught, and often with situations where more than one language is used in classroom talk. Finally, language classroom research is a little like anthropology in some ways, where researchers try to understand what is going on in particular social or cultural settings. Although language classroom research has only occasionally looked at cultural differences, the individual classroom can be considered (and studied as) a cultural entity.

So language classroom research has its own distinctive tradition. But it is not an entirely novel tradition. The backdrop to be described in Part I is in fact based to a considerable extent on a history of borrowing and adapting from other research traditions. This history has led to a research framework that is still evolving. What it has already achieved is a strong (and still growing) awareness of the tremendous depth and richness of the language classroom as a site for the investigation of language teaching and learning.

1 The development of classroom research

Before we begin to present the findings of classroom research, we need to acknowledge that it has a chequered history. To put the findings in proper perspective, we shall, first of all, loosely define the field and present a brief survey of the different themes that have characterised the last twenty or so years of classroom research on language teaching and learning. Our intent is to show how some themes have retreated into the background in spite of their early promise, and how new ones have come forward to take their place. It is a research field still really in its infancy, still working on major breakthroughs, but at the same time already well established and already making a distinctive contribution to our understanding of classroom language learning and teaching.

1.1 What is classroom research?

Classroom-centred research is just what it says it is – research *centred on* the classroom, as distinct from, for example, research that concentrates on the *inputs to* the classroom (the syllabus, the teaching materials, etc.) or on the *outputs from* the classroom (learner test scores). It does not ignore in any way or try to devalue the importance of such inputs and outputs. Instead classroom research simply tries to investigate what actually happens inside the classroom. At its most narrow, it is in fact research which treats classroom interaction as virtually the only object worthy of investigation.

This conception of classroom-centred research is far too narrow for our purposes here, however. We shall want to include studies that focus on classroom language learning in many different ways, and we shall want to refer to some that do not directly investigate classroom interaction at all.

We take 'classroom-centred research' (or simply 'classroom research' hereafter) as a cover term, then, for a whole range of research studies on classroom language learning and teaching. The obvious unifying factor is that the emphasis is solidly on trying to understand what goes on in the classroom setting. Examples of the types of issues that have been studied so far include how teachers respond to learners' errors, how interaction occurs in classrooms, the type of linguistic input provided in classroom settings, the feelings of teachers and learners at various points during or after lessons, and so on. Most of these topics will be discussed in some detail in Chapters 5 to 10 of this book.

1.2 How is it done?

Basically research on classroom language learning involves a good many different procedures. As with any other sort of research, the starting point will involve getting as well informed as you possibly can on the issue you wish to investigate. We can call this consulting 'expert opinion', and it will include catching up with the speculative and theoretical literature as well as with earlier research.

Consulting expert opinion in this way does two things. First of all, it tells you what issues have already been thought about and investigated, and should lead you to sort out more precisely whatever you eventually decide to investigate yourself. Second, it should tell you how related questions have been investigated in the past, so that you can make a more informed decision about how to start doing your own study, and about the procedures you will eventually use.

Doing the actual research is essentially a matter of data collection and analysis. Typically you need some sort of a record of what happened in a particular classroom or classrooms, so that you can analyse the record (your data) and describe the classroom processes in whatever terms interest you. There are, broadly speaking, two different ways of getting such a record.

The first and most obvious way is to develop a data base (the record) by direct observation. You could observe the classroom processes by sitting in the classroom and taking notes. To make your record more focused you may decide in advance what you are going to be looking for, make an observational schedule with the categories you consider appropriate, and then record what happens under those category headings. If, for example, you are interested in seeing whether boys or girls do more of the talking in class, you might have just two categories ('boys' and 'girls') and then make a tally in the appropriate column on your observation sheet whenever a child speaks. For more complicated enquiries, and so that you can have a more complete record anyway, you may prefer to audio-record, or even video-record, what goes on, so that you can go back in detail to what was said, by whom, in what tone of voice, and so on. For that you will probably need to transcribe the interaction from the tape, so that you will end up with a comprehensive written record of the lesson to analyse, as well as the original tape itself.

Direct observation is not always the most appropriate way to gather classroom data. Sometimes it seems too risky because of the likelihood that being observed will change people's behaviour. Can a teacher really be expected to carry on just as usual with an observer sitting at the back of the room, or with a video-camera there, or even with just a modest audio-cassette machine sitting on the desk? Furthermore, there are many interesting aspects of classroom processes that are not actually observable in any very reliable or measurable way. If we want to know what makes people anxious in class, for example, then just looking at them will not tell us everything we want to know. Sometimes people do look anxious, of course, but a lot of people who in fact feel very anxious may be able to cover it up very convincingly in class. If we want to investigate anxiety, then, some other way of eliciting the data will be necessary.

The second way, the obvious alternative to direct observation, is simply to ask, to give people an opportunity to report for themselves what has happened to them and what they think about it. The traditional way of getting such 'self-report' data is to conduct surveys, usually through interviews or by written questionnaires. Although we must not assume that such survey questions are always answered truthfully, or even carefully, we can try asking people to tell us what has happened to them in class, and treat their replies as our basic data, or at the very least as data to consider alongside whatever we have been able to observe directly. Survey data collection techniques normally involve working out in advance the categories you are going to use for your investigation (but this time for your questions rather than your observations – what you are going to ask about). For this reason, you need to think very carefully about the wording of your questions so that nobody can say you got the answers you did just because of the way you posed the questions.

The problem with observation schedules and with surveys is precisely, however, that someone has to decide in advance what to look for, or what to ask questions about, and that someone is most often a researcher who is not typically directly involved in the classroom being investigated. Such relatively 'closed' techniques may easily miss the insights that could be provided by the participants themselves, the teachers and the learners, beyond anything the researcher has thought to build into the data collection procedures.

To capture these sorts of insights, alternative forms of data collection are needed – some more 'open' form of self-report, for example, where the participants themselves, without specific prompting on specific issues, try to record their experiences and perceptions for the researcher. For example, a learner's diary may reveal aspects of the classroom experience that observation could never have captured, and that no one would have thought of including as questions on a questionnaire. The relationship of competitiveness and anxiety in language classrooms has been explored this way (see Chapter 10 for further details), through the analysis of a number of diaries by different learners in different classes. They were not asked to write about competitiveness or anxiety, but these proved to be important issues for many of them, given what they did write, unprompted.

The desire not to prejudge the importance of events observed has led some researchers to consider the procedures and philosophies of ethnography as a viable approach to collecting and interpreting classroom data (see van Lier 1988; Watson-Gegeo 1988; Watson-Gegeo and Ulichny 1988). 'Ethnography' has been variously defined, but basically it is a collection of procedures (and an attitude) used predominantly by anthropologists who attempt to document and understand the behaviour of people in cultures. Originally, ethnographers studied exotic cultures, but in recent years, ethnography has been used to study people in many diverse but everyday settings, including restaurants, urban street gangs, schools, etc.

Ethnography has gained considerable support as an approach to classroom research in education in general (Wilson 1977; Erickson 1981; Green and Wallat 1981), as well as in studies of language teaching and learning. For example, van Lier (1988) makes a convincing case for ethnography as potentially the most useful means to study classroom phenomena. He stresses a point which is relevant here, namely, to understand what happens in classrooms, researchers must try to get at the meaning given to these events by the participants themselves.

Thus, the main tools of the classroom research trade are observations (including recordings), surveys, and other forms of self-report. These are tools that set classroom research apart from research in the so-called 'hard' sciences and which draw from social science and ethnography. There is a further tool that classroom researchers often utilise: test data. Of course, the use of test results is in no way special to classroom research. Although there is a lot that can be studied without anyone worrying about whether or not a particular teaching point has been successfully taught (that is, learned), in the long run we must all be interested in the notion of effective learning, and we want to know whether the particular issues we study (sex differences in participation, or classroom competitiveness, or whatever) are important in relation to effective learning. So classroom researchers, like most others, need from time to time to collect test data (and/or other sorts of performance data – spontaneous conversations, essays, and so on) along with information gathered from their observations, their surveys, or students' and teachers' self-reports.

1.3 Where did classroom research come from?

Classroom research is certainly not unique to language teaching and did not even originate among language-oriented researchers. In fact, it took language teaching some time to even begin to catch up with the rest of the educational world in this respect.

Modern classroom research began in the 1950s, among teacher trainers, in response to the problems involved in helping student teachers in subject-matter classes by giving them feedback about their perform-ance in class during their teaching practice. The trainers realised that they needed to investigate what constituted effective teaching, and then find a way of incorporating their findings into effective teacher training. As we shall see, the first of these issues – what constitutes effective teaching – has proven to be so complex and so fascinating a research problem that teacher training itself has slipped gradually into the background.

1.4 How has it developed?

Just as teacher training provided the earliest concerns, which centred on the attempt to determine what constitutes effective teaching, so teacher training also provided the basic tools of classroom observation – the 'observation schedules' themselves. Researchers such as Flanders (1970) had used direct observation to study teaching, and had developed observation schedules – essentially lists of the categories of teacher and learner behaviour thought to be most closely related to successful teaching. (See Appendix A for a copy of Flanders' system, sometimes called 'FIAC', for 'Flanders' Interaction Analysis Categories'.) These observation sheets were used to help teacher trainees to see just how well (or how badly) their teaching behaviour matched the patterns that research (or consensus) had suggested would be most effective.

Unfortunately the early, almost euphoric, confidence in the findings of such research did not survive many years of scrutiny by an increasing number of researchers who found classroom behaviour altogether too complex to be reduced to a few categories. It seemed that applications in teacher training were therefore premature, and that a major effort should first be put into trying to unravel the enormous complexities of classroom behaviour.

One probable reason why the language teaching profession came late to classroom research was that, just when teachers of other subjects were losing confidence in their methods, language teachers were enjoying a period of unprecedented confidence in theirs, with audiolingualism very widely used and intellectually accepted, especially in the United States. The audiolingual method was related to highly developed theories in linguistics and behaviourist psychology, and had apparently proved its practical worth by its success in military language training programmes during World War II. However, in 1959 the confidence in audiolingual-ism as a theory was seriously undermined, by Chomsky's (1959) all-out attack on Skinner's (1957) behaviourist views on language and language learning. And in practical terms audiolingualism was further damaged by reports that learners were not only bored by the repetitious drills that occupied so much of their time, but were not really learning any more than they ever had. Nevertheless there was no immediate loss of confidence in the concept of method itself, since an alternative method to audiolingualism was quickly found. In fact, the alternative drew from cognitive psychology (hence the new method's rather odd name – 'cognitive code') and used arguments from that field to bring together some ideas that were genuinely new and some from the already well-established but otherwise outmoded grammar–translation method.

At that time (the early 1960s) language teacher training, naturally enough, revolved around the issue of which of the major competing methods one should prescribe to beginning teachers. Had Chomsky really succeeded in refuting Skinner and the whole theoretical apparatus of audiolingualism? Had audiolingualism really failed in the classroom, or did we just need a much more imaginative approach to drill writing? The underlying assumption was still that what mattered was finding the right method. In effect, what happened in the classroom, and therefore what was learned, was thought to be completely determined by the choice of method.

Unfortunately for the methodologists, however, the major experiments conducted in the 1960s to decide between the main competing methods proved miserably inconclusive. Scherer and Wertheimer (1964), working at university level in Colorado, compared what was at the time the modern audiolingual method with traditional grammar–translation teaching and found no significant differences overall, for a two-year trial period. Soon afterwards came the massive Pennsylvania Project, where, this time at secondary school level, audiolingualism was now being compared with traditional teaching informed by the latest 'cognitive' ideas. After a total of four years of teaching, this experiment (Smith 1970) also failed to demonstrate the expected superiority of either of the methods being compared, although the 'traditional' method yielded better results on some tests of reading skills.

1.5 What has happened to the early concerns?

In the long run, the ultimate loser in this inconclusive battle was neither audiolingualism nor its cognitive rival but the very notion of making global methodological prescriptions. It no longer made sense to imagine that any one method would ever prove in some absolute way to be superior to its competitors. No one method could therefore be prescribed, like some patent medicine, with absolute confidence in its global, universal, effectiveness.

Grittner (1968:7) summed up the situation at the time by suggesting: ' ... perhaps we should ask for a cease-fire while we search for a more productive means of investigation'. Some researchers decided to move a step down in the Approach, Method, Technique hierarchy described by Anthony (1963) and do small-scale research at the level of technique instead of large-scale research at the level of method. (In Anthony's terms, the 'approach' was the philosophy of language and learning that provided the theoretical underpinnings of language teaching. The 'method' was a systematic collection of activities and procedures which were derived logically from the approach. The 'techniques' were the various activities implemented during a lesson, which stemmed, in turn, directly from the method chosen.)

Researchers on the Gothenburg English Teaching Method Project (which is often referred to by its Swedish abbreviation, GUME) compromised by working at the level of technique but still in the hope of establishing the validity of such comparisons. (See Lindblad 1969.) They were in fact hoping to test the usefulness of grammatical explanations framed according to Chomsky's 1957 version of Transformational Generative Grammar. In essence, this meant trying to test an 'approach' (Chomsky's theory) by experimentation with 'techniques' (in this case the provision of certain types of grammatical explanation as compared with no explanation at all). The results were again inconclusive, at least until the researchers switched from children to adults, who did seem to learn better from explanations and practice than from practice alone. Even these positive findings, however, did not amount to verification of the absolute validity of any global methodological prescription. The mere fact that they had obtained different results with children and with adults damaged any truly global claims. And, in any case, the relatively small-scale nature of the GUME project – in terms of the number of lessons involved, the number of teaching points covered, the fact that the teaching was not live but on audiotape, and so on – would suggest that we ought to be very cautious about drawing global conclusions from this research.

Meanwhile, in the United States, Politzer (1970) had already conducted and reported upon a seminal study in which he videotaped a number of secondary school French classes. He recorded the frequency with which certain techniques (mostly different types of structural pattern practice) were used, and related the frequencies to learner achievement in the different classes. His results were complex and make very interesting reading. However, they add up to strong evidence that small-scale research at the level of technique was by no means ready to support a prescriptive approach to teacher training. In fact, Politzer retreated from prescriptivism himself when he articulated his 'principle of classroom economics': he noted that the value of any technique depends in part on the relative value of other techniques that could have been used in place of the one actually selected by the teacher.

Politzer concluded that 'the very high complexity of the teaching process makes it very difficult to talk in absolute terms about "good" and "bad" teaching devices' (1970:43). It was becoming increasingly clear that language teaching is vastly more complicated than that. Even now, over two decades after Politzer's study was first published, teacher trainers are not in a position to tell their trainees just which techniques to use and which ones not to use – not in a position, that is, that can be justified by solidly established research results.

Having already retreated from a focus on 'method' to one on 'technique' it therefore seemed necessary to retreat at least one step further back into the unknown. In fact two moves were involved. First, it meant retreating from prescription altogether in favour of a descriptive approach, and second, it meant retreating from 'techniques' to 'processes'.

These two moves, taken together, meant trying to find ways of describing classroom processes to find out what actually happens in language classes. We could no longer assume that all that happens is that a particular method, or a particular set of techniques, is simply implemented. Instead, we began to feel that something below the level of technique (something more interactive and less obviously pedagogic) takes place, and that this interaction (that is, whatever actually happens in the classroom) is likely to provide a fruitful topic for investigation.

In the pursuit of these two retreats, first from *pre*scription to *de*scription, and then to the description of classroom processes, two somewhat different viewpoints have emerged in the last decade. Some researchers (those with more of a sociological outlook on education, in fact) have tended to look at the language lesson as a 'socially-constructed event', which all the people present produce through their interactive work. Put more simply, such researchers have stopped looking at teaching as if everything of importance came from the teacher, and have instead started looking at the way people interact in the classroom to collectively produce the learning opportunities that arise there. For example, one of the present authors (Dick Allwright) has gone from looking at how teachers correct errors (see Chapters 5 and 6) to investigating how teachers and learners together determine each learner's level of participation in classroom activities (see Chapters 7 and 8). He has now moved on to investigating how learners' contributions to classroom interaction affect the syllabus the teacher is trying to teach, and therefore what learners can get from lessons.

One viewpoint, then, has stressed the importance of social interaction.

The other viewpoint is the one adopted by more directly language-oriented researchers who have chosen to look at the classroom as a setting to study how language might be acquired from the input provided by the teacher's talk (see section 8.1). Language-oriented investigations have also examined the language produced by learners in classroom settings.

As we shall see in the remainder of the book, these two viewpoints (the sociological orientation and the linguistic orientation) can be viewed as complementary, rather than as being in competition with each other. For example, the 'sociological' interest in the way learner behaviour affects the syllabus can easily be related to the 'linguistic' interest in the nature of the language the learners are exposed to in the classroom. In fact the two viewpoints *must* come together if we are not to miss what might be valuable insights into classroom language learning.

1.6 What has happened to the basic tools?

In the move from teacher training to more fundamental research, typified both in the move from prescription to description and in the moves from method to technique to process, what has happened to the basic tools of classroom research? You will recall that they were originally borrowed from general educational research, and consisted mostly of techniques for using observation schedules (lists of categories) for the classification of teacher behaviour. (Relatively little attention was paid to *learner* behaviour at the time, given the focus on *teacher* training.) These observation schedules had to be modified to make them appropriate to the obvious complexities of language teaching, where language is the content as well as the medium of instruction, where more than one language may be used, and where, as in pronunciation practice, all the learners may need to have a chance to try to produce the same answer to exactly the same question, sometimes simultaneously.

The starting point for many people was Flanders' pioneering work on 'Interaction Analysis' (1970). Flanders used this term for his ten-category observation schedule, which is reprinted in Appendix A. He designed it for general educational purposes, to be relevant to a variety of lessons, rather than for any subject in particular. In his work he combined a politically powerful idea with a very practical simplicity. The powerful idea was that teaching was more or less effective depending on how 'directly' or 'indirectly' teachers influenced learner behaviour. Flanders' was a pro-democratic, anti-authoritarian position that therefore looked for a positive relationship between a 'democratic' teaching style (that is, using indirect rather than direct influence) and learner achievement. He built this general idea into his ten categories, so that some would be used to record direct influence (for example, 'criticising or justifying authority') and some to record indirect influence ('accepting learners' ideas', for example). He then developed a simple way of analysing the resulting observations to give teachers scores reflecting the 'directness' or 'indirectness' of their teaching styles.

Moskowitz (1967, 1968, 1971, 1976) produced the best known and most widely used modification (for language pedagogy) of Flanders' Interaction Analysis Categories. She called her version 'FLint' (*Foreign Language int*eraction – see Appendix B). Moskowitz expanded and refined Flanders' categories and then used FLint both as a research tool, to pursue the issue of what constitutes 'good' language teaching, and as a feedback tool in teacher training. She trained student teachers to analyse their own teaching behaviour using the FLint categories so that they could have more objective feedback and a firmer basis for comparison in their later attempts to behave differently in class.

In another important contribution in this area, Fanselow (1977a) made major modifications to and elaborations of Bellack's pioneering analytical system (see Chapter 6) to produce 'FOCUS' (Foci for Observing Communications Used in Settings – see Appendix C). FOCUS was an observation schedule developed with language teacher training in mind, but as a descriptive system applicable to research on any example of human interaction. Fanselow's system, therefore, does not have separate categories for teachers and learners, but instead has general categories that can be used regardless of who the participants are or what role they play in the interaction.

These refinements of the basic tools (the observation instruments) seem not to have caught on quite as much as one might have expected, however. One possibility is that some researchers cannot bear to use anyone else's observational schedules. There may be some truth in this position, and certainly some researchers have called attention to the proliferation of marginally different observational systems, but there is another, more intellectually responsible possibility that deserves consideration.

It is possible that there is something inherently problematic about trying to keep the close link between fundamental research and teacher training. Fundamental research needs fully developed, reliable observational instruments and analytic systems. Teacher training, on the other hand, can do very well with relatively crude instruments, ones that can be taught quickly to novice teachers and then used by them in their own teaching, without spending inordinate amounts of time transcribing and analysing recorded data. (It takes researchers about twenty hours to produce a good working transcription from a tape-recording of an hour-long classroom language lesson, and that is before they really start on all the analytical work. It would be virtually impossible to justify that use of time on a teacher training course.)

Another issue, of course, is that existing instruments, particularly those developed for teacher training purposes, are not necessarily appropriate tools for some types of classroom research. For example, four researchers working in Mexico (Long, Adams, McLean and Castaños 1976) wanted to investigate the language produced by university level Spanish-speaking students of English under two conditions: in full classroom interaction and in dyads (pairs). These researchers considered the available observation schedules and found that none were appropriate for their purposes, so they invented a new classification system, which they dubbed the 'Embryonic Category System', in order to reflect its developmental nature. (See Appendix D for a copy of this coding system.) This system was used to code the communicative variety in transcripts of speech produced by learners – a focus which none of the earlier teacher-oriented systems had embodied. In this sense, the proliferation of instruments is an almost automatic result of refinement and progress in our research: as new avenues of investigation are discovered, new analytic tools are invented to pursue them.

One important recent development in classroom research on language teaching and learning reflects the emergence of discourse analysis as a field of linguistic enquiry. Indeed, the analysis of classroom discourse transcripts may supersede the practice of using category systems in 'real time'. Many researchers, concerned over the potential invalidity of category systems, over the problem that they necessarily have to prejudge what is worth paying attention to, and over the crude category distinctions that such instruments typically involve, have turned to transcriptions of recorded classroom events as their prime data base. (We will examine the role of discourse analysis and transcription in more detail in section 4.1.)

While transcription is a time-consuming process, it provides a detailed account of the linguistic interaction in classrooms. This sort of account can be explored in many different ways. For instance, Sinclair and Coulthard's (1975) analysis of transcripts of British classrooms enabled them to draw up a hierarchy of units of interaction, units that might be identifiable in classroom settings anywhere in the world. Their largest unit was the lesson itself, made up of units they called 'transactions', themselves made up of 'exchanges', made up in their turn of 'moves', which were made up of the smallest interaction units, 'acts', which could be further analysed into linguistic units like words and phrases. (See Appendix E for a copy of Sinclair and Coulthard's category system.)

Yet another stimulus for change and development in the basic tools has come from teaching itself. Changes in pedagogic theory have led, naturally, to changes in the questions asked of observational data. And the data collection procedures have had to change in order to provide appropriate material for the researchers to analyse. A clear example of this sort of addition to the catalogue of observational instruments is the COLT system (Allen, Fröhlich, and Spada 1984; Fröhlich, Spada and Allen 1985). COLT stands for 'Communicative Orientation of Language Teaching' (see Appendix F). This instrument was developed in hopes of distinguishing communicative language teaching classrooms from those that are more teacher-centred and form-focused: COLT's categories were designed 'to measure the extent to which an instructional treatment may be characterized as communicatively oriented' (1985:29). Issues gleaned from the literature which influenced the researchers' design of the instrument included the use of authentic materials and groupwork, functional emphases in meaning-based lessons, and attention to the discoursal and sociolinguistic features of the language under study. As you can imagine, these kinds of issues were not matters of concern when Flanders first devised his two-part system of direct and indirect teacher behaviours in general education. And so, as teaching has developed – language teaching in particular – the research tools have had to develop apace and have become somewhat more sophisticated in the process.

Given such very different demands on the basic observational tools, we can see why we should expect research and teacher training to drift apart, and why researchers should feel a strong need to develop original observation instruments. Of course, this position implies that teacher training cannot afford the time to use the more elaborate and highly developed research tools that might come somewhere near reflecting the full complexities of the language classroom; that, in essence, observation in teacher training has to risk being relatively superficial because it must necessarily be more concerned with immediate practicalities. But this idea also suggests that the value of an observational schedule depends directly and exclusively on the reliability and validity of its categories. This may be true in basic research but in teacher training we should not forget the potentially very significant value, for novice or experienced teachers, of the whole process of obtaining observational feedback on their classroom behaviour. It can act very effectively to stimulate highly productive thinking about what goes on in the classroom. Experience suggests that the quality of such thinking does not depend on the demonstrated reliability and validity of the categories used as a starting point. In fact, as a starting point, categories devised by teacher trainees themselves may suffice very well to provoke fruitful thought and even helpful behavioural change.

This issue is basic to one of the main purposes of this book – to encourage teachers to look upon themselves as explorers in their own classrooms. The business of doing classroom research, of looking carefully into classrooms, can be extremely fruitful for the people doing the looking. And in many cases, the teacher who is already in the classroom, who already has the day-to-day experience of working with learners, is

B

surely in a particularly privileged position to decide what needs to be investigated.

Research on classroom language learning, then, has shifted away from teacher training as a central focus, not only in its moves from prescription to description and from technique to process, but also in its search for the most appropriate observational tools. The aim is still to end up with something helpful to say to teachers and teacher educators, but we have been retreating on all such fronts, in the hope of being able to return some day with things really worth saying. Meanwhile researchers have retained the basic idea of classroom observation as central to data collection procedures, and have concentrated on developing analytical tools for particular purposes. Researchers have also gone beyond classroom observation in the use of surveys, transcription methods, discourse analysis, and self-report procedures as viable research techniques.

1.7 Summary

In this rapid overview, we have deliberately presented a summary of themes, rather than of findings. (These will be dealt with in Chapters 5 to 10.) We have done this in order to trace the origins of classroom research on language teaching and learning, and to trace the various changes it has gone through in the development of its central concerns and of its research methods. As we have seen, the history of classroom research on language teaching and learning has been one of retreat from the simplistic optimism that we now find in the earliest attempts both to determine what constitutes 'good' language teaching, and then to train language teachers accordingly. It has been a history of movement in general away from traditional pedagogical concerns (the best method to adopt, the best technique to use) towards other areas (for example, the classroom interaction process) that promise insights of value to language pedagogy – a retreat to what may reasonably be called fundamental research, which has brought us much closer to other educational researchers and notably close to people working in the psycholinguistic field of second language acquisition. It is also, perhaps surprisingly, a retreat that can bring researchers nearer again to classroom teachers themselves, since it is now abundantly clear that language classroom research must focus on what actually happens in the classroom, and not on testing other people's prescriptions for what they think *should* happen there.

In Chapter 2 we will pursue this issue by looking in more detail at the classroom as a setting for language learning and teaching. But first we hope you will work through our *Discussion starters* and *Suggestions for further reading*, as well as the suggested *Mini-project*: 'Sizing up the instruments', as a way of gaining more first-hand awareness of these issues.

DISCUSSION STARTERS

1 Which of the topics mentioned in this chapter as being part of the classroom research tradition are most interesting to you? Which, if any, are related to matters that concern you in thinking about your own teaching?
2 Would you rather collect data by direct observation (recording lessons, say) or by self-reports (by asking people to talk to you about lessons, perhaps)? Why? What kind of data do you trust the most?
3 Does it make sense to you to suggest that there are no 'absolutely good' and no 'absolutely bad' teaching techniques? Whichever way you answer, what are the implications of your position for language teachers and for teacher educators?
4 Have you ever consciously tried to teach following a particular method? If so, did you find that your choice of method actually gave you a clear way of dealing with all the pedagogic decisions you had to make during language lessons? How?
5 Do you think, from what you have read so far, and from what you know already, that researchers gave up too easily on their search for the best method? Were researchers justified in moving from prescription to description? What research results would you accept as evidence that there was, in fact, a 'best' method?

SUGGESTIONS FOR FURTHER READING

1 Several reviews of language classroom research are now available. Some of the most accessible are those by Allwright (1983), Gaies (1983a), Bailey (1985), and Mitchell (1985). A full-length book, Chaudron's *Second language classrooms: research on teaching and learning* (1988a) gives an in-depth literature review of classroom research.
2 Allwright's book, *Observation in the language classroom* (1988a), provides a representative selection of observational studies and instruments, organised in a historical framework, with accompanying commentary.
3 The reports of the early comparative methods studies are interesting accounts of attempts to apply the rigour of controlled experiments within existing educational institutions. See, for example, Scherer and Wertheimer (1964) and Smith (1970) for reports on the Colorado

research and the Pennsylvania studies, respectively. Otto (1969) wrote about the teachers' point of view in the Pennsylvania Project, and Clark (1969) discussed some of the problems in that same study.

4 For more information about the GUME Project, see Lindblad (1969), and Von Elek and Oskarsson (1973).

5 Anthony's (1963) hierarchy of approach, method, and technique was widely used for many years. In 1983, Richards, and later Richards and Rodgers (1986), made an argument for rethinking the concept of method as consisting of approach, design and procedure.

6 Politzer's (1970) account of his videotape research with high school classes of French as a foreign language is still very well worth reading. While many teachers no longer emphasise the drill types which formed the bulk of his analytic categories, Politzer's thoughtful conclusions are still important, regardless of the instructional method(s) a teacher uses.

7 Long's article, 'Inside the "black box": methodological issues in classroom research on language learning', contains an extensive comparison of the observational instruments used in classroom research up until its first publication in 1980. (It was reprinted in Seliger and Long 1983.)

8 A book called *Classroom interaction* (Malamah-Thomas 1987) sets out many of the observation schedules introduced in this chapter, including COLT, FIAC, FLint, and Sinclair and Coulthard's approach to discourse analysis. The author includes numerous tasks for familiarising teachers with these tools.

9 Leo van Lier's book, *The classroom and the language learner: ethnography and second language classroom research* (1988) is a fascinating and detailed account of the conceptual arguments leading up to some of our present methodological orientations in language classroom studies.

MINI-PROJECT: SIZING UP THE INSTRUMENTS

The appendices of this book contain reprints of several of the observation instruments that have been used in classroom research on language teaching and learning. As you compare them, you will note many similarities and many differences.

This Mini-project will involve you in some speculation. It is designed to help you gain an armchair familiarity with some of the 'basic tools'. We suggest the following steps, preferably to be done in small groups.

1 Skim over the instruments in the appendices. For each one, you can ask yourself the following questions. First, what are the general principles of *language teaching* embodied in this instrument? Second, what are

the assumptions about *language learning* that it reflects? Generally, how can such implicit assumptions be identified?

2 Compare your answers to these questions across the various instruments. If you are working with a group of people, compare your answers with theirs.

3 Given these initial comparisons, without actually having used the instruments in classroom observations, try to assess your own reactions to the various systems. Are there any that you would particularly like to use as an observer? Any that you would prefer not to use? What about if you were the teacher being observed – are there any instruments which you would either like or would rather not have used by observers in your classroom?

4 Again, if you are working with a group, compare your reactions to your peers' responses to the questions posed above. Where there are differences of opinion, what is their source? For instance, do the varying opinions arise out of really different teaching philosophies, or are they simply a question of which tools seem the most convenient to use?

5 Before researchers use these instruments to collect data in classrooms, they normally go through some sort of training. The purpose of such training is to ensure the accurate and consistent use of the procedures and to provide a clear understanding of the various categories. Since you have now considered (but not used) these instruments, what sort of training course might you suggest? Plan a series of tasks to familiarise novice researchers with the instrument of your choice. Compare your proposed training procedures with those devised by your classmates or colleagues. What similarities and differences arise in your approaches? Finally, discuss how you would decide when you had done enough training.

6 Now go to the original source for the instrument you chose. Read the authors' explanation of how the instrument was intended to be used. What additional training procedures would you need to develop, based on the authors' objectives?

2 Why focus on the classroom?

In this chapter we will turn to the setting of classroom research – a setting with which we are all familiar, given our experience as teachers and our years as learners. But what exactly do we mean by 'classroom', and why is it important to focus specifically on this educational setting in conducting language learning research? These and related questions provide the structure for Chapter 2.

2.1 The classroom is the crucible

The classroom, as the term is used in this particular research tradition, has been defined as 'the gathering, for a given period of time, of two or more persons (one of whom generally assumes the role of instructor) for the purposes of language learning' (van Lier 1988:47). The breadth of this definition allows us to consider group work and tutorial meetings, with as few participants as one learner and one instructor, as well as larger, more traditional educational contexts.

As Gaies has noted (1980), the classroom is the crucible – the place where teachers and learners come together and language learning, we hope, happens. It happens, when it happens, as a result of the reactions among the elements that go into the crucible – the teachers and the learners. They do not, however, go in 'empty-handed'. The learners bring with them their whole experience of learning and of life in classrooms, along with their own reasons for being there, and their own particular needs that they hope to see satisfied. And the teacher brings experience, too, of life and learning, and of teaching. The teacher also brings into the classroom the syllabus, often embodied in a textbook. But no matter what they all bring, everything still depends on how they react to each other (learner to learner as well as teacher to learner) when they all get together in the classroom. 'React' may seem a little dramatic, perhaps, but it is not just a matter of their initial reactions to each other (although these may be of lasting importance). It is more a matter of their constant *inter*action – the fact that every time they come together they somehow have to get along, and in a way which actually helps the learners to learn.

The success of this constant interaction in the classroom cannot be taken for granted, unfortunately, and it cannot be guaranteed just by exhaustive planning either: if the interaction is totally planned in advance then the result is a play-reading, rather than a lesson. Interaction, in class or anywhere, has to be managed, as it goes along, no matter how much thought has gone into it beforehand. Even more important for teachers, though, and for language teachers in particular, is the fact that it has to be managed by everyone taking part, not just by the teacher, because interaction is obviously not something you just do *to* people, but something people do *together*, collectively. In a classroom, of course, it is usually considered normal for the teacher to 'run the show' – to make many of the managerial decisions about who should talk, to whom, on what topic, in what language, and so on, but none of this alters the fact that everything depends on the learners' co-operation. In choosing to co-operate (or not, as the case may be), the learners make a significant contribution to the management of the interaction that takes place in the classroom. And these contributions are crucial to the success of the interaction, and to the success of the lesson itself as a social event in the lives of both teachers and learners. We all know how easy it is for one or two unco-operative learners to spoil everything, to make a classroom a miserable place to work in. In a sense, the learners have power of veto over any of our attempts, as teachers, to manage interaction as if we were in sole charge, and their power is still there even if they choose, for the most part, not to use it.

2.2 The management of interaction in the classroom

In this special sense interaction is a sort of 'co-production' and it is worth spending some time on the complications this idea involves. The main problem is that successful interaction in the classroom, or any-where, involves everybody managing at least five different things, at the same time, all the time. These five factors are listed below as questions, along with the labels they are usually given in the classroom research literature:
1 Who gets to speak? (participants' turn distribution)
2 What do they talk about? (topic)
3 What does each participant do with the various opportunities to speak? (task)
4 What sort of atmosphere is created? (tone)
5 What accent, dialect, or language is used? (code)
(For a more detailed discussion of these and other variables related to the context of classroom research, see van Lier 1988:5–12.)
   What makes it even more complicated is the fact that these five aspects of interaction are means as well as ends. This suggests that if teachers of, say, English as a foreign language want a particular learner to say

something, they have a variety of possibilities open to them. They can do the direct thing, and simply ask the learner to answer a question, for example:

'Pierre, what's the time, please?'

Alternatively, they may simply change the topic to something they know the learner in question is especially interested in, and hope he or she will be interested enough to contribute to the discussion:

'OK, let's talk a little about French food. Does anyone have any favourite dishes?'

Another possibility is to change the task that the learners are asked to do in such a way as to ensure that Pierre is the only person likely to be able to answer:

'Does anyone know who won the Tour de France last year?'

If a learner is particularly shy or anxious, teachers may have to work towards a generally more relaxed atmosphere before they can expect the learner to be willing to speak in public. Finally, if all else fails, teachers may have to use the learner's first language (French, in this case) just so that Pierre will at least feel confident that he knows what is wanted of him. And all of this will have to happen in front of the whole class, of course, since the management of interaction in classrooms is necessarily a public affair.

Although some of these possibilities are no doubt somewhat remote, they do still exist as possibilities, and it is important to remember that, very often, teachers, just like people outside classrooms, prefer to adopt an indirect approach to the management of interaction, since directness can have unfortunate overtones of authoritarianism and plain bossiness, as noted by Flanders in his Interaction Analysis work. (Indirect control is still control, of course, and possibly all the more sinister for being deliberately hidden; but that is a moral issue we must let individual teachers resolve for themselves.)

Given such complications it is hardly surprising that successful class-room interaction cannot be taken for granted. As language teachers, though, we can be more positive and reflect that using another language successfully, for most people, involves being able to manage interaction successfully in that language. ('Manage interaction' may sound pompous, but even buying a postage stamp in a foreign country calls for skills we can think of as basically a matter of interaction management.) Perhaps we should be grateful that the classroom gives our learners constant opportunities to practise their interaction management skills, especially if we actually conduct our lessons wholly in the language under study, although simply using that language as the medium of instruction does not guarantee that the learners get management opportunities, especially if the teacher is very controlling.

Of course, we might discover, through our reflections, that we were not really making very good use of the opportunities classroom interaction could in principle offer to our learners. If that were the case, we could then try to do something about it, and with a little goodwill and some ingenuity we could probably improve things quite quickly.

2.3 The management of learning in the classroom

If we think too much about the management of interaction in the classroom, however, we may lose sight of the fact that what is much more important is the management of *learning*. We do not manage interaction purely for its own sake. We manage interaction in the language classroom for the sake of giving everyone the best possible opportunities for learning the language. In fact, everything we do in the classroom, any of us, can make a difference to what anyone else in the class could possibly learn from being there. In this way, managing interaction and managing learning come together. So every time the teacher asks a particular learner to say something in front of everybody else, then all the learners can pay attention to what happens, if they wish, and perhaps learn from it, as in the following fictional example:

Teacher: When's your birthday, Alvaro?
Alvaro: Fourteen September.
Teacher: **The** fourteen**th** of September. Again?
Alvaro: The fourteenth of September.
Teacher: I should hope so. Now when's **your** birthday, Miko?

What the learners can learn from such an exchange depends in part on what they know already, of course. But an attentive newcomer might learn something (if he or she can be bothered to pay attention) about how the teacher asks questions (in this case, by not saying who is to answer until after the question itself has been stated), how the teacher deals with errors (by telling Alvaro what he should have said, and then giving him another chance to do it himself), and how the teacher reacts if the student does eventually get it right (by being unpleasant about it, instead of just letting him know that he finally made it). The newcomer will have had an opportunity to get a feeling for the general classroom atmosphere, to get used to the teacher's voice and generally practise listening, and last but not least, we hope, to learn something about discussing birthdays in English. Sadly it seems that many learners do not bother to pay very much attention to what is happening to their fellow learners, but, nevertheless, in deciding not to pay attention they are playing a part (albeit a negative one) in managing their own learning. In this sense we all manage, for good or ill, our own learning, and that of everybody else, just as we manage interaction, not as individuals in sole charge of it, but certainly as contributors to it, however passive our participation might be. (We will return to these issues in Chapters 7 and 8, where we will focus specifically on classroom interaction.)

None of the above should blind us to the obvious fact that in most teaching situations it is considered to be the teacher's job (largely what the teacher has been trained for and is being paid to do) to plan a sequence of lessons and bring them to life effectively in the classroom. The point here, though, is simply that no matter how well the teacher does his or her job, what any one learner *can* learn from each lesson will depend on what happens in the course of classroom interaction, and on whether or not that learner bothers to pay attention to the different learning opportunities that arise.

2.3.1 Three aspects of classroom language lessons

Generally speaking, teachers plan, more or less explicitly, three major aspects of their lessons. First, they plan *what* they intend to teach – the 'syllabus', in other words. Many teachers may be able to rely on a syllabus drawn up for them by people in authority, and perhaps simply embodied in a textbook. Other teachers will be used to making their own decisions about what to teach. In any case most learners will take it for granted that thinking about the syllabus is not their job. The same is typically true also for the second aspect – 'method'. Teachers normally go into the classroom with a predetermined plan for *how* the syllabus is to be taught, and it is seen as an obvious part of their job to do so. The third aspect is not so clear-cut a matter, but it does seem fair to suggest that most teachers have a good idea of the sort of 'atmosphere' they would like to have in their classrooms, and do their best to plan to set up such an atmosphere (whether they want it to be relaxed and friendly, or brisk and business-like, or whatever). In recent years this aspect of teaching has begun to receive much more attention than it used to (thanks particularly to the work of Stevick), but it is clearly seen as a much less precisely plannable aspect of teaching than either the syllabus or the method, because a social atmosphere is just that – social – and so it is much more obviously dependent on co-operation from all concerned than are the syllabus and the method.

It is one thing to have plans, though, and quite another to bring them to life in the classroom precisely as intended. The language teacher, as we have seen, has to interact with the learners to implement any plans, and this inevitably means that even the most detailed and carefully worked out plans will give rise to slightly different lessons each time they are used. The end result, each time, is not just that a certain bit of the syllabus is taught, or a certain planned method is used, or that a certain planned atmosphere is created, just like that. Instead, the outcome in all three respects will be the result of interactive processes, and therefore necessarily different from any plans. To reinforce this point we can use three different terms to describe the different outcomes of the three major aspects of lessons, introduced above. These outcome terms are 'receptivity', 'practice opportunities', and 'input'.

2.3.2 Three outcomes of classroom language lessons

One way of looking at the outcomes of a lesson is to say that a lesson, as it unfolds, offers innumerable learning opportunities, some that more or less directly reflect the original planning, and others that arise out of the interaction itself. Each learning opportunity can be associated with a degree of receptivity, corresponding to the classroom atmosphere that accompanies it, although of course learners' perceptions of classroom atmosphere may vary, even within a single class.

Learning opportunities can also be seen as being describable in two different ways: as opportunities to *do* something with whatever one is trying to learn – 'practice opportunities'; or simply as opportunities to *encounter* what one is trying to learn – 'input opportunities'. Very often these two types of learning opportunities occur together, of course, but it may help to distinguish between them at this stage.

Whatever the teacher plans in terms of classroom atmosphere, as mentioned above, the end result can be better discussed in terms of the state of receptivity (or, negatively, of 'defensiveness') of the learners during the lesson. By receptivity we do not mean merely a passive acceptance; rather we mean an active openness, a willingness to encounter the language and the culture(s) it represents. As van Lier has pointed out (personal communication), receptivity as a psychological state is probably a range on a continuum of attitudes and purposeful behaviour, whose two poles could be labelled as 'reactive' and 'proactive' behaviour.

For teachers (and for classroom researchers as well), the question is whether the learners are receptive to the language and to the learning situation in general, or whether they are putting up defences against the learning we are trying to help them with. Whatever the answer, we can be certain that it is the result of virtually everything that happens in the class (and possibly outside it), and not just of the teacher's efforts to implement a specific plan concerning the most desirable classroom atmosphere. (These themes will be explored in more detail in Chapters 9 and 10.)

Similarly, the way the learners actually go about learning during the lesson is not simply a direct reflection of the teaching method the teacher employs, even though the method may be the most obvious influence. In the course of classroom interaction the learners get all sorts of practice opportunities. Many of these may arise incidentally, perhaps because of the questions learners ask or the errors they make (as we saw in the 'birthdays' example). Two sorts of practice opportunities arise in this way: opportunities to practise with bits of the language (saying them, writing them, listening to them being said, putting them into sentences, and so on), and opportunities to practise language learning techniques. This last is a rather neglected area but there is some research to suggest that we could usefully pay more attention to the opportunities learners get (or do not get) to develop as language learners, rather than just as repositories of more and more bits of a new language. In fact 'learner training', as it is called, is a developing field of considerable promise, aided by the recent publication of some 'learners' guides' to language study.

Finally there is the outcome that relates most clearly to the bits of the language that the teacher plans to teach – the syllabus. Here again it is not very difficult to see that, in the course of a lesson, all sorts of 'bits of the language', in addition to those the teacher actually planned to teach, might become 'available to be learned', especially if the lesson is actually conducted in the language under study. The best term for all such things seems to be 'input', and there are two basic types of input to consider. First, there are the 'bits of the language' already mentioned, and second, there are all the bits of information any attentive learner could get *about* the language, and about everybody's attempts to speak it, by listening to the teacher's explanations, for example, and the teacher's reactions to anything the other learners say. 'Guidance' seems the best word for these last 'bits of information'. Guidance can take the form of explanations, as when the teacher answers a learner's question about the language, or it can occur as feedback, when a learner makes a mistake (or gets something right) and the teacher reacts accordingly.

The three 'outcomes' just described (namely, learners' receptivity, their practice opportunities, and the input) refer to what actually happens in the classroom, regardless of whatever was planned to happen. For this reason we can expect them to relate closely to the actual learning that we hope also happens, more closely than the relatively remote concepts of the *planned* classroom atmosphere, method, or syllabus – concepts we have come traditionally to regard as central to our success or failure as teachers. Figure 1 depicts the dynamic interaction among these three aspects of language lessons and the various outcomes which may result.

PLANNED ASPECTS   THE LESSON   CO-PRODUCED OUTCOMES

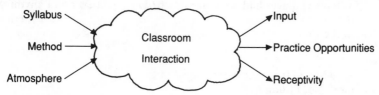

Figure 1   The relationship between plans and outcomes

2.3.3 Co-production of a classroom conversation

It is likely that every language teacher has had the experience of having something unexpected occur during a lesson. Whether it leads to a derailment of the lesson or a contribution to learning is often largely a matter of how the teacher reacts to the unexpected, and the extent to which the co-production is encouraged or stifled.

Given below is a portion of transcript from an ESL (English as a second language) lesson for a lower intermediate class of heterogeneous adult learners in California. The teacher and learners knew the class was being audio-recorded. Two stereo microphones had been suspended from the ceiling of the classroom, and one observer was present, functioning as the teacher's aide. There were nine people enrolled in the class (numbered S1 to S9 in the transcript, for the sake of confidentiality), but on this particular evening, S4 was absent. The planned lesson had been about the English present perfect, with learners supplying the auxiliary *have* or *has* and the correct participle of the verb given in isolated, sequential sentences listed in the textbook.

After the lesson had begun, one learner entered the classroom late and somewhat flustered. She announced that her husband's car had been broken into and she did not know yet what had been stolen. The teacher and her classmates expressed their surprise and their sympathy, and then the class talked about car robberies for a few minutes.

We begin the transcript at the point where the teacher took up the topic of stealing, temporarily abandoning the textbook lesson. In the transcript, brackets indicate the observer's commentary, while parentheses indicate a possible, though uncertain, transcription. The letter 'T' represents the teacher and 'A' the aide, while 'FS' stands for the voice of any unidentified female student. (In British and American classrooms, the word 'student' does not carry the connotation of a young learner.) Indentations indicate partially overlapping turns, and curly brackets in the left margin indicate turns which overlapped completely. A dash at the beginning of a line, preceding the speaker symbol (for example, –T), indicates the completion of a continuing utterance which has been interrupted or overlapped. An 'xx' indicates unintelligible speech.

Why focus on the classroom?

Transcript 1: Have you ever had anything stolen?

T: But have you ever had anything stolen? Have you ever had anything stolen?

S9: Here in the United States?

T: Yeah.

S9: No.

T: I– whe– where? Have you ever though? In

S9: In France? No, I (didn't).

T: No? Never? Nothing. You're lucky.

⎰S3: What about you?

⎱S9: (I have nothing to, to take.)

T: Mhm.

S3: What a– what about you?

T: xx   Yes, this summer. (Very), I had four robberies.

FS: xx here, in Los Angeles?

FS: Four?

S3: You had good luck. You had good luck. [Laughing]

T: Yeah, (four). They, they, within a month, they

FS: xx

–T: took my bicycle, they took a tape-recorder out of my car, they broke into my house and stole all my money, checks and IDs, and then I went to the beach and they

FS: Wow.

–T: stole my knapsack.

FS: xx

FS: Oooh!

T: A knapsack, it's, it's a bag for putting books in

FS: xx

–T: that you can put on your back.

S3:   Yeah.

FS: Oh, ah.

S9: Oh, people in the laboratory where my husband w– w– works, to me, no (he's) there is no trouble, and we have never xx nothing like that.

T: (Oh.)

T: Lock your house. Lock your car. [One student laughs.]

S9: Oh.

T: Who else? Have you ever had anything stolen?

Ss: No.

T: No?

S3: I just lost a lot of things. [One or two students talking.]

T: Oh, you lose it. You don't need to have anything stolen. [T and S3 laugh.]

FS: xx stolen.

S3: Stolen.

T: Oh yeah! [S8's name said twice] had a robbery just recently.

S3:   xx
     [One student laughs.]

T: Right? What did they take?

S8: They took a branches, uh, a (gold)

T: xx

26

S3: xx
T: A pin?
S8: Uh, not pin. A xx [French?]
S3: xx
A: Brooch.
T: Brooch?
S8: Oh yes, brooch.
T: Brooch? xx
(T):   That's a type of pin? Yeah.
S8: A brooch and, uh, a camera and television.
S3: xx [Laughs, along with T and other Ss.]
S8: xx
FS: xx
⎧ T: xx
⎩S8: I had a robbery in Iran, too. They [Class laughs.]
S3:   No!
S8: They took my television. [Laughs. Some general murmuring and laughter.]
T: Again.
S8: And uh, yes, my husband   a raincoat and a xx
S3:   (The husband) [Laughing.]
Ss: [Loud laughter.]
T: His raincoat?
S3: xx to your husband.
T: Oh my goodness.
S8: And the, shaver.
T: A shaver?
FS: (Shaver.)
S8: xx
T: Uh, an electric shaver.
S8:   Electric (shaver).
T: Electric shaver. Huh.
   Maybe the, the, the thief was a, visitor in town, tourist or something (and
   he wanted) stuff for travelling. That's really strange. Who else has had
   something stolen? (What about) [S5's name]? No?
FS: xx
T: Yeah.
S7: xx it was not mine, but, uh, in Italy, we xx something in the, back seat?
T: Mhm.
S7:   And (they), they took it.
T: [S6's name]? [said with rising intonation.]
⎧S6: Never.
⎩ T: Never?
S6: Never.
T: You're very lucky, very lucky ...

Transcript 1 is a portion of the data used by Allwright in his (1980) study of turns, topics and tasks in language classrooms.

Several interesting things occur in this brief segment of a lesson. Specifically, we can see an example of the lesson foreordained by the syllabus and the textbook (the English present perfect) giving way to a new topic, having things stolen. The unexpected topic was introduced by a student, whose reaction to being robbed provided the class with a lively topic for conversation. In the process, the practice opportunities shifted away from the planned focus on the grammatical structure (although the teacher still uses the present perfect in her questions to the learners). In this co-produced classroom conversation, the learners have opportunities to practise taking turns while listening to and answering questions about information previously unknown to the group. (We will return to the continuation of this lesson at the end of Chapter 3.)

2.4 Summary

We have looked at how the classroom, or rather what happens in the classroom, is crucial to language learning because what happens determines what learning opportunities learners get. We have seen how teachers and learners together manage the classroom interaction and at the same time manage these learning opportunities. In the process plans give way to reality. Learners do not learn directly from the syllabus. They learn, partly, from whatever becomes of the syllabus in the classroom, but they can learn from other things that happen too. Finally, we have argued that whatever actually happens in language lessons can best be described in terms of three outcomes: the 'input' provided for learning, the 'practice opportunities' provided, and the effects on the 'receptivity' of the learners.

If we are right in thinking that such outcomes are the things that really matter, then we can be equally certain that if we want to understand them better (and how else are we, as teachers, going to learn to do our jobs better?), then we must study the processes that are responsible for what happens in our classrooms. One goal of this book, then, is to present what we have learned so far from studying language classroom processes, to see how far we can draw any useful practical conclusions from the years of language classroom research, and to see how teachers themselves can use the techniques of classroom research to explore what is going on in their own classrooms.

The developments discussed in Chapter 1 and the concerns summarised in Chapter 2 have brought us to a state of considerable diversity and healthy controversy. In our present state, unresolved (and perhaps unresolvable) methodological issues are a key concern (but hardly a major worry, except for those with a very low tolerance for uncertainty in their lives, who still expect quick and easy answers to all questions). It is to these methodological issues that we now turn, to end this introduction to the field of classroom research, and to lead into the concerns of the remainder of the book.

But first, there are some *Discussion starters* you may find helpful, especially if you are able to work with a few other people, and some more *Suggestions for further reading*. There is also another *Mini-project* that should help you develop your understanding of the points made in this chapter.

DISCUSSION STARTERS

1 Do you find it easy to accept the view that language lessons are 'co-productions', in the sense suggested in this chapter? Why or why not? Can you think of an example from your own experience, either as a teacher or as a learner?
2 Can you find examples, from your experience, of the five aspects of the management of interaction described in section 2.2? They are listed below to refresh your memory:
   a) Who gets to speak? (participants' turn distribution)
   b) What do they talk about? (topic)
   c) What does each participant do with the various opportunities to speak? (task)
   d) What sort of atmosphere is created? (tone)
   e) What accent, dialect, or language is used? (code)
   If you are working in a group, compare your examples with those of your colleagues or classmates.
3 Think of a class (in which you were a student, a teacher or an observer) where a sudden change of atmosphere occurred. What brought it about? Who creates atmosphere? How does it happen?
4 Look over Flanders' categories in Appendix A. Given his orientation, which do you find preferable – a direct or an indirect approach to the management of interaction in the language classroom? Why? Are there times when one or the other would be more appropriate?
5 Can you think of striking examples from your own teaching (or learning) of how the management of interaction in the classroom can affect learners' opportunities for learning, and in so doing contribute to the management of learning itself?
6 Have you taught, or been taught, in a situation where learners came to the classroom with strong views on what should be taught, how, and in what sort of classroom atmosphere? Was it a help or a hindrance to the work of the class? Why?
7 It is very important in our thinking that what *happens* to plans when they get inside the classroom is more significant than the plans themselves, because it is what happens inside the classroom that determines the learning opportunities each learner gets. We are not against planning, though. Where do you stand? Can classroom

interaction be planned without reducing the lesson to a sort of play reading? Do you have any specific ideas about what can and cannot usefully be planned in advance?

SUGGESTIONS FOR FURTHER READING

1 Stevick's work (mentioned in section 2.3 as having influenced teachers' and researchers' thinking about atmosphere) is very readable and readily available. Three of his best known books are *Memory, meaning and method* (1976), *Teaching languages: a way and ways* (1980), and *Teaching and learning languages* (1982).

2 Materials are among the things teachers bring with them to the language classroom. For two contrasting but not incompatible perspectives on the types of materials needed and the roles materials play in language teaching, see Allwright (1981) and O'Neill (1982).

3 Littlejohn (1983) has written an article entitled 'Increasing learner involvement in course management'. It describes his experiences in working with a group of Arabic-speaking adults learning English as a foreign language. The learners were given major responsibilities for developing tasks, locating materials, correcting errors, and setting class rules.

4 Long (1983a) has conducted a review of the research literature to answer the question, 'Does second language instruction make a difference?' (This is also the title of the article.) We are pleased to say that his tentative answer is 'yes', but you may enjoy reading his findings for yourself.

5 If you are interested in seeing some learners' guides, you could consult Rubin and Thompson (1982), Dickinson (1987), Wenden and Rubin (1987), Ellis and Sinclair (1989), or Brown (1989).

6 Allwright's (1988b) paper, 'Autonomy and individualization in whole-class instruction', describes how what learners do in class effectively makes each lesson a different lesson for each learner. The paper ends with a suggested activity for teachers to work through, by looking in detail at a transcribed extract from a language lesson.

7 In a diary study, Bailey (1980:60–1) has described a very tense situation in a French classroom following what the learners considered to be an unfair test. The journal entry shows the role learners may play in directing the course of a lesson, and indeed, in resolving serious classroom problems.

MINI-PROJECT: PLANNED ASPECTS AND CO-PRODUCED OUTCOMES

In this chapter we considered three planned aspects of classroom language learning and their concomitant outcomes (see Figure 1). Do the relationships depicted in Figure 1 make sense to you? This Mini-project is designed to help you examine these relationships more closely.

Think back on your own experience (if you have some) as a language teacher. You could also consider your history as a language learner. In your opinion, to what extent do students' attitudes and behaviours influence the planned aspects of lessons in generating the co-produced outcomes? To what extent are these variables under the teacher's control? Does your answer differ from one language class to another? Do you think the answer would differ depending on the culture (or cultures) of the learners being taught?

Given this backdrop, it could be constructive to check out these hypothesised relationships by observing a class. You should begin by getting permission from a language teacher to visit a class for one lesson.

During the lesson, focus your attention on just one or two learners, to see if you can see the lesson from their point of view. Pick out for special attention one or two people who seem to be taking a very active part in the lesson. Watch what happens when one of the active learners says something. Ask yourself the following questions:

1 Does the learner's utterance change the input? Does it, for instance, cause the teacher to focus, even if only for a moment or two, on a point that was not in the original lesson plan?
2 Does it change the practice opportunities? Does what one learner says make a difference to the skills the other learners get to practise, for example?
3 Does the learner's comment or question change the atmosphere? Does the learner's contribution affect the tone of the lesson? Does it make it more light-hearted, or perhaps more business-like? Does it seem likely to encourage others to pay more attention to what is going on, or to lead them to believe that there is no point in bothering with the lesson any more?

Use these questions to help you form a learner's view of the lesson, and then write a description of the lesson from that perspective. Try to sum up the observation in terms of the input that actually became available during the course of the lesson, in terms of the sorts of practice learners actually got involved in, and in terms of the class-room atmosphere that actually developed. Then, and only then, ask the teacher for his or her opinions about the lesson, so that you can compare your picture with the teacher's original intentions. Here are some questions you could ask the teacher to elicit his or her ideas about the class you observed:

Why focus on the classroom?

1 What did the syllabus say about this lesson? What specifically did you plan to cover in this class?
2 What method(s) did you plan to use? How did the choice of method influence your choice of activities at the technique level?
3 What type of atmosphere did you hope to create in this class?

With the teacher's permission, you could also ask the students about their view of the lesson. For example, you could ask the learners themselves to describe the atmosphere of the class.

Finally, it would be interesting to see if your interpretation of the events, as an observer, differed from that of the teacher (or the learners). Here are some questions you could consider in developing such a comparison:

1 What sort of input did the students receive in this lesson? How much of the input that actually occurred was a result of pre-planned decisions and how much was spontaneously generated as the lesson progressed?
2 What sort of learning opportunities occurred? Which ones (and what proportion) were structured by the teacher and which did the students negotiate? Which were opportunities to encounter the input for the first time, and which were practice opportunities?
3 What observable signs of receptivity did you see among the learners? How, in your opinion, was this receptivity (or defensiveness, if that's what you witnessed) influenced by the teacher's plans for the class atmosphere and subsequent behaviour during the lesson? How much of it was a product of the learners' personalities and interaction styles?

When you have made your comparison, turn back to Figure 1 to see if your observations confirm our analysis that what actually happens in language classrooms is best seen not as the simple product of the teacher's plans, but as the complex product of the interaction among the people in the classroom.

If, on the other hand, you do in fact find what looks like a very simple direct relationship between the teacher's plans and the resulting input, the practice opportunities, and the receptivity aspects of the lesson, consider whether or not this is the best possible state of affairs for language learning.

Of course, if you are currently teaching a language class, you could modify this activity to involve an investigation of one of your own lessons. When you are planning the lesson, decide specifically what you hope to accomplish in terms of the input, the practice opportunities, and the atmosphere of the classroom. Make some written notes to yourself about your goals. Then tape-record the ensuing lesson, and after the lesson, listen to the tape to see to what extent you achieved your goals. Where the lesson did not go exactly as planned, what accounts for the modifications? What role did the learners play in co-producing the outcomes? Were you, as the teacher, able to be flexible when the learners' behaviours weren't exactly what you expected? And finally, to what extent do you view the unexpected parts of the lesson as irrelevancies, temporary derailments of the lesson plan, or interesting new developments which generated unpredicted opportunities for learning?

Part II Classroom research: principles and procedures

Before we start looking in detail at what research has so far revealed about classroom processes and about how we can best investigate them, we should take a little time to think about some of the decisions that must be made by anyone doing classroom investigations. These are decisions that will become important in the following chapters as we describe research projects and their findings. They will come up again in the *Discussion starters* and suggestions for practical activities at the end of each chapter. Readers who work their way through all these should end up well able not only to read published research reports critically, but also to design and carry out their own classroom investigations. We hope that by raising such matters systematically throughout this book we will be able to offer the reader a practical introduction to classroom research.

In the two chapters included in this part of the book, we will be dealing with both philosophical issues and practical concerns. These are matters that can get very technical, but we have concentrated on trying to give the reader a sense of what it means to get involved in classroom investigations. For readers who wish to delve into these problems in more detail, key citations are given in the *Suggestions for further reading* at the end of each chapter.

If you are in a hurry to get to the chapters that talk about findings, then you may wish to go straight on to Part III, but we hope that if you do, you will come back to this section later. In any case, you may find you need to have read it to make the most sense of the findings as we gradually unfold them in the chapters that follow. And certainly these methodological issues will concern you when you begin to do your own original classroom research.

3 Getting started – the question of approach

In this chapter we will deal with the background issues and the first steps to be taken by anyone conducting language classroom research. We will first look at the decision of what to investigate and whether to take a theory-driven or a data-driven stance with regard to this question. Then we will discuss three important approaches to language classroom research: experimental studies, naturalistic enquiry, and action research. Finally, we will consider three key standards in research (reliability, validity, and generalisability), and then look briefly at the issue of generalisability in the three approaches to research.

3.1 How do you decide what to investigate?

If you are interested in exploring what's going on in a language classroom, how do you decide what particular issue to focus on? If you are a teacher-in-training and are not yet working with a group of learners, it may be most sensible to start by reading reports of earlier classroom research. Reading these studies (many of which are summarised in the remainder of this book) should give you ideas about how to replicate those that interest you. In doing so, it is perfectly acceptable to utilise research plans, questionnaires or observation instruments from published documents to conduct your own research, provided you give credit to the original authors. Furthermore, replication of existing studies is an important way in which research progresses: it is part of the refinement process.

Direct replication is very rarely possible, however, if only because each project must try to learn from earlier mistakes. For this reason, it is usually more appropriate, in our field, to talk of 'follow-up studies' rather than of exact 'replications'. For example, Day (1984) followed up on Seliger's study of interaction patterns among ESL learners (Seliger 1977, 1983a) using refined procedures with learners from different cultural groups. Day obtained very different results from Seliger. His findings thus help us to be more cautious in our interpretation of Seliger's results. (These two studies will be discussed in more detail in section 7.4.)

If you have access to a class you can observe, or if you are an in-service teacher with your own classroom, then watching language learners can be a rich source of ideas for investigation. Be alert for interactions that intrigue you, and for apparently puzzling behaviours that may arise. If you notice any patterns, or any anomalies, in the currents of classroom discourse, these can suggest interesting topics for research. On a practical level, then, you can either decide what to investigate on the basis of previous research and/or theory, or you can start from your own observations.

On a more philosophical level, there is a dynamic tension between these two opposing points of view on how to determine the topic of an investigation. The first position, which is associated with experimental science, holds that a researcher should decide in advance what to investigate, on the basis of predictions generated by theory. A formal hypothesis or research question is posed at the outset of the study, and the processes of data collection and analysis are planned specifically to test the hypothesis or answer the research question. In the second view, that more commonly associated with ethnography, the research questions and hypotheses arise from the data that are collected.

Watson-Gegeo (1988:584, using categories from Hymes 1982) has described three stages in this ethnographic sequence:
1 the comprehensive stage, in which the ethnographer collects all potentially pertinent data;
2 the topic-oriented stage, in which the research topic is narrowed via focused observations; and
3 the hypothesis-oriented stage, in which hypotheses are tested and research questions answered, through in-depth interviews, more focused observations, discourse analysis, etc.

This data-first approach is valuable in developing 'grounded theory' (Glaser and Strauss 1967) – that is, theory which stems from data rather than from logic alone. (See Watson-Gegeo 1988 for further discussion of this point.)

Some theorists would argue that *any* hypotheses or research questions, by definition, ought to come directly from a theory which makes predictions that can be empirically tested by some sort of classroom investigation. The theory thus provides the rationale for deciding what to measure or observe. This position, which is derived from the theory-first procedures of the 'scientific method', assumes that the main point of research is to test theories by finding out if the theory correctly predicts what actually happens. For example, if a theory predicts that language learners will learn better when their errors are corrected immediately, then research should test this prediction to see if it holds. If the results do not bear out the prediction, then it is possible that the theory is wrong, or at least that it needs modification, as long as the research findings cannot be shown to have been unduly influenced by problems in the study's design or data analysis. So, for instance, if we found that immediate error correction did not give good results in our particular study, the theorist could perhaps defend the theory by arguing it had not been properly interpreted in practice – if, for example, the immediate error treatment had been handled in a humorous and light-hearted way that might have affected the learners' ability to concentrate. Failure to control this aspect of the teacher's behaviour in the study would be considered a design problem.

While the theory-first position is often a reasonable source of research ideas, there are two problems with this way of looking at where research questions come from. First, the theories of language learning which our field has developed to date do not always lend themselves to making directly testable predictions. For instance, Krashen's idea that language acquisition is an unconscious process has been criticised by McLaughlin (1978) and Gregg (1984) as being untestable in the classic experimental tradition. It is 'untestable', in part, because in practice we cannot operationalise non-conscious learning. That is, we cannot define 'unconscious process' in such a way that we can cause one group of learners to learn a language (or portions thereof) unconsciously and then compare them with another group of similar learners who have consciously learned the same bits of language. Thus, the prediction made by the theory cannot be tested.

Furthermore, some researchers (for example, van Lier 1988) feel that classroom lessons are such complex affairs that it is virtually impossible ever to control the number of different variables that could bias the results of any attempts to test a particular theory-driven prediction. For these reasons, among others, the classic experimental design procedures may not be as useful in classroom research as they have been in other fields of scientific enquiry. For example, we used to think that if a theory predicted that a new method would be more successful than an old one, then we should be able to test that prediction by running an experiment comparing the two methods in practice. That, as we saw in Chapter 1 (section 1.4), simply did not work and we had to think again about the whole issue of what sort of research made sense in our field.

The second problem with putting theory first is that it misses the point that theories themselves have to come from somewhere. In the field of language teaching it is common for classroom experience to suggest issues for research and this research helps build up a theoretical position. From this point of view, new research does not *test* theories so much as it illuminates the field and therefore helps to *develop* emerging theories.

But classroom research does not always have to concern itself so directly with theories at all, whether to test them or to illuminate them. Instead, classroom research can be directed at trying to understand and deal with the immediate practical problems facing teachers and learners. Any thoughtful teacher will be curious about what is going on in the

37

classroom – why treating errors seems to be ineffective, perhaps, or why some learners never want to join in, or why some join in but never seem to learn much anyway. Such problems can provide the starting point for some highly specific classroom exploration. The term for this sort of work, aimed as it is at investigating and dealing with immediate practical problems, is 'action research'. (We will return to this concept in section 3.2.3.)

This highly practical approach is clearly the first to consider when you come to selecting from the Mini-projects and Major projects we will recommend after each of the following chapters. If you can find one that corresponds to an immediate practical problem facing you, then that will be an obvious one to choose. Of course, it is perfectly possible, even quite likely, that dealing with an immediate practical problem will generate all sorts of ideas that may illuminate the field and help us develop a better theoretical understanding of classroom language learning and teaching, but that does not have to be the reason for doing the action research in the first place.

Whether you begin from the data-first or the theory-first position, it is important to have a specific issue in mind, a particular problem to think about, because there is a strong risk of wasting a lot of your own and everyone else's time if you begin a research project with no clear idea of what you are going to do. As an example, after keeping a journal of her experiences in a college French class, one of the authors (Kathi Bailey) decided she would use the journal entries as data to examine the issue of error treatment from the learner's perspective. After outlining a paper on this topic, she began searching through the data, only to find that there were basically no references to error treatment in her diary. Even though this topic had fascinated her as a researcher, error treatment apparently had not been important enough to her as a language learner to be recorded in the journal entries. What she found instead were numerous references to competitiveness and anxiety (Bailey 1983a), a topic that arose from the data rather than from any preconceived hypothesis or theory of classroom language learning. This topic turned out to be a productive focus in itself, but a certain amount of frustration arose and time was lost in the search for the learner's reactions to error treatment – a topic for which there were no pertinent data in the journal.

The point may seem obvious but there is often a temptation for novice researchers to collect the data first (just because it looks as if it would be interesting to do so) and ask the questions later. The data-first sequence can work out well, but sometimes the questions that come to mind later on cannot really be properly explored with the original data, so you have to start again to collect truly relevant information. Of course, even if you start out with a specific research question you are likely to find yourself modifying it as you go along, refining and reformulating it progressively, and even raising new questions, as you become more familiar with the situation you are investigating.

Given these opposing viewpoints on the research sequence (data-first versus theory-first), it would probably be best for you, as a new classroom researcher, to start off with at least a general issue you want to investigate, and to use your thinking about that issue to help you to decide what sorts of data you will need. Of course, the more precise your original question, the more specifically it will guide your collection of data. (For example, if you want to find out about a teacher's use of gestures during a lesson you'll probably need a videotape-recorder, but if you want to study learners' pronunciation, an audiotape will suffice, as long as the microphone is placed properly to pick up all their voices.) You should expect to continue refining your issue as you go along, but you also need to stay alive to the possibility that in the process of collecting and studying your data, new research questions will emerge that may point you in some quite new direction.

Another aspect of the decision about what to investigate is the understandable temptation to look at the most visible things only, the things that are easiest to observe, to record, and to count. It is relatively easy to determine the number of different people who speak to the teacher during a lesson, for example, and extremely difficult, perhaps impossible in principle even, to detect all the occasions when each person is attending to the lesson. And yet how well learners are attending to what is going on may be much more important than how often they speak to the teacher. This problem is especially a dilemma for researchers who prefer to work with numerical data, since they risk being seduced by the potentially trivial things which are relatively easy to count or measure. This temptation may go a long way towards explaining the relative wealth of classroom studies dealing with turn taking and with teacher speech (see Chapters 7 and 8), compared with the relative dearth of studies dealing with learner speech, which is much more difficult to record satisfactorily, or with learners' receptivity, which is much more difficult to observe and measure in any reliable way (see Chapters 9 and 10).

Two problems arise in this area of deciding what to investigate. First, the overall picture we have of classroom language learning from research so far is already distorted by this bias towards the visible. We only know about what we have looked at, and what we have looked at over the last two decades consists largely of whatever has been easiest to observe. Second, this bias towards the easy things to investigate is a luxury that action researchers at least cannot usually afford – not if they are going to address immediate practical problems.

3.2 **The problem of approach**

When you have decided on an issue to investigate, what next? We have already suggested that any one problem is likely to call for a variety of factors to be investigated, and we now need to face the probability that no one person could cope with all the problems that are likely to arise. This likelihood obviously suggests teamwork, and teamwork offers the possibility of covering a number of different perspectives. In this way, for instance, an investigation might be able to cover both the linguistic and the sociological approaches mentioned earlier (section 1.5), instead of having to choose between them.

If you are unable to work with a team, then your choice of approach will probably depend on your personal preferences, but it is important to remember that, to a large extent, your approach will determine your findings. The approach you adopt really needs to be based on a well-informed opinion about what is most likely to contribute to the sort of understanding you want of the issue you are investigating. For instance, if you adopt a linguistic approach to something that is essentially a sociological problem, then you will get a linguistic answer, but it probably will not be very helpful. If, for example, you study the verbal expressions a teacher uses to encourage learners to speak during lessons, but fail to take into account the cultural mix of the class members, you may discover that some expressions seem more effective than others, although what is really going on might have very little to do with the actual language used and much more to do with culture-specific rules about speaking out or not speaking out in a group.

You will recall from Chapters 1 and 2 that the field of language classroom research is defined primarily by its setting. The classroom provides the focal point for the types of data collected. However, as noted in Chapter 1, a wide variety of approaches are used to obtain and analyse the data, and the choice of approach depends upon many factors – the researcher's philosophy, the issue to be investigated, the constraints inherent in the situation, etc. Broadly speaking, however, the problem of approach can be addressed in terms of potentially opposing viewpoints on how research should be conducted. The differences between these perspectives hinge primarily on differing attitudes towards intervention and control. In 'experimental studies', the researcher exerts a high degree of control and purposefully intervenes in the setting, to determine the effect of the intervention. In 'naturalistic enquiry', the researcher tries not to intervene in the research setting and does not try to control naturally occurring events. In yet another approach, that of 'action research', there is typically direct intervention with only limited possibilities for control. We will briefly consider each of these approaches before moving on to other specific issues in data collection and analysis.

3.2.1 Experimental studies: intervention and control

In the context of experimental research, 'intervention' is by no means a negative thing. Instead, it is simply a technical term which refers to the 'treatment' administered to some subjects (the 'experimental group') in order to test a hypothesis about a cause-and-effect relationship. This treatment is withheld from other subjects in the study (typically called the 'control group'). If the researchers are careful in setting up the study, these two groups can be presumed to be virtually identical in all respects, except that one gets the treatment (a new teaching method or set of materials or a particular type of feedback, for example), and the other does not. After the treatment has been implemented, a test of some sort is usually administered to both groups and their results are compared. Then various mathematical procedures are used to determine whether or not there are statistically significant differences in the test scores of the two groups. From the results, the paradigm claims, we can infer that the treatment either did or did not cause a measurable change in behaviour or learning (the hypothesised effect).

This model of experimental science has been applied to language classroom research with varying degrees of success. For example, (as we saw in section 1.4) the Pennsylvania Project (Smith 1970), Scherer and Wertheimer's (1964) study in Colorado, and the GUME Project in Sweden (Lindblad 1969; Von Elek and Oskarsson 1973) all used control and experimental groups to test their hypotheses about the effects of implementing a particular methodological treatment (the intervention) in language teaching. However, none of these studies demonstrated very clear superiority for any one method. The use of the experimental method should not itself be blamed for such inconclusive results, of course, since they could represent the true state of affairs (that is, perhaps 'method' is not an important variable). Critiques of these studies (see Clark 1969, and Allwright 1972), however, have brought out the enormous difficulties involved in implementing the experimental method satisfactorily in the natural setting of public education. These critics have also argued that given these difficulties, it would not be safe to assume that the results obtained were valid.

3.2.2 Naturalistic enquiry: seeing what happens

In contrast with those who espouse the experimental method (and in some cases as a result of its apparent inapplicability in the classroom setting), other classroom researchers have taken a non-interventionist stance. They have purposefully tried *not* to influence the normally occurring patterns of instruction and interaction, because they wished to describe and understand these processes rather than to test specific hypotheses about cause-and-effect relationships. This mode of research is often referred to as 'naturalistic enquiry'. While it may include comparison groups and can involve the collection of both quantitative and qualitative data (see section 4.3), it does not use the experimental concept of a 'treatment'. Nor does the researcher create special groups for the purposes of experimentation or observation. Instead, naturally occurring groups become the focal point (Watson-Gegeo 1988). For this reason, regularly scheduled classes are likely sites in which to use the naturalistic enquiry approach.

Experimental research and naturalistic enquiry can be viewed as contrasting poles on a continuum of research intervention. Relatively few 'true experimental designs' have been carried out in classroom research on language teaching and learning, partly because of this desire to understand what goes on in naturally occurring classes, but also partly because we have discovered, over the years, that it is virtually impossible to control all the factors that should be controlled in order to replicate the laboratory conditions called for by experimental research. (Many observational classroom studies can be classified as non-interventionist by design, and several of these will be discussed throughout this book.) Figure 2 (opposite) illustrates these relationships and demonstrates the variety of approaches available to researchers, depending on whether they are interested in 1) measuring, 2) controlling, 3) watching, or 4) asking and doing.

3.2.3 Action research: intervention and observation

Whereas experimental research involves intervention and a high degree of control over variables, and naturalistic enquiry is typically non-interventionist and non-controlling, another approach, that of 'action research', involves an intervention but a low degree of exerted control. Although it can take many forms, action research in classrooms basically involves taking an action and systematically observing what follows. So, for example, if a language teacher in a large class wanted to encourage more learner interaction in the language under study, it would be possible to implement small-group tasks and observe the apparent results. Will the learners resort to their mother tongue, or will they actually use the language under study to accomplish the assigned tasks? A carefully controlled experimental design is not needed to answer this question in a local context.

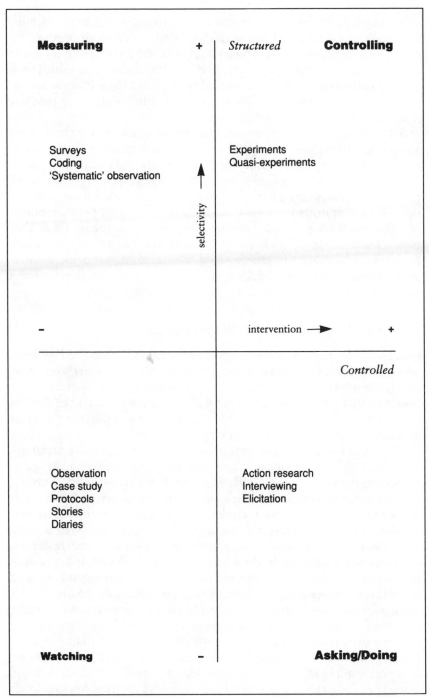

Figure 2   Types of research (van Lier 1988:57)

Action research has been defined as 'a form of self-reflective enquiry undertaken by participants in social situations in order to improve the rationality and justice of their own social or educational practices, as well as their understanding of these practices and the situations in which these practices are carried out' (Kemmis and Henry 1989:2). It is characterised as being a participatory, self-reflective and collaborative approach to research.

Action research in classrooms follows a series of repeated steps. Strickland (1988:760) discusses the following sequence: 1) identify an issue, interest or problem; 2) seek knowledge; 3) plan an action; 4) implement the action; 5) observe the action; 6) reflect on your observations; and 7) revise the plan. The cycle then begins once more, with the revisions incorporated in a new action, which is itself observed, and so on. This process allows teachers who wish to investigate events in their own classrooms to take constructive steps towards solving immediate problems, systematically reflecting on the outcome. Thus the goals of action research are achieving local understanding and developing viable solutions to problems.

3.2.4 Combined approaches to research planning

Of course, very few studies can be confidently characterised as being purely experimental (+ structured, + controlled, in van Lier's terms) or purely naturalistic (− structured, − controlled). In fact, in recent years observational procedures from naturalistic enquiry have been used to document the process variables involved in implementing the treatment in product-oriented experimental research.

The process–product distinction is familiar in general educational research, but it has been discussed most frequently in second language classroom research by Long (1980a, 1984). In a pure 'product study' the researcher focuses on comparing learning outcomes, often in the form of test scores (the outputs from the classroom mentioned in section 1.1), usually from two or more classes, without documenting what actually went on in the classrooms. In a pure 'process study' the researcher describes what went on in the classrooms, by collecting and analysing interaction-based data, but does not document the learning outcomes. In a 'process–product study' the researcher tries specifically to describe the classroom processes and relate them to the documented learning outcomes.

While there are not many process–product studies available yet in the language classroom research literature, some have been attempted. For instance, Bailey *et al.* (1990) reported on methodological research comparing language test scores of students who received Suggestopedic instruction (the experimental group) with those taught via a more traditional method (the control group). This study was conducted with students of Russian as a foreign language. While the research project was clearly designed as an experiment with an intervention (Suggestopedia), it used classroom observers to document the instructional processes (particularly the method variables and the teacher variables) in the control and experimental groups.

Not surprisingly, the observers found that the use of the two different teaching methods led to two different sets of emphases in the classroom. In the traditional classes, error treatment was constant across all activities, the teachers stressed accuracy, and the activities themselves were largely non-interactive. In the experimental classes, instructional goals encompassed both fluency and accuracy, error treatment was selective, and the activities were predominantly interactive. What was surprising, however, is that although there were some clear-cut methodological differences, the observers noted strong similarities in teacher style (for example, in turn distribution and use of humour) which cut across the methods (Bailey 1986).

The observational component of the process–product study also helped to explain the test results. The learners in the control group outscored those in the experimental groups on tests of listening and reading, but based on the classroom observations, the researchers suggested (Bailey *et al.* 1990) that these tests were more appropriate for measuring the types of skills practised in the control group classes than in the Suggestopedia classes. This point raises the issue of carefully selecting fair post-course measures in product studies or process–product studies (Beretta 1986).

While there are as yet relatively few examples of this combined approach, the report by Bailey *et al.* (1990) demonstrates that it is not only possible but also valuable to combine procedures of naturalistic enquiry and experimental research, if experimental results are to be interpretable. Furthermore, it is becoming increasingly clear in general educational research (though research on language teaching and learning has lagged behind somewhat in this area) that action research is often a viable alternative, and one which offers immediate rewards to teachers and learners. Having considered these three approaches and the possibility of combining elements of them, we turn now to questions of quality control – that is, to the criteria by which we assess the value of various kinds of classroom research.

3.3 Reliability, validity, and generalisability

In any discipline, concerns for quality control are characteristic of an emerging or established sense of professionalism, and the field of

c

language classroom research is no exception. As a profession, we have borrowed three standards from experimental research – sometimes comfortably, sometimes less so. The labels given to these standards are 'reliability', 'validity' and 'generalisability'. Since you are very likely to encounter these concepts as you read classroom research reports, and since their technical use varies somewhat from their lay meanings, we will spend some time here explaining and illustrating their importance.

3.3.1 Reliability: the concern for consistency

If you investigate classes using an observation instrument, or if you count linguistic structures in transcripts, or code incidences of behaviour in field notes, it is important to know that your observational system, or your determination of the structures to be counted, or your coding categories do not change from one day to the next. That is, the research procedures must be consistent, both over time and across the variety of people who might use them. The technical term for this desired consistency is 'reliability'. It applies to both the data collection and data analysis phases of classroom research.

One area of obvious concern about reliability is in situations where more than one observer is involved in trying to count or code the same things. Clearly if the observers do not agree with each other (if one finds that the teacher corrects ninety per cent of the errors and the other puts it only at seventy per cent, for example), then their findings are not reliable, and therefore not usable. Given these discrepancies, we cannot tell if the first observer was nearer the mark, or the second. In fact, they could both be off somewhat.

The degree of reliability between observers can in fact be calculated, and of course steps can be taken to train observers to improve their 'inter-observer agreement' figures. In general, before going ahead with the coding of a large corpus of data, classroom researchers strive for at least eighty-five per cent agreement among observers or raters. This figure is called 'inter-observer agreement' or 'inter-rater reliability'. It typically represents the consistency with which different members of a research team use a category system to code, or a rating system to evaluate, the same set of data. The percentage is sometimes derived by taking the number of agreed-upon cases that have been coded and dividing it by the total number of cases coded. Another matter for concern is the percentage of 'intra-observer agreement' – that is, the extent to which a single observer or coder, working with the same data, codes or categorises the data consistently after a lapse of time.

The following quote details the procedures used to determine inter-coder agreement by researchers at the University of Hawaii in coding transcripts of classroom data:

Four pages of two transcripts were coded according to the guidelines by three coders who reached consensus on the codes. Three- to four-page segments of four additional transcripts were coded separately by two of these coders until 90% agreement was reached, and the remaining differences were used to establish modifications and clarifications of the guidelines and a standard set of codes for the entire set of training transcripts. The first two transcripts were then discussed in a group with all the coders to assure understanding of the guidelines.

Each coder then independently coded one segment of a transcript at a time, until 85% agreement with the standard codes was reached on a given training transcript. After reaching this criterion of reliability, and discussion of the remaining differences in coding, each coder proceeded to code, to the extent possible, the classroom transcripts that he or she had transcribed. (Chaudron 1988a:24)

While this procedure may sound somewhat technical, the description does give a sense of how classroom researchers systematically try to achieve acceptable levels of reliability before analysing their data.

Sometimes intra- and inter-observer reliability figures are reported as a correlation coefficient. (See Brown 1988:126–46 for information on how to calculate this statistic.) These figures range from 0 to 1.00, with decimals nearer to 1.00 representing greater consistency in the observers' use of the categories. For example, in Seliger's turn-taking study previously mentioned (1983a:254), the inter-observer reliability indices ranged from a low of .917 to a high of .984, which means that the various observers were using the category system very consistently. In studies where two or more observers collect or analyse the data, it is important to look for some indication of their consistency.

3.3.2 Validity: the concern for truth

A related concern, especially in experimental research, is the issue of validity. When researchers talk about validity they give special meanings to the term.

As a technical construct in experimental studies, validity takes two important forms. First, there is the notion of 'internal validity'. A study is said to have internal validity if the outcomes of the experiment can be directly and unambiguously attributed to the treatment applied to the experimental group, rather than to uncontrolled factors. For example, in section 3.2.1, we reported on the 'failure' of large-scale methodological comparisons to show consistent superiority for any one method. This could have been a valid finding, but as suggested earlier, critics disputed its validity, drawing attention to problems in the implementation of the experimental design. Specifically, in the case of the Pennsylvania study, it was argued (Clark 1969) that there was evidence to suggest that teachers in the experiment had not kept strictly to the method they had been allocated to teach. If that was the case, then the whole experiment was obviously not a valid test of the methods being compared. Thus internal validity relates to the extent to which the results of an experimental study can be reliably and unambiguously related to the treatment which was implemented.

Other terms related to validity appear in observational research. Chaudron (1988b) has discussed three types of validation which relate to classroom research. The first is 'construct validation', which involves trying to determine, usually through the use of two different measurements of the same underlying concept or trait (the 'construct'), that the construct has some psychological reality – in other words, that it is verifiable and can be 'captured' through various measurement procedures. The second is 'criterion-related' validity, in which some form of measurement (usually an established and accepted instrument or test) is used to measure a trait along with another form (the procedure to be validated), and the latter is judged by how well its results correspond to the measurement derived from the former. A third type of validation which is important in observational studies is called 'treatment validation'. This focus is closely related to the process component of process–product studies; the researcher tries to document that the treatment was in fact implemented and that it was identifiably different from whatever it was being compared with. Thus 'treatment validation', as the term is used in observational research, is very close to the concept of 'internal validity' in experimental research.

3.3.3 Generalisability: the concern for applicability

The other form of validity in experimental research, to set against the internal kind, is of course 'external validity'. This concept is so important that it deserves a special section to itself here, under its more familiar name: generalisability. As the name implies, this issue involves the extent to which the findings of a study can be generalised, or applied, to other (external) situations. You will recall that in experimental science, researchers try to control the factors that might influence the outcome of the experiment. However, 'laboratory conditions' are seldom found in the real world, so there is always a concern that the findings of such studies will not be repeated in actual classrooms.

Generalisability is connected to the concepts of 'population' and 'sample'. In experimental science, the population is the entire group of subjects of interest – in our case, typical learners – whether it be all the children acquiring two languages simultaneously, or all the adult learners attending English classes, etc. The 'sample' is that smaller group which is actually studied by the researcher. Because experimental researchers usually hope to generalise their results beyond the immediate group they have investigated, they often try to select the sample at random from the population, in the hope that it will fairly represent the larger group. So in trying out a new set of listening comprehension materials, for instance, we would want to know if they would be helpful to all the learners in the course, and not just to that subset of learners who happened to be selected for the original research project.

Sampling is a major problem in our field if we move outside the frame of reference of a small institution, but still want to make claims about a whole population. If we are dealing with a whole country, for example, and wish to know how learners are likely to react to the introduction of a new textbook, how do we choose a sample school in which to pilot the text? It will probably be easier, from a purely practical point of view, if we choose a city school, but the outcome might not be at all valid for rural students, or for other city schools in different sorts of neighbourhoods.

An alternative view on sampling, and one implied of necessity in most action research, is that generalisability has to remain more a matter of apparent similarity of groups than a matter of statistics. So much of our research can only be conducted on very small samples, and we so often have to rely on friendship networks and accessibility for help in obtaining volunteer teachers and classes, that, in the end, we can only hope to establish internal validity in any technically adequate way.

Generalisability is nevertheless a key issue in experimental research, precisely because the researchers want to know if the treatment used in the study will work in other settings. Experimental science has well established procedures for dealing with this problem (based on inferential statistics and the laws of probability), but they are procedures that are often not easy to apply fully in the normal classroom situation. This is because we are seldom able to select learners randomly to be in one class or another, or to control all the variables that might influence the outcome of a study. Furthermore, it is not always ethical to withhold instruction (a set of promising new materials, say) from some learners while offering it to others.

We should also point out that one of the main tenets of experimental research is that reliability and validity are intertwined, and importantly so. If the results of an experiment are not reliable, they cannot be applied to other contexts. Furthermore, in experimental research terms, there can be no 'external validity' (generalisability) without 'internal validity'. The reasoning behind these maxims is that if the findings of an experiment cannot be reliably determined to have been caused by the treatment (if there are problems in measurement, say), then there is no point in trying to apply that treatment in other settings.

So far we have looked at generalisability from the point of view only of researchers doing experimental studies. Clearly experimenters must look for generalisability, since the experimental situation is, by definition, artificial. We do not just want to know what people do in artificial situations; we want to know whether their behaviour in artificial situations is likely to be repeated in real life.

As teachers reading research reports, we will naturally want to know whether or not the findings would hold true with our own learners. For this reason, it is important to know something about the background of the sample of learners investigated in the study. Most researchers include background information about their subjects, so that the readers can compare them with their own clients, students, teachers-in-training, employees, etc. This information is sometimes given in prose descriptions, or in lists of facts, and other times as 'descriptive statistics' which summarise the learners' age, language proficiency, reading test scores, and so on. When such information is presented in numerical form, it is common to see 'mean scores', which are simply mathematical averages, and 'standard deviations'.

The standard deviation is a statistic which indicates how much variety there is in a group of scores. It is a measure of the average distance of the scores in a group of scores from the average score of that group. (See Brown 1988:69–71 for a clear explanation of how the statistic is computed.) If the standard deviation is small, say, for a set of reading test scores, it means the learners in the group performed rather similarly to one another on the reading test. If the standard deviation is large, relative to the range of possible test scores, it means that there was considerable variation in the learners' performance. This same sort of information is sometimes given as the 'range' of test scores. The range shows the distance between the highest score and the lowest score, but it does not tell how the other scores were distributed between the two extremes. As a reader, you can use these and other descriptive statistics to help you judge how similar the people in the study are to learners you are concerned about. This similarity can then help you judge whether or not the findings of the study might generalise to your own situation.

3.4 Generalisability and the different approaches to classroom research

Experimental research aims at investigating a situation without changing it in any way other than the treatment, while action research deliberately aims at bringing about changes for the better in the specific situation being investigated. Another major difference between experimental research and action research is that action research – by definition – can afford to confine itself to looking for local solutions to local problems, whereas experimental researchers are committed to trying to develop the sort of understanding that will apply much more globally.

Usually experimental research seeks generalisability. One of its goals is to be able to claim that research results are valid not just for the local situation but for all similar situations. People who work in this tradition can apply quite rigorous and well established statistical techniques to their data, and can therefore come up with conclusions (generalisations) that, statistically speaking at least, are presumed to be valid beyond the immediate settings of their research studies. The goals of action research, in contrast, are to gain local understanding and to solve specific problems. For this reason, the issue of generalisability is not so crucial in the tradition of action research.

In naturalistic enquiry similarly, and again in contrast to experimental research, generalisability is not always such a primary focus. Recall that naturalistic enquiry is non-interventionist and uses naturally occurring groups, rather than artificially designed or randomly selected groups representing some wider population. In language classroom research, which is a relatively new field, van Lier has argued that generalisability cannot be a major goal because 'the first concern must be to analyse the data *as they are* rather than to compare them to other data to see how similar they are' (1988:2). Thus the goal in naturalistic enquiry is to understand what happens in the individual classroom, which is itself a potentially unique social context. It may be more or less similar to other classrooms, but understanding the interaction must precede generalising its patterns to other settings.

Classroom researchers working within a tradition of naturalistic enquiry often deal with matters of opinion and interpretation. Along with action researchers, they also have largely to take their chances both in terms of the sample of learners and teachers they work with, and in terms of what actually happens to these learners and teachers. Therefore, they cannot simply use the statistical techniques experimenters have developed to deal with the issue of generalisability. (This is because such procedures are predicated upon the theory of probability and depend on assumptions of random sampling and large sample sizes.) But then the whole issue of generalisability looks very different to anyone doing research in the naturalistic tradition. Instead of claiming that whatever has been discovered must be true of people in general, a naturalistic enquirer will claim that whatever understanding has been gained by an in-depth study of a real-life classroom may illuminate issues for other people. For example, a diary study of just one learner by herself (Bailey 1983a), as we saw in section 3.1, gave rise to productive thoughts about competitiveness and anxiety among adult second language learners. This was not a generalisable finding from an experiment, but an illuminating insight from a case-study approach to the analysis of eleven learners' diaries.

Naturalistic enquirers can also appeal to the intuitive nature of human experience, and may point out that poets, for example, contribute to our understanding of human affairs not by assembling incontrovertible generalisations but by offering us unique perceptions of our world, perceptions that are neither true nor false but that simply seem insightful to their readers. Relating research to poetry may seem odd, but the main points are that all basic research is aimed at improving our understanding, and that there are alternative viewpoints concerning the sorts of understanding we can most usefully seek.

3.5 Summary

In this chapter, we have considered, first, the problem of deciding what to investigate in classroom research. We saw that there is a dynamic tension between theory-driven and data-driven ideas about getting started on a study.

We also considered three different approaches to conducting classroom research: experimental studies, naturalistic enquiry, and action research. These three approaches involve varying attitudes towards the degree of control over variables and the desirability of intervention in a research project. We want to make it clear that each of these approaches to understanding has its place and its value, and that choosing the appropriate means of addressing an issue is much more productive than adhering rigidly to one or another approach.

Following the *Discussion starters* and *Suggestions for further reading* that accompany this chapter, we will provide, in the Mini-project, a segment of transcript for your consideration. It is a continuation of the transcribed lesson which was excerpted in section 2.3.3. You may use this transcript as data for an exercise in deciding what to investigate if you start from a data-first position. Then, in Chapter 4, we will turn to additional issues in data collection and analysis, after which we will return to Transcript 2 once more to compare quantitative and qualitative approaches to data analysis.

Important note. Throughout this book we have used samples of transcript material from real lessons. We have not chosen the extracts to provide models of good teaching practice, but simply to make our points about what goes on in language classrooms. The result is a bias towards teacher-centred extracts. This is in some ways a bias introduced by the very idea of collecting classroom recordings, as it is in practice very much easier to record lessons well when they are teacher-led. The bias may also reflect the history of our subject, which started with a focus on the investigation of teacher behaviour. Some readers may nevertheless be disappointed that our extracts do not illustrate more learner-centred teaching styles. We recognise the problem, and can only hope that enterprising readers will very soon be gathering all sorts of data from all sorts of classroom settings.

DISCUSSION STARTERS

1 What puzzles you about classroom language learning? Brainstorm with two or three other people, if you can, and produce a list of possible research topics. Now look back over the list and try to prioritise these items. Discuss your priorities and decide what makes some topics more interesting or important than others.

2 Take your three top priorities from 1 and consider whether each one would be best investigated from a theoretically motivated position, or by the collection of data first.

3 Alternatively, take your three top priorities but consider which of the following approaches you would find most appropriate as a way of investigating the topic:
a) an experimental study;
b) naturalistic enquiry;
c) action research;
d) a combination of procedures from these three approaches.

4 Finally, take just one of your top priorities and try to establish how the issues of reliability, internal validity and generalisability could best be addressed in your proposed study. A lot will depend, presumably, on the decisions you took in 3.

5 Find a classroom research study that interests you. After reading the paper, decide whether or not you could replicate the study, given a) the information in the paper, and b) the resources you have to work with. If you were to try to conduct a follow-up study on the same topic, what would you do differently? Which of the original authors' procedures would you utilise? (It may be useful to have several people read the same study and compare their answers to these questions.)

6 Can you place the study you read in responding to 5 in terms of Figure 2? That is, is the study locatable along van Lier's axes of control and structure? If not, what features of the study make it difficult to categorise?

7 If you are familiar with any theories about language learning and teaching, what research topics do they suggest to you? Which of these topics would be amenable to research in a classroom setting?

SUGGESTIONS FOR FURTHER READING

1 Long's paper about getting 'inside the black box' (1980a reprinted in 1983) reviews a number of observation systems and discusses the roles of anthropological and interaction analysis traditions in classroom research. His discussion parallels our comparison of experimental studies and naturalistic enquiry.

2 Long was influenced by Ochsner's article (1979) entitled 'A poetics of second language acquisition'. Ochsner argues forcibly for a kind of scientific bilingualism – avoiding being rigidly stuck in one research tradition or another. While this article is not easy reading, it pulls together a great deal of information about the philosophy and history of science, as they relate to language research.

3 Working in a similar vein, Bellack (whose work inspired the development of Fanselow's FOCUS system) has written an interesting paper on 'Competing ideologies in research on teaching' (1978). While not specifically directed at language researchers or language teachers, many of Bellack's ideas are pertinent to our concerns. Likewise, Guba's (1978) monograph on naturalistic enquiry is readable and relevant to the issues raised in this chapter.

4 Many ideas that are related to the issues dealt with in this chapter are covered by van Lier (1988). He criticises the use of the experimental method in language classroom research and calls into question the traditional notion of generalisability, as the term is used in experimental science.

5 Long (1980a, reprinted in Seliger and Long 1983) discusses the traditional research sequence, in which descriptive studies are viewed as hypothesis-generating and are followed by hypothesis-testing experimental studies. However, van Lier (1988) argues that ethnography should not be limited to hypothesis-generating endeavours in classroom research.

6 Watson-Gegeo (1988) has written a succinct and informative article explaining the characteristics of good ethnography and contrasting ethnography with other terms (for example, 'qualitative research' and 'naturalistic research') which are often confused with it. See also Watson-Gegeo and Ulichny (1988).

7 Two important papers on the use (and misuse) of ethnography in general education research are by Wilson (1977) and Rist (1980).

8 Chaudron's book (1988a), particularly Chapters 1 and 2, gives thorough coverage to the issues raised in this chapter.

9 For an in-depth discussion of inter-observer agreement and reliability in observational research, see Mitchell (1979). Many of her ideas are pertinent to classroom research, but some additional background in

research design (beyond the brief introduction provided in this chapter) would be useful in reading her article. For a more technical statistical treatment of observer agreement and reliability, see Frick and Semmel (1978).

10 Several books on action research are now available. These include work by Nixon (1981), Carr and Kemmis (1986), Hustler, Cassidy and Duff (1986) and Goswami and Stillman (1987). Two good papers on this topic are by Strickland (1988) and Wallat *et al.* (1981).

11 Leona Bailey's (1975) critique of Moskowitz's means of calculating observer reliability is well worth reading. Portions of her paper were reprinted in Allwright's (1988a) book on observation in language classrooms. (See especially page 117 regarding the issue of observer agreement indices.)

12 Many texts are available now for teachers who would like to learn more about statistics and research design. Three books that have been written specifically with language teachers in mind are by Hatch and Farhady (1982), Woods, Fletcher, and Hughes (1986), and Brown (1988). (The Woods *et al.* text is somewhat more technical than the others.) In the field of general education, Tuckman (1978) is widely used and deals with a variety of methodological topics, although its coverage of statistics is limited to one chapter. Shavelson (1981) is more technical, but very clear, with numerous example problems and an answer key. Jaeger's book (1983), which has clear explanations and illustrations, is designed specifically for people who wish to read and interpret research findings, rather than conduct their own studies.

13 Hammersley (1986) has written an interesting book entitled *Controversies in classroom research*, which deals with issues raised in this chapter.

14 For an introduction to teacher research, see Nunan 1989.

MINI-PROJECT: A DATA-DRIVEN ANALYSIS

In this Mini-project you will have an opportunity to see some transcribed classroom interaction. In section 2.3.3 we gave a partial transcript of an ESL lesson for lower-intermediate adult learners. As you may recall, the lesson the teacher had planned was about the English present perfect. But one learner's experience of being robbed quickly led to a discussion of who in the group had ever had anything stolen. Following the end of the segment given in 2.3.3, there was some joking about a thief who had been caught near one learner's home. That idea led to the interaction which is transcribed below.

Getting started

THE GENERAL TASK

As you read Transcript 2, try to decide (from a data-driven perspective) what topics you could explore, using this transcript. To guide you, we have posed some questions (below) and made a suggestion for the development of a background information questionnaire which could (hypothetically) be administered to the learners in this class.

THE TRANSCRIPT

You will probably remember how most of the transcription conventions are used. The letters 'T', 'A' and 'FS' represent the teacher, the aide, and any unidentified female student, respectively, while every other learner is represented by 'S' and a number. Only one learner, S3, was a male. (S4 was absent.) Indented lines indicate partially overlapping speech, as when S3 says, 'I should change my house' while the teacher is saying '... very secure ...' (see lines 9 and 10 of Transcript 2). Curly brackets in the left margin indicate wholly overlapping utterances. A dash at the beginning of the line, preceding the speaker symbol (−T, for example), indicates the completion of a continuing utterance which had been interrupted or overlapped. Parentheses in the transcript indicate a probable though uncertain transcription, while information given in square brackets represents the transcriber's gloss. The lower-case 'xx' indicates garbled speech that could not be accurately transcribed, and in this particular transcript there is one long unintelligible utterance indicated by 'xx' followed by elipses and 'xx' again. In addition, you will notice that phonetic symbols have been used to represent the utterances of some participants (for example, S2). These data provide an illustration of why transcripts of second language learners' discourse are often more difficult to produce than transcripts of native speakers: the varying accents contribute to the already existing complexities of natural speech. We pick up the lesson at a point where the teacher checks to see if the learners know the meaning of 'Peeping Tom':

Transcript 2:   You ever seen a flasher?

```
  T:  Do you know what a, do y– do you know what a Peeping Tom is?
  S3: Yeah.
  FS:        Yeah.
  T:         xx They caught a Peeping Tom at my apartment a
  S3:                                    Yeah.
 −T:  month ago.
  S3: Tsk, tsk, tsk. [Others gasp or giggle.]
  T:  (Well) I feel very secure xx [Writing on board.]
  S3:                 I should change my house, I should change my house.
```

S7: Qu'est-ce que c'est, ça? [= What does that mean?]
 T: A Peeping Tom. It's a person who comes and he looks in the window.
S7: Oh, my xx
S3:   (He's) peeping.
FS: Where do you live? [T. laughs.]
⎰S3: Why Tom?
⎱ T: xx xx   by a house at, um, I live very close to campus, on [street name].
 (Do) you know where the tennis courts are?
S1: Yes.
 T: OK, I live over there.
FS: Oh.
 T: And they caught him. He's been coming there off and on for a year and
 they'd never been able to catch him until last month. [Two students
 chuckle.] So anyway xx
S2: Hmm. It's called Peeping Tom?
 T: Peeping Tom. Peeping Tom, I don– I don't know
S3:   Why Tom?
 [One student laughing during last two utterances.]
⎰S3: (Maybe the first one.)
⎱ T: (OK, people didn't know his name.) [Loud laughter.]
S9: What does it mean?
 T: Tom, Tom is a very neutral, a neutral name.
 OK, a very common name. I do– I don't know
S3: John's better.   Peeping John.
–T: the origins of it. Pardon?
⎰S3: Peeping John is better.
⎱S9: Peeping.
 T: xx [Laughter.]
S9:   What does it mean, Peeping Tom?
 T: 'Peeping' means to look. OK? Like a, like a secret
S3:   Somebody like xx
FS: xx
–T: look. All right, no one knows. Hidden.
S2: (I heard a word) xx (children) xx (/bɛru/)[= bathroom] xx say I wan'
 make peepee, and xx confuse me.
 T: Like a bird?
S2: No, no, no. When the little boy xx go (/bɛrum/), [S3 begins to laugh] xx
 say I (want to) make peepee.
 [Laughter.]
S3: That's something else.
 T: No. [Laughing.]
S2: (This is) why I said, 'What's this?' I (think) this is the word.
 T: Ah! [Laughter continues.]
S2: xx peepee. [Laughing.]
 T: No, this is different. This means to look.
 [Laughter continues.]
S2: Well, the kid(s) speak English, you know, and uh, and
 T: Yeah.

−S2: I just, I (said), 'Oh.' That's why you write uh right now
    and I xx
  T: Here's, here's another useful word. [Writing on the blackboard.]
    Have you ever heard of a flasher?
  S3: Yeah, yeah.
  FS: Yeah, I (/hɛda/) [= heard of] flasher.
    [One or two students laughing.]
  T: [S8's name], what's a flasher?
  S3: It's like a flash. [Laughter.]
  T: What's a flasher?
  S8: (Flasher?)
  S1: Somebody /ət/ takes pictures.
  T: No. [Laughter.]
  S3:   No.
  T: xx. What's a flasher? You ever seen one? You ever seen a flasher?
  S3: Somebody that flash.
  FS: No.
  T: OK. [Aide's name], you know. [Aide laughs.] (You) want to tell
    them xx
  A: Somebody who shows off, uh, all the parts of his body.
  S6: [Gasps.] Oh, xx!
  T: A flasher, a flasher is like a person who has nothing on and
    maybe a raincoat.
  S3:   Nude?
  S7:   Exhibitionist?
  T: OK, flash is uh flash is a quick movement, right?
  S3:   Streaker?
⎧ A strea–   A streaker?
⎩ T: xx   OK, well. A streaker has absolutely nothing
⎧ on. A flasher shows himself for a second or two.
⎩S7: Exhibitionist.
    [Laughter.]
  T: xx Like he'll, [above laughter] he may have a raincoat on or
    something or a coat and he comes up to
  S3: Why?
−T: you and he goes [Shows movement of someone opening a coat quickly.]
  S3: Why? [Laughing. General laughter.]
  T: And then he runs away. OK?
  S3:   He should be out of his mind.
    [Some laughing continues.]
  FS: xx........................xx
  T: That's a, that's a flasher. Anyway.
  S3:   xx
    [Some whispering.]
  T: Oh, dear. OK.
  S3:   It's a job? It's a job?
  T: Pardon? It's a job? No, it's not a paying job. No.
  S3:   It's a job?   Flasher.
    [S3 laughs. Mumbling continues.]

T: OK, why don't you take a short break since we've kind of been fooling around today? [Laughing a little.]
OK? So take a short break, five minutes.

This transcript is a portion of the data used by Allwright in his (1980) study of turns, topics and tasks in language classrooms.

DATA COLLECTION PROCEDURES

The classroom interaction documented in this transcript was collected by stereo audio-recording with an observer/aide present in the classroom, who took notes on the interaction as it progressed. The audiotapes were subsequently transcribed by another researcher and then checked by the observer/aide for completeness and accuracy of speaker identification. The researchers did not implement a treatment, nor did they exercise any control over the teacher, the learners, or the lesson content. Thus this transcript presents data collected via the non-interventionist approach of naturalistic enquiry.

COMMENTS ON THE TRANSCRIPT EXTRACT

Transcript 2 clearly illustrates a point made in section 2.3.3 – that language lessons are always co-productions, the result of the interaction of all the people present, and not just the direct result of the teacher's lesson plan. In fact, lessons seldom go exactly according to plan. This comment should not be viewed as a condemnation of the teacher – far from it. By being flexible and responding directly to one learner's experience of being robbed (in Transcript 1 – see section 2.3.3), the teacher involved the learners in lively target language interaction in which they could all comment on their experiences, if they wished.

In this segment of transcript, the teacher departs even further from the original focus of the lesson (the English present perfect) as she discusses several current lexical items with the class. You will recall that these are all adult learners of English, living in Los Angeles, a setting where the target language is spoken. As a result, they encounter many words in the surrounding environment about which they are curious (for example, S2's confusion about 'peepee' and 'peeping'). This particular teacher was flexible enough to let the conversation take its own course, rather than struggling to stick to the grammatical point of the original lesson.

In fact, a curious thing happened to use of the present perfect as the discourse developed. As the interaction became more conversational, the teacher used a syntactic pattern characteristic of casual speech when she said, 'You ever seen a flasher? You ever seen one?' This ellipsis of the auxiliary verb *have* is not ungrammatical. Instead, it is typical of casual spoken English in Los Angeles (see Vander Brook, Schlue and Campbell

1980:68, for a discourse-based analysis). Here the teacher got so caught up with the newly established conversational topic that she left behind the very point of the original lesson plan!

SOME QUESTIONS TO CONSIDER

This co-production raises several questions. How do topics get nominated in this class? Who has the right to suggest things to talk about? How are misunderstandings clarified? Who contributes to the management of learning in this lesson? Can you answer these questions by examining the data? You can also try to get a feel for the interaction by reading the transcript as if it were the script for a play, with each learner's role being played by a member of your group. This procedure might give you some useful insights into each participant's role in the co-production.

DESIGNING A QUESTIONNAIRE

This lesson may or may not be typical of lower-intermediate adult ESL classes in California. What sorts of background information would you want to have about the learners to be able to judge how similar they are to the ones you work with?

Try drafting a background information questionnaire which you could administer to the members of such a class, in order to elicit self-report data. Your questions might include information about the learners' purposes for studying English, the length of time they have been in the country, their previous exposure to the language, their years of formal education, and so on. Remember to respect concerns for confidentiality.

Keep in mind also that these learners have lower-intermediate proficiency in English, so your questionnaire would need to be worded accordingly. If you are working with a group, compare your questionnaire draft with those of your colleagues. Do some of them have items which you would find useful to include? If you have access to a group of learners, try administering your background information questionnaire to them, to see what sorts of information they are actually able to provide.

Finally, it would be useful for you to discuss and document what you have learned about questionnaire design through this experience. We would like to suggest that you keep your draft and your notes so that you can use them later.

4   Issues in data collection and analysis

Language classroom research to date has been characterised by the tremendous diversity of its data collection and analysis procedures. As we noted in Chapters 1 and 2, the history of classroom research has been one of rapid evolution of concerns, and as a result a wide range of research procedures has also developed.

In the early days of language classroom research, when the focus was more squarely on teacher training, observation instruments were used which focused primarily on the teacher's behaviour. But as language classroom research has become more deeply involved with issues in language learning, a clearer focus on the learners, and on the interaction among learners and teachers, has superseded the earlier emphasis on teacher behaviour. One result of this shift in focus has been a decrease in the use of observation schedules and an increase in the use of discourse analyses of transcribed data.

4.1   Discourse analysis and transcription

'Discourse analysis' refers to a variety of procedures for examining chunks of language, whether spoken or written. In the case of classroom research, discourse analysis usually involves the analysis of spoken language as it is used in classrooms among teachers and learners. Van Lier (1988:122) describes it as 'an analysis of the processes of interaction by means of a close examination of audiovisual records of interaction'. However, the term is very broad: it covers many analytic processes, from coding and quantification to more qualitative interpretations.

The focus on stretches of oral discourse in classroom interaction leads us naturally to units of analysis which are different from the concepts of sentence, clause, or phrase, as these terms are used in syntactic analyses. Instead, discourse analysts, who are interested in the way talk is structured, have investigated concepts such as utterances, repair strategies, topic nomination, and turns. (Many of these analytic units are extremely important in the analysis of classroom discourse, and they will arise again as we summarise the findings of some classroom research.)

Discourse analysts typically use transcripts and audiotaped or videotaped interactions as their data base (van Lier's 'audiovisual records').

Some use transcripts and accompanying videotapes in order to document the nonverbal channel of communication. Transcripts are written records of interaction in which the researcher copies down, verbatim, the utterances of the participants. Transcripts vary widely in their level of technical complexity. They may use standard orthography or detailed phonetic representations of speech, depending on the research goal. (An example of a somewhat detailed transcript, entitled 'You ever seen a flasher?', was given at the end of Chapter 3.) Throughout this book, you will encounter various transcripts derived from classroom observation. These data will be presented in the original transcript format of the researchers' published reports unless otherwise stated. The guidelines to one form of transcription for classroom discourse are given in Appendix H.

One thing to keep in mind, both as you read reports of classroom discourse analysis and as you begin your own research, is that producing a high quality transcript is a time-consuming business, even if you use standard orthography. Transcribing native speaker dyads normally takes about five times the length of the interaction (that is, it takes about five hours to transcribe a one-hour conversation). It takes even longer to transcribe the speech of pairs or small groups of non-native speakers interacting in their second language. Transcriptions of classroom inter-action, where there are large numbers of speakers whose voices and accents may be similar, where voices often overlap, and where some speakers will be heard more clearly than others, can be a very time-consuming process indeed. (In our experience, one hour of language classroom data can take up to twenty hours to transcribe accurately.)

Nevertheless, verbatim transcripts, which display all the hesitations, false starts, pauses and overlaps of natural speech, are extremely valuable records of interaction. Transcripts show us, in ways that coded data and frequency counts often mask, how classroom interaction develops, as a dynamic phenomenon. For this reason, many classroom researchers prefer to conduct discourse analyses with detailed transcripts, rather than using other data collection procedures which may be easier to do, but which also run the risk of obscuring important information.

These dual issues (first, data collection via transcriptions of recordings, and second, a data analysis focus on discourse) lead us here to themes of both theoretical and practical import. Language classroom researchers, like researchers who investigate language in other defined settings, are concerned with concepts which may at first sight appear to be dichoto-mies, or at least polar opposites – issues such as objectivity and subjectivity, and quantitative versus qualitative approaches to data collection and analysis. We hope to show, in the sections that follow, that these concerns may be more fruitfully considered as continua rather than as dichotomies. We also want to demonstrate that, while these are indeed weighty issues of theoretical concern, they have an immediate practical impact on anyone who begins to do classroom research.

4.2 Objectivity and subjectivity

A source of seemingly endless controversy in research circles is the issue of 'objectivity' versus 'subjectivity'. These are difficult terms to deal with for at least two reasons. One is that many people start off by assuming that 'objectivity' is a good thing and that 'subjectivity' is therefore somehow bad. Originally, 'objectivity' meant 'conformity with the object' or 'independence from the subject' (Maquet, 1964:53). 'Subjectivity' referred to qualities or attitudes belonging to the thinking subject, as opposed to the object of thought. But as anthropologists know, 'the content of knowledge is never entirely independent from the subject; rather it is the result of the meeting of the subject and the object' (ibid.).

In the experimental approach predominant in the physical and biological sciences, objectivity is paramount. Researchers intervene by applying a treatment but they try not to influence the measurement of events in any way. However, we hope to show that, in research on human learning, especially in naturalistic enquiry and action research, both objectivity and subjectivity have their respective roles, and that in practice the two can be combined.

The second reason these are difficult terms to deal with is that they can be applied to different aspects of any investigation. For example, most people would probably agree readily enough that the amount of time a teacher spends talking during a lesson is an objective matter, whereas what the learners think of what the teacher says is clearly a subjective matter. But if you are investigating these two issues, then your processes of data collection and analysis could themselves be more or less objective, or more or less subjective. For example, you could audio-record the lesson and then calculate the amount of time that the teacher's voice was heard on the tape. These would be relatively objective data collection and analysis processes; other people could replicate them with good hope of reaching the same conclusion about the number of minutes the teacher talked in that particular lesson. Alternatively, you could attend the lesson (as many teacher trainers and school inspectors have no doubt done) and form your own opinion about the quantity of teacher talk, without actually counting the minutes. This would clearly be a subjective process, and many researchers would probably say it was an unsatisfactory one.

On the other hand, if you were trying to find out what the learners thought of what the teacher said, you could collect and analyse their undoubtedly subjective opinions in a relatively objective way if you wished. You could, for example, ask the learners to respond to a carefully prepared multiple-choice questionnaire at the end of the lesson. This procedure would give a written record of their opinions and you could then tabulate the data in an objective way, simply by counting the number of times the learners' different subjective opinions were expressed. Overall, this objective collection and analysis of subjective data would be more satisfactory than attending the lesson and forming an opinion of the learners' views by simply noting the looks on their faces while the teacher was talking. However, the choice of what items to include on the questionnaire may itself be a subjective process (that is, determined more by the researcher's taste and interests than by the object of enquiry). Furthermore, the apparently 'objective' multiple-choice format might not include as an option some of the learner's opinions, and would thus, conceivably, overlook potentially important information. So, there are advantages and disadvantages to both subjective and objective approaches to data collection and analysis.

The appeal of trying to be objective is fairly obvious. If you can deal with incontrovertible facts, then you are on safe ground. Other people may challenge your interpretation of the facts but at least they will have to agree on what the facts are, and that gives both sides something solid to argue about. The problem is that human endeavours such as classroom language learning cannot simply be reduced to a set of incontrovertible facts without missing out on a great deal of what is humanly interesting and probably pedagogically important. For example, whether learners work well or not in class may depend on their perception of how much the teacher cares about how well they work. It may not matter very much what the teacher really thinks. Instead, what matters might be the necessarily subjective issue of what the learners *believe* the teacher thinks. Thus we can see that there is a limit to how far objectivity will take us, if we try to stick only to 'incontrovertible facts'.

The issues of subjectivity and objectivity often arise when devising observation schedules for recording classroom data. In constructing such instruments, researchers distinguish between 'low inference' and 'high inference' categories of analysis (Long 1980a). Low inference categories include things that can be counted or coded without the observer having to infer very much (the number of times a certain student raises his or her hand, for instance, or the frequency with which the teacher uses the learners' names). 'High inference' categories, on the other hand (factors like the learners' attention, or the social climate), demand that the observer make a judgement that goes well beyond what is immediately visible. Generally speaking, in developing a coding procedure, it makes sense to use low inference categories wherever possible, and to try to document all the evidence that leads you to make broader inferences. A universal problem for classroom researchers, then, is one of finding low inference means of investigating non-trivial aspects of what happens in language classes.

4.3 Quantitative versus qualitative issues

Before we move on, we will try to deal with the terms 'quantitative' and 'qualitative', since these are often taken, wrongly, as simple alternatives to 'objective' and 'subjective'. From the preceding example, we saw that 'objective' and 'subjective' can be applied not only to the content of an investigation but also to the processes of data collection and data analysis. In practice, this means that different combinations of 'objectivity' and 'subjectivity' are not only possible but often desirable as well.

The terms 'quantitative' and 'qualitative' are also applied to both the data collection and data analysis phases of an investigation. That is, the data themselves can be quantified, as when an observer counts the frequency of certain behaviours (hand raising, for instance), or when a researcher uses learners' test scores as an outcome measure in a process–product study. Any sort of measurement that yields numerical information generates quantitative data. On the other hand, some data are not the product of measurement or counting and thus do not result in numerical information. These sources of data can include prose descriptions, photographic records, life histories, school records, diaries, interviews, audio- and videotapes, and transcripts. Given this diversity of data types, it is appropriate to talk about the use of both quantitative and qualitative approaches to data collection in classroom research.

Likewise, once we have collected data we can analyse them by counting or measuring (quantitative analyses), or by directly reflecting upon and trying to interpret them (a qualitative analysis). For example, once we have produced a transcript of a classroom lesson (qualitative data), we could count all sorts of things – the amount of teacher talk, or of learner talk, the frequency of use of certain words, the number of instances of learner error, and so on, depending largely upon what interests us. Alternatively, we could treat the lesson transcript more like a literary text, and try to understand it by close textual analysis that need not involve counting at all. The third possibility is that the quantitative and qualitative approaches to data analysis can be combined, as when Allwright (1980) counted the number of various turn-getting moves found in transcripts of ESL classes – a quantitative analysis of data that were originally qualitative in form. He then offered an in-depth interpretation of one segment of transcript – a qualitative analysis. (See section 7.3 for a more detailed discussion of this study.) Of course, even a numerical analysis has to be treated qualitatively at some stage, since the researcher must decide how to interpret the figures.

Various combinations of quantitative and qualitative data collection and analysis are possible, as shown in Figure 3. Like Figure 2 (from van Lier, 1988), this model involves two intersecting continua – one for the

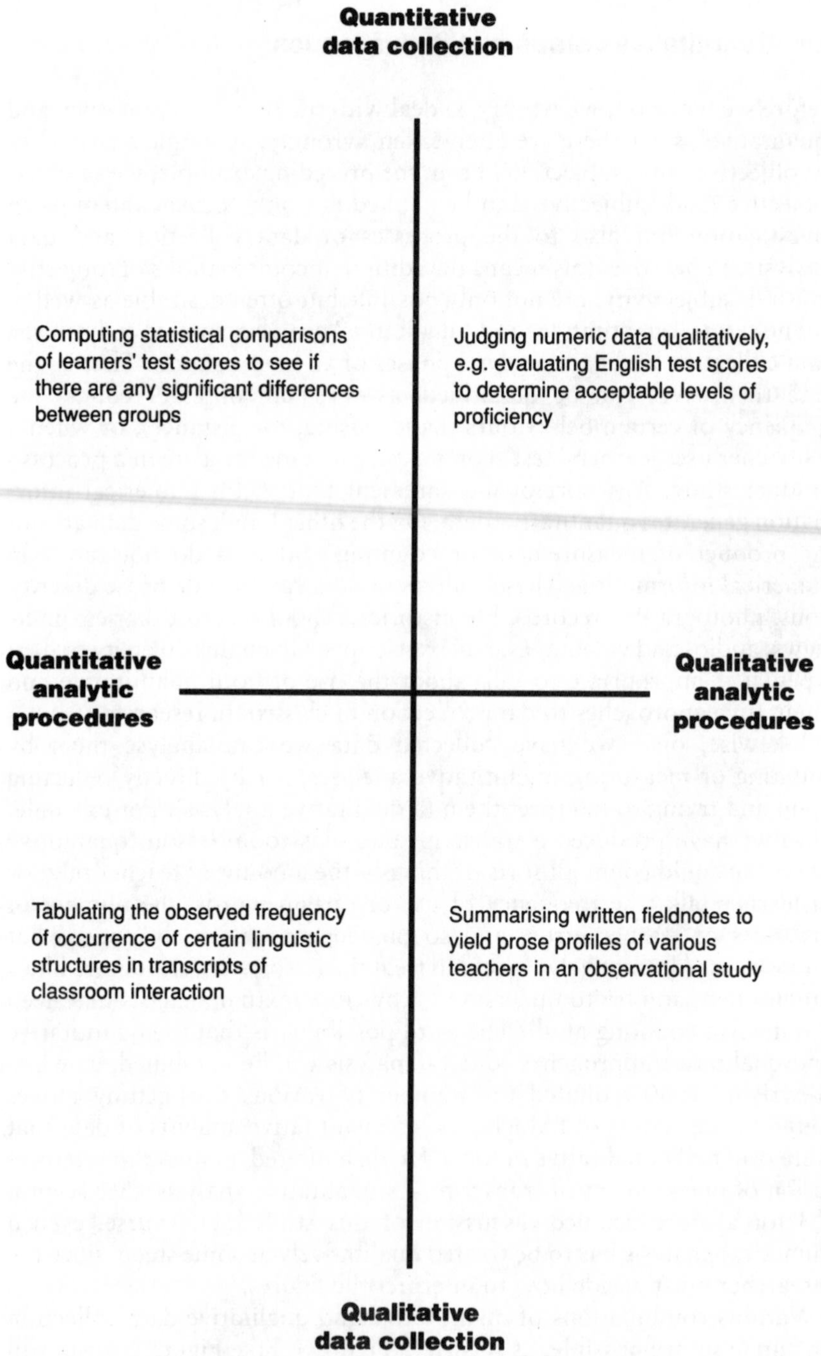

Quantitative
data collection

Computing statistical comparisons
of learners' test scores to see if
there are any significant differences
between groups

Judging numeric data qualitatively,
e.g. evaluating English test scores
to determine acceptable levels of
proficiency

Quantitative
analytic
procedures
————————————————
Qualitative
analytic
procedures

Tabulating the observed frequency
of occurrence of certain linguistic
structures in transcripts of
classroom interaction

Summarising written fieldnotes to
yield prose profiles of various
teachers in an observational study

Qualitative
data collection

*Figure 3   Examples of qualitative and quantitative procedures in
data collection and analysis*

type of data collected, and one for the type of analytic procedures used in a study.

There is clearly a connection between qualitative and quantitative approaches to data collection and analysis, and what people think of as objectivity and subjectivity. Qualitative data, such as a set of diaries kept by learners, would typically be considered subjective, a record of opinions and perceptions, rather than (or in addition to) 'facts'. For some researchers, learners' diaries are of interest not because they hold the 'truth' about something, but precisely because they are a record of opinions and perceptions important to the learners – ideas which cannot easily be tapped in other ways.

Quantification has a similar appeal to objectivity, in that if you can count things then you can subject them to rigorous statistical analyses using procedures set out in statistical manuals. If you get the procedures right, people can challenge you on your interpretation but the figures themselves cannot be denied. The problem here, of course, is that not everything can be counted or measured adequately, and therefore numbers cannot tell the whole story. Some vital element may be missing. Also, there is the difficult problem that statistical procedures are themselves the subject of endless controversy. Even deciding on a unit of analysis for counting can be very tricky. For instance, when Seliger (1977, 1983a) set out to investigate the role of classroom participation in language learning, he counted the number of verbal turns learners took in ESL classrooms. Any utterance, from a single word to a multi-word response, was coded as a single turn. Seliger was later criticised on the grounds that his definition of a turn did not reflect the different types of practice that different sorts of turns might yield. (See section 7.4 for further discussion of Seliger's work.) While no one disputed his figures, people took exception to the information that may have been masked by his decision of *how* to count. As this illustration reveals, what in principle should be incontrovertible findings often turn out to be highly controversial.

4.4 Combined approaches to data collection and analysis

From all that we have said on the topic, it should be clear that we see most value in investigations that combine objective and subjective elements, that quantify only what can be usefully quantified, and that utilise qualitative data collection and analysis procedures wherever they are appropriate. Unfortunately, many researchers seem to see these various viewpoints as mutually exclusive and see themselves as needing therefore to join one or the other of the 'opposing' sides. We hope this book will help people see that arguing over such matters is not likely to be productive.

There is, of course, no compelling reason why both quantitative and qualitative ways of collecting and analysing data should not be deliberately combined in any one research project, and every reason why both approaches should be harnessed at all times. In practice they are not kept rigidly separate anyway, whatever the researcher's intentions may be, although individuals tend to have very strong preferences for one or the other, and those researchers holding opposing views can rarely be found working together on a team. Some researchers have, however, successfully combined both approaches in one study, in what Ellis (1984) has called 'hybrid research'. For instance, Bailey (1984) made multiple observations of twenty-four non-native English-speaking teaching assistants, which she documented in field notes (qualitative data). She summarised these data to generate prose profiles, which resulted in a typology of the teaching assistants (a qualitative analysis). These profiles were then related to learners' numerical evaluations of the teaching assistants (quantitative data) in order to produce a rank-ordering of desirability of teaching assistant types (a quantitative analysis).

Increasingly, it appears, language classroom researchers are calling for judicious selection and combined approaches, rather than rigid adherence to one approach over another (Ochsner 1979; Long 1980a; Ellis 1984; van Lier 1984, 1988). However, as late as 1985, after conducting an exhaustive review of the available language classroom literature, Mitchell wrote that the two 'approaches to classroom research are active and developing, but there is little sign of any coming together of the two in some overarching, grand methodological design' (1985:345–6). We have yet to see whether such a marriage of approaches is going to happen on a wide scale. The two points to be made here are that, first, readers of classroom studies should be aware of the researchers' biases, and should be able to judge whether the procedures of data collection and analysis employed were appropriate for the purposes of the study. Second, if you undertake a classroom study of your own, you need to be ready to face these kinds of decisions from the very beginning, because they will influence your planning, before you even start to collect data.

4.5 Dealing with teachers and learners

Classroom research of any kind is very likely to be a sensitive business, however carefully it is done, because being investigated in any way is anxiety-provoking, to say the least, and being closely observed, recorded and analysed is enough to put anyone on the defensive. Typically researchers are encouraged to cope with this problem by getting written permission, before they start, from all the people involved, so that everybody at least has some idea of what is going to happen, and a real opportunity to get out of it altogether if they want to. Thoughtful researchers will also guarantee the confidentiality of their data, and the anonymity of all participants in any published reports. These preliminary steps are very important parts of 'gaining entry to the field' – securing the permission, as well as the confidence, of the people whose classrooms you are about to investigate. (For specific guidance on the issues involved, and some practical suggestions for getting written permission, you can read the TESOL association's 'Guidelines for ethical research in ESL', reprinted in the *TESOL Quarterly*, 1980:383–8.)

This cautious approach is necessary and entirely appropriate for all research, but for action research the emphasis is likely to be placed much more directly on establishing and maintaining the willing, active and productive co-operation of all concerned. This process is not easy in itself, since it requires a maturity and openness to scrutiny and discussion that cannot be taken for granted, either in learners or in their teachers.

4.5.1 Participants' anxiety as a factor in classroom research

Anyone attempting to investigate what goes on in classrooms needs to be well aware of the practical problems involved in trying to avoid raising anxiety levels. Anxiety is an occupational hazard for teachers, and at times for learners as well. How do you walk into a lesson without worrying the teacher and the learners that you are somehow testing or evaluating them, no matter what you say to reassure them? And if they *are* worried about what you are doing, then their lesson risks being less effective. The risk may seem rather trivial to you as the visitor, but many teachers find it extremely uncomfortable to have another person in the room, and consider it a most unwelcome threat to the very delicate but crucial relationship between the teacher and the class. (In some instances, it appears that teachers are more nervous with visitors than are learners. In a sense, the learners are already giving public performances in class anyway, but the observer may be perceived as posing an unusual threat to the teacher's power base.) Of course, you can always hope to find a willing and welcoming teacher who likes visitors, but such teachers are likely to be uncommon, and their lessons may be unrepresentative of the sort of teaching provided by their less welcoming (and perhaps less self-assured) colleagues.

We are now well beyond the purely practical issues and well into the ethical ones. The usual justification claimed for intrusive research is that the risk to the people directly involved is less than the potential benefit to mankind of the new knowledge that is expected to come out of the research project. In this way, scientists can justify trying out a new cancer treatment on patients even though it might have some harmful side effects, because the benefits of finding a new and successful form of treatment are obvious.

Nothing is quite so clear in the field of classroom research, however. The danger of physically harmful side effects may not be there, but the risk of psychological damage is a real and humanly important one. For example, anyone publishing a report on a diary study has to be sensitive to the possibility that other people in the class, including the teacher, will recognise themselves, however well confidentiality is preserved, and suffer a blow to their self-esteem as a result, if the report carries negative overtones. Many teachers, in state school systems in particular, feel their self-esteem under considerable threat from their daily classroom encounters with unwilling and unco-operative school children, and they certainly do not need the extra burden of unflattering published reports, even if they are alone in being able to identify themselves. The example may seem relatively trivial, and it is indeed trivial compared with some of the dangers of medical research, but that gives us no excuse to put teachers or learners at psychological risk in any way. This concern is all the more important because, unless we are working in the action research tradition and therefore focusing directly on the solution to an immediate practical problem, it is difficult to point with any confidence at all to real benefits for either the teacher or the learners involved in any particular study.

There are no general propositions that will enable a researcher to eliminate totally the possibility of provoking anxiety in teachers or learners. It is clearly much too personal a matter, but at least anyone undertaking an investigation can be aware of the potential problems, and be constantly on the look-out for ways of defusing the situation should anxiety levels rise. One generally reliable piece of advice is to demonstrate, from the beginning, that you have thought about such matters, that you have proposals for preserving confidentiality, and so on. You should be aware, however, that if you over-emphasise such matters, people may begin to suspect that the risk is greater than you have said.

4.5.2 Reactivity: the 'observer's paradox'

Teachers' and students' anxiety during observations can have repercussions for researchers too, as the following example illustrates. When one of the authors (Kathi Bailey) was observing apprentice instructors teaching in university physics labs in English (their second language), she failed to establish proper rapport with one particular teacher before visiting his class. When she entered the laboratory, the young man interrupted his own lecture with the comment, 'Uh-oh, here comes the spy.' Of course, the physics students were somewhat puzzled by this remark. As the teacher went on with the lesson, Bailey began taking notes, but then the instructor said, 'Uh-oh, you are making me nervous.' At that point Bailey ceased her note-taking efforts and simply observed for the remainder of the class period. Thereafter she took more care to make sure the teachers being observed understood the general purpose of the study and the procedures used to collect data before she began her observations (Bailey 1982, 1983b, 1984).

The example given above illustrates a phenomenon that anthropologists call 'reactivity' – an alteration in the normal behaviour of a subject under observation, due to the observation itself. In sociolinguistics this problem is called 'the observer's paradox' – a phrase coined by Labov (1972), who realised that by getting people to speak or to focus on their speech, sociolinguistic researchers often trigger alterations in speech patterns – the very data they are trying to collect. (This change occurs because people adjust their speech, often in a more formal direction, when they become aware of it.) Whether we refer to 'reactivity' or to 'the observer's paradox', minimising this problem is a major headache for classroom researchers – but one that can be overcome with patience. If you make repeated visits to the classroom, familiarise your subjects with any intrusive data collection devices (such as videotape recorders), make yourself available before and after observations, and maintain an openness to the people involved in the study, they will probably grow accustomed to you.

Your chances of succeeding in this effort are probably greater to the extent that you do not need to keep any secrets from the teachers and learners you observe. There is a dilemma here, however: if you let everyone know the focus of your investigation, then they may well try to make their behaviour fit whatever pattern they think you are looking for. If you keep it a secret, they may find it that much more difficult to believe that you do not pose any sort of threat to them. One way of coping with this dilemma, if secrecy about your purpose is an essential part of your investigation, is to make this clear to the participants, apologise for the awkwardness it causes, and promise to reveal the purpose as soon as it becomes possible to do so. An alternative we would not recommend is to attempt to deceive, to lay claim to an innocuous purpose in order to camouflage your real one. Deception is not recommended because it is deception, and because, as such, it can only serve to reinforce any feelings of distrust between teachers, learners, and those who wish to investigate classroom language learning. Deception might, in the short term, appear to be a sensible policy, but in the long run it must be counter-productive.

4.6 The role of learners in classroom research

Another related point to be considered at an early stage is the role of the learners in the classroom under study. Depending on the researcher's attitude and plan, the learners in the study can be viewed as anything from passive observees to actively involved participants. In any given classroom study, the researcher must decide if the learners are going to be treated like subjects in a classical psychology experiment and kept uninformed about what the experimenter is investigating, or – at the opposite end of the continuum, as in the action research paradigm – if they are going to be involved as full collaborators from the start, helping to define problems, deciding how to approach them, and so on. Very often it seems as if the learners are not thought of as participants with anything to offer beyond their role as unwitting providers of raw data in the form of recordings or test scores. The usual objection to involving the learners in any more human way is that it will 'ruin the experiment'. This claim may be true, if a fully controlled experiment is being attempted, but fully controlled experiments, as we have already noted, are rarely possible in classroom research (and may not always be desirable). Many classroom investigations could benefit greatly from the insights the learners themselves might be able to provide.

The question of whether to involve the learners directly in the classroom research is related to the concepts of 'emic' and 'etic' analyses (terms which were originally borrowed from Pike's distinction between 'phonemic' and 'phonetic' analyses – see Pike 1982). As these terms are used in anthropology, an emic analysis or interpretation uses categories, concepts or frameworks derived from within a particular culture. Etic analyses, in contrast, utilise theories or belief systems that come from outside the culture being investigated. As van Lier (1988) and Watson-Gegeo (1988) have pointed out, in order to meet the emic criterion, which is vital to ethnography, the participants' perspectives must be considered. Thus, the learners' ideas and interpretations of events are more likely to be sought in an ethnographic approach to classroom research than in an experimental approach. By the same token, incorporating the learners' ideas would be consistent with the philosophy of action research, given its emphasis on collaborative enquiry and reflection.

An illustration of emic information can be found in an example from research on first language classrooms. A teacher was listening to the learners as they individually read their homework essays aloud. After one boy's skimpy rendition the teacher commented about the learner not having accomplished very much and said, 'Is that all you've done?', at which point another boy commented, 'Strawberries, strawberries.' This remark was followed by laughter from his classmates. While classroom observers could certainly agree on what the learner had said, they might be hard pressed to know how to interpret the comment. When the researchers later asked what 'strawberries' meant, they were told that the teacher often criticised the children's work for being like strawberries: 'good as far as it goes, but it doesn't last nearly long enough' (Walker and Adelman 1976, cited in van Lier 1988:11). As a result, *strawberries* had taken on a local (emic) meaning, which was part of the shared classroom culture, but was unknown to the observers.

4.7 Triangulation: the value of multiple perspectives

As language classroom research procedures have become more sophisticated, we have come to recognise the value of multiple perspectives in data collection and analysis. Learner collaboration is one way of ensuring a variety of perspectives on the situation being investigated. An important methodological concept here is that of 'triangulation'. Anthropologists have borrowed this term from land surveying to suggest that at least two perspectives are necessary if an accurate picture of a particular phenomenon is to be obtained. In the practice of classroom research these perspectives (typically the researcher's and the teacher's, or the researcher's and the learners') do not guarantee accuracy, but at least they counterbalance each other and make it much more difficult to believe in the absolute truth of data taken from any single perspective. Where such triangulation has not been achieved (and it rarely has) it makes sense to ask who has been left out, and what difference this omission might make to the picture obtained.

Actually, triangulation can take several different forms (Denzin 1970: 472). One of them is 'data triangulation', which means using a variety of sampling strategies. Another is 'investigator triangulation', in which more than one observer contributes to the findings. 'Methodological triangulation' refers to using different methods (for example, observation, analysis of transcripts, and self-report surveys) to collect the data. Finally, 'theoretical triangulation' demands that the researchers approach the data analysis with more than one perspective on possible interpretations.

4.8 Getting baseline data

How special is the language classroom? For very many learners a language lesson is just another lesson, more or less like any other subject in the daily school routine. At the same time, many language teachers have been trying to make language lessons different by bringing into the classroom activities that will give learners opportunities to experience language as it is used out of class, in so-called 'real life'. This is an interesting area for classroom research, because we cannot take it for granted that classroom activities based on out-of-class experience will in fact reproduce that out-of-class experience accurately. We need therefore to document carefully what happens in language classes where such activities are introduced.

At the same time, however, we cannot take it for granted that we know very much about 'real-life' behaviour. That too needs to be carefully documented as comparison, or 'baseline' data. For example, in an ethnographic classroom research project on the discourse of engineering Shaw (1983) observed selected meetings of several university engineering courses, and actually attended one course for an entire semester. His field notes and audio-recordings provided him with the baseline data for making reasonable curricular suggestions about what should be taught in an engineering English course for non-native speakers.

The term 'baseline data', then, refers to information that documents the normal state of affairs. It provides the basis against which we make comparative claims about how different or unusual the phenomena we have seen may be. For example, if we want to determine whether language teachers ask more and/or different sorts of questions, compared with teachers of other school subjects, we need to be sure we understand the questioning behaviours of the other subject teachers in order to make this comparison. Such an understanding comes either from reading the research literature about teachers' questioning patterns, or from doing our own research with comparison groups of language teachers and teachers of other subjects.

We are not denying that language classrooms and other kinds of classrooms are, in fact, different in many ways. We have already made the point that language classroom research is complicated, in part, because language is both the object of and the medium of instruction. However, language classrooms and other classrooms are also very similar in many ways, and these important similarities should not be dismissed or overlooked, especially if comparative claims are to be made. For this reason, we want to encourage you, as you read the published reports or the summaries of classroom research in the chapters that follow, to be aware of the use (or absence) of baseline data.

Anthropologists sometimes use a very similar phrase, the 'base line', to refer to the pre-existing framework researchers bring with them to an observational setting (van Lier 1988:5). As researchers, we need to be aware that our previous training, experiences, and attitudes all contribute to the way we view the events we observe. This awareness is especially important to keep in mind in doing classroom research, because virtually all researchers have themselves been learners, and most have also been teachers. And when we, as teachers, get involved in doing classroom research, of course we cannot divest ourselves completely of our attitudes as teachers. Thus, it is important for all classroom researchers, especially those who are also teachers, to be aware of their own predispositions, their 'base line', before they begin to collect and analyse classroom data. It will be helpful to keep this point in mind as you analyse the transcripts given throughout this book.

4.9 Summary

Having set the historical scene and made our case for classroom research in Chapters 1 and 2, we tried, in Chapter 3, to develop the framework for the rest of the book by reviewing the major sorts of decisions that classroom researchers need to consider in their work, from the most basic and practical issue of deciding what to investigate, to the more philosophical problem of choosing among research approaches.

In Chapter 4 we have looked at issues in data collection and analysis, focusing first on the objectivity–subjectivity debate. This sticky problem led us to consider the possible usefulness of both quantitative and qualitative approaches to data collection and analysis. We considered the perennial problem of the 'observer's paradox', and the question of what role learners should play in classroom research projects. Finally, we dealt with the point that language teaching researchers have to be careful to collect baseline data if comparative claims about language classrooms are to be made. Language classrooms are undoubtedly special in some ways, but we may learn as much from focusing on their similarities with other settings as on their differences. The most important thing is that classrooms are fascinating places to study, and we hope more people will realise just how rewarding it can be to investigate what happens in them.

It is time, however, to move from the framework to the findings, while these methodological issues are still fresh in our minds. In the rest of this book, we will present the results of a number of research projects from the last two decades. The organisation will follow history in its move from studying the treatment of error (in Chapters 5 and 6) to studying classroom interaction itself (Chapters 7 and 8), and, finally, to studying learners and their receptivity to language and language teaching (Chapters 9 and 10). As before, however, there are *Discussion starters, Suggestions for further reading*, and project suggestions for you to consider before you continue.

DISCUSSION STARTERS

1 What is meant by a quantitative or a qualitative approach to class-room data collection and analysis? Do you have a personal preference? If so, can you say why? Can you identify the advantages and disadvantages of each approach? If you are working with a group, you may find it fruitful to divide into two smaller groups, one to argue for a quantitative approach and the other for a qualitative one, regardless of personal preferences. (Make sure each subgroup has enough time to prepare its case.)

2 Which approach do you find the more congenial, the objective or the subjective? Why? Can you see ways to combine the two in a research project of your own?

3 Try to find an article in a professional journal which is related to your research interest. Some likely places to look, depending on the topic, would be the *TESOL Quarterly*, *Language Learning*, the *Modern Language Journal*, *Studies in Second Language Acquisition*, the *English Language Teaching Journal*, or any of the references given at the end of this book. After you have read the article, try to characterise the study in terms of the continua depicted in Figure 3. In other words, see if you can locate the study in terms of its data collection and data analysis procedures as represented in Figure 3. Was the research more quantitatively or more qualitatively oriented? Did the authors use a combination of data types and analytic procedures?

4 Again, with regard to the study you selected, were there any concepts that were unfamiliar to you? If so, were they concepts related to the topic of investigation (to error treatment, or interaction, for instance), or were the unfamiliar terms part of the metalanguage of research (for example, statistical procedures)? Try not to be discouraged if much of the reporting language seems unfamiliar. Like all cultures, the sub-culture of classroom research has its own rules and its own jargon. Both will become more familiar as we go along. If you are reading this book with a group, it would be helpful if each person created a vocabulary list of unfamiliar items for his or her article, and then the group could compile a common list of these new terms and be on the alert for them in the chapters ahead. As an alternative, you could check their meaning in the *Dictionary of Applied Linguistics* (Richards, Platt, and Weber, 1985), or in a research design text.

5 In the article you read for 3 and 4, was there any mention of reliability, validity, or generalisability? Did the situation call for reliability indices – if, say, two or more people coded or rated the data, or if there were two or more observers working in the data collection phase? Do you think the findings of the study would generalise to the population of learners that interests you the most? Why or why not?

6 In classroom observations you have conducted (or on occasions when you have been observed), were you aware of anxiety, or 'reactivity' affecting the teacher or the learners? If so, what steps could you have taken to overcome this problem? Thinking ahead to the next time you are an observer, what could you say to the teacher and the students to help overcome any anxiety they might experience as a result of the observation? What could you say to yourself if you feel anxious when you are being observed?

7 Think about the topic you identified as your first choice for an original investigation in the discussion starters at the end of Chapter 3. What would be the ideal role of the learners in your research project? Should they be actively involved in some way, or will you simply observe their behaviour without initially discussing the project with them? Are there insights they might offer if you asked them, either before or after the observations? Could their input or that of the teacher help you provide triangulation in your proposed study?

8 Choose at random any of the transcripts provided in this book. Having established a topic you would like to investigate – perhaps the first one on your rank-ordered list – see if the transcript offers any data which are pertinent to the investigation of your topic. If not, would it be worthwhile to get more transcribed data, or would you need to collect different sorts of data instead?

SUGGESTIONS FOR FURTHER READING

1 Chaudron has written widely on the issues raised in this chapter. His book (1988a) is a very complete source of information. He has published an article about the interaction of quantitative and qualitative approaches to research (1986a), and a paper about different types of validation in classroom research (1988b). For a review from outside the field of language pedagogy, see Hammersley (1986).

2 If you would like to know more about discourse analysis, there are several sources you could consult. Three of the most accessible books are by Sinclair and Coulthard (1975), Coulthard (1977), and Brown and Yule (1983). Hatch and Long (1980) wrote an article which deals specifically with discourse analysis in second language research, and a paper by Crookes (1988) discusses the functional units of discourse analysis used in classroom research.

3 Mitchell (1985) has compiled a broad overview of language classroom research, including many European studies. Her paper is organised in sections according to the sorts of methodological issues raised in this chapter.

4 For a cogent discussion of triangulation in second language classroom

D

studies see Chapter 1 of van Lier (1988). His (1984) paper raises several important issues about discourse analysis in language classroom research. Adelman (1981) and Sevigny (1981) also deal specifically with triangulation in classroom research.

5 Most published research studies make it sound as if everything always goes smoothly. This is not the case. There are many false starts, problems, delays, and outright mistakes in classroom research, as in most human endeavours. Bailey (1983b) has written a brief paper which talks about some of the things that can go wrong in classroom research. Before you begin any of the major projects suggested later, it may be helpful to read that paper so you can hope to avoid some of the typical pitfalls associated with observing people in classrooms.

6 Information on qualitative research procedures is more commonly found in general education references than in language pedagogy. Spradley has written two very useful books – one about the procedures of ethnographic interviewing (1979) and one on ethnographic observations (1980). Both are very practical introductions and highly readable. Bogdan and Taylor (1975) is often viewed as the classic introduction to qualitative research methods.

7 In this chapter, and in the project for Chapter 3, we have mentioned questionnaire design. We have not given you any specific guidance in this process, but questionnaires are often used as additional tools in classroom research. Four helpful references on questionnaire design and use are Babble (1975), Cohen (1976), Tuckman (1978 – especially Chapter 9), and Wolfram and Fasold (1974). The last deals specifically with language research.

MINI-PROJECT: ANALYSING CLASSROOM DISCOURSE

We will now suggest several tasks that can be carried out, using Transcript 2 ('You ever seen a flasher?') as the data base, to illustrate some of the topics raised in Chapter 4. The data are amenable to a variety of qualitative and quantitative analytic procedures.

STAGE ONE: A QUANTITATIVE ANALYSIS OF CLASSROOM DISCOURSE

One of the topics which has been investigated in language classroom research has to do with teacher talk and student talk. We can address this issue in purely quantitative terms to begin with. Using the data presented in Transcript 2, try to decide who talks the most frequently.

Turn distribution

You can start by trying to calculate the number of turns taken by each participant. Before you begin your analysis, however, you will have to come up with some definition of a turn. Will any utterance count as a single turn, whether it consists of one word or several? (This was the problem that Seliger faced – see section 4.3.) How will you code interrupted turns, and discourse maintenance moves, such as 'Uh-huh' or 'Yeah' (said while the original speaker is still talking, probably to indicate the listener's attention)? When you have decided what constitutes a turn, write down your definition so that you can refer to it again, if tricky cases arise, and so that you can share it with others if you are working in a group.

You can set up a grid, such as the following, to tabulate the frequency of each person's speech attempts:

Participant	*Number of turns*
T	
A	
S1	
S2	
S3	
S5	
S6	
S7	
S8	
S9	

(S4 was absent.)

Word counts

When you have completed the turn distribution tally, it will be instructive to use a specifically linguistic unit of analysis – the word. How many words does each participant utter during this segment of interaction? Here you must decide what a word is, in speech, and what to do about untranscribable utterances, indicated by xx in the transcript. Many of these were very quiet utterances, hushed comments from one learner to another, or private remarks which the learner apparently did not intend to make to the group at large – practice repetitions, perhaps, or egocentric speech. How will you count these? Again, you can use a grid such as the one you used before, or you can just add a column for the word count to your original grid.

Integrating the figures

You can use your figures to make statements about the relative frequency of the group members' overt verbal participation. First, rank order the participants (that is, list them in order from the person who spoke the most to the person who spoke the least) and then try to answer the following questions:

1 Did the teacher speak more than the students (individually or combined)?
2 Which learners spoke most often? Is there a clear rank order, from most frequent to least frequent speaker, among the participants?
3 Does the word count yield information which was not provided by the turn count (or vice versa), or do the two quantitative analyses provide essentially the same information?

Cross-checking with other data

Next you could go back and conduct the same analyses for Transcript 1 (given in section 2.3.3), which represents an earlier portion of the same lesson. Do the same findings obtain, or has the rank order changed in some noticeable way?

Inter-coder agreement

If you are working with a group, it would be appropriate at this point to check your reliability, in terms of the data analysis. Compare your tally of the turn frequencies and word counts with those of your colleagues. See if you can come up with a coder agreement index above the usual 85 per cent criterion.

Those people working in groups can also consider the validity of their category system. How similar was your definition of a turn to those of your colleagues? Can the entire group agree upon a single definition of a turn which everyone would use in coding the data? If so, how does this a priori consensus affect your coder agreement levels?

Drawing conclusions

Finally, it is worthwhile to look back at your quantitative analyses to see what conclusions can be drawn from the data. What generalisations can be made about this group of learners, assuming this lesson is characteristic of their interaction patterns? What conclusions can you *not* draw? In other words, what would you like to know about this lesson that is not revealed by the quantitative analyses alone?

STAGE TWO: A QUALITATIVE ANALYSIS OF CLASSROOM DISCOURSE

Now, without counting anything, let's take a closer look at this transcript. In Chapter 2 we described 'atmosphere' as one of the planned aspects of language lessons, and learners' 'receptivity' as one of the co-produced outcomes. How would you describe the atmosphere in this class? Do the learners strike you as particularly receptive or defensive? Is there any language learning going on here, or is this part of the lesson (as the teacher says) an example of just 'fooling around'? What is your evidence for these conclusions? Try to locate the data in the transcript which support the inferences you draw.

Participant perspectives

Imagine that you had just transcribed these data, after hours of listening to the audiotapes of the class. If the class were still meeting, you could speak to the teacher, the aide and the learners, to get their emic interpretations of the transcript. (This step would provide some triangulation on your etic interpretation of the events.) Devise a list of specific questions that you would like to ask each participant. The questions may have a linguistic focus, or a sociological focus, or a combination of the two. Compare your questions with those of your colleagues, if you are working with a group.

Next steps

Ethnographers often keep an ideas file, in which they enter notes about issues to follow up on in future observations or interviews. If Transcripts 1 and 2 had been derived from your initial observations in a long-term study of this class, what issues would you wish to explore in subsequent visits? Again, it might be productive to compare your ideas with those of your colleagues, if you are working with a group.

Part III The treatment of oral errors in language classrooms

In this section, we will discuss the findings of many (though by no means all) of the classroom research projects completed to date on the topic of learners' oral errors. We have selected studies which we feel are important or representative, and in most instances, easily accessible. In a volume of this size, we could not do justice to the complexities and subtleties of the studies described in this chapter. Interested readers will be guided to primary sources by our citations and our *Suggestions for further reading* at the end of each chapter. And, of course, the bibliographies of those studies will also provide a wealth of references for further exploration of the topics introduced here.

We will begin with some theoretical background on the concept of error (in Chapter 5) and then move directly to what classroom research has revealed about teachers' reactions to learners' errors (in Chapter 6). We want to stress that, while many of these studies were conducted several years ago, the field of language classroom research is still in its youth, if not its infancy. Many of these findings are inconclusive, and most of the studies would bear replication. Some have generated specific results which can be immediately useful to teachers; others have yielded testable models that inform us about the observable patterns found in classrooms. Certainly, all these results demand close scrutiny, as do the findings of any young science. While we have made progress, there is still a great deal of work to be done, and much of it could be done by teachers working in their own classrooms.

We can, of course, learn from the methods researchers have used as well as (perhaps even more than) from their findings. This will be a recurrent theme throughout the remaining chapters. We hope you will see, in the discussion of findings which follows, how the three approaches to classroom research (experimental studies, naturalistic enquiry, and action research) have been used, or could have been used, to explore the topic of error and its treatment. We will also deal with studies using a variety of quantitative and qualitative procedures in their data collection and analysis phases. Our purpose throughout Part III will be fourfold: 1) to acquaint you with the theoretical background and the findings (however tentative) of the classroom research on error; 2) to familiarise you with the most common research procedures; 3) to offer information that may be helpful to you in your own teaching; and 4) to encourage you to attempt some exploratory investigations of your own.

5 Oral errors: the general picture

Some of the early observational research in second language classrooms examined teachers' responses to learners' errors. This focus is not surprising, given the observability of learners' errors and teachers' reactions, but it also follows logically from the shift in emphasis from contrastive analysis to error analysis in the late 1960s and early 1970s. Contrastive analysis generated predictions based on comparisons of the mother tongue and the foreign language. Teachers and researchers, however, knew from classroom experience around the world that the errors which learners commonly made in class were not necessarily always the ones predicted by contrastive analyses. There were errors that could not be explained simply by noting the differences between the languages involved, and sometimes the errors that a contrastive analysis did predict were not found in practice.

Error analysis differed from contrastive analysis in that it studied the errors actually made by learners, and in so doing it raised a number of interesting issues. It became clear to researchers and teachers alike that language learners inevitably make errors. Of course, this fact alone raises many questions. What causes people to make errors? Are errors really a problem, or are they an important part of learning itself? How do teachers react to learners' errors? Do teachers' responses make any difference to the learners' progress?

The purpose of this particular chapter is to present the background to thinking about oral errors in the language classroom. This chapter will not deal so much with classroom research, therefore, but will introduce other lines of enquiry (from first language acquisition and from studies of out-of-class talk) that are important if we are to be able to interpret properly the findings of oral error research in the language classroom. The other lines of enquiry will also provide us with some suggestions about how investigations can best be conducted, in or out of the classroom setting. First of all, however, we will need to deal with the concept of error itself. Contrary to first assumptions, the notion of 'error' is not at all a simple one.

5.1 Problems in defining 'error'

What is an error in language learning? Typical definitions include some reference to the production of a linguistic form which deviates from the correct form. The 'correct' version, in turn, is often identified as the way native speakers typically produce the form. This is called the 'native speaker norm'.

However, the practice of using departures from the native speaker norm to define error is too narrow and certainly inadequate for our purposes. For one thing, it does not take into account the possibility that the target language model the learner is exposed to may not be the native speaker norm. A great deal of the world's foreign language teaching is done by non-native speaking teachers, who provide a non-native model of the target language. (The 'target language' here refers to the language the learners are studying – the model they are aiming at.) Thus the language the learners are taught in classrooms may itself actually deviate from the native speaker norm in a number of systematic ways, depending, in part, on the target language proficiency of the non-native speaking instructor. In some parts of the world (for example, India, Singapore, Hong Kong, West Africa), the situation is further complicated by the fact that there is a perfectly acceptable alternative norm (such as Educated Indian English, or West African English) which serves as the language of wider communication.

Likewise, sociolinguistic research has shown that second language learners living in the target culture and acquiring language naturalistically (outside the classroom, without instruction) do not always adopt a native or a 'standard variety' of the target language as their model. For instance, research conducted in New York City has shown that some Puerto Rican children use Black English as their target model (Goldstein 1987). Other studies have revealed the variation with which even native speakers of a particular dialect produce the same linguistic forms in different settings. Thus, sociolinguistic research has profoundly influenced our conception of correctness.

Changes in pedagogy have also influenced our attitudes towards error and its treatment. With the recent advent of the communicative approach to language teaching, less emphasis has been placed on formal accuracy than was formerly the case, and more importance given to the question of communicative effectiveness. Language learners' speech usually deviates (to some extent) from the model they are trying to master, and these deviations or discrepancies in form have typically been viewed as errors. But teachers who adopt the communicative approach are often more concerned with second language learners' ability to convey their ideas, get information, etc., than with their ability to produce grammatically accurate sentences. Some feel that it is more important for learners to accomplish their communicative goals than it is for their sentences to be perfectly well formed. Thus many teachers consider the degree of pupils' communicative success when reacting to their output, in both speech and writing: whether or not the learners' language is accurate, does it *work* in a communicative sense? Research on error treatment to date has been limited largely to accuracy errors, which are relatively easy to identify, but clearly we will not be able to say we know very much about error treatment until the treatment of communication errors has also been well studied.

In formal classroom instruction of second or foreign languages, the teacher's response to students' utterances may be the most important criterion for judging error. Indeed, one definition states that an error is a form unwanted by the teacher (George 1972:2). In looking at transcripts of classroom discourse, we find that learners' responses are sometimes rejected by teachers – not because they are wrong but because they are unexpected. Fanselow (1977b:585) has observed lessons in which the teacher's apparent goal was for the student to respond to questions 'in a way the teacher had planned with no variation allowed'. Nystrom (1983:171–2) has documented an example of this phenomenon in the following transcript excerpt. (Observations about nonverbal behaviour are given in parentheses. The observer's comments are recorded between slashes. P stands for *pupil* and T for *teacher*.)

Transcript 3: 'I see a pig'.
T: I want you to look at this and tell me ONE THING that's going on in this picture. Tell me in a complete sentence. Okay, Dione?
P: (Gasps / wants to be called on /)
T: Dione.
P: A pig.
T: (Looks out of the corner of her eye / uncertainly /). A pig. Can you tell me that in a complete sentence? You need to say more than just, 'a pig'. You need to see, say, 'I see a pig' or you need to say, uh, 'The pig is doing something'.
P: A goat?
T: Okay, Tony?

Transcript 3 is reprinted (with transcription conventions adapted) from Nystrom 1983:171–2.

As Nystrom points out, the answer 'a pig' is very sensible: it is factually correct and it reflects the natural oral discourse pattern of speaking in phrases (rather than complete sentences) when sufficient context is provided. However, the teacher does not accept the utterance because the student has committed an error of classroom discourse: 'not using a complete sentence as the teacher required' (ibid.:172).

In a study of teachers' reactions to children's errors made in French immersion classrooms in Canada, Chaudron also discussed various ways of defining error. Chaudron defined errors as 1) linguistic forms or content that differed from native speaker norms or facts, and 2) any other behaviour signalled by the teacher as needing improvement. Chaudron also used the concept of 'corrective reactions' – defined as 'any reaction by the teacher which transforms, disapprovingly refers to, or demands improvement of, a student's behaviour or utterance' (1986b:66). The categories of error he studied included phonological, lexical, morphological, syntactic, discourse, and content errors. Chaudron summarises the problems faced by researchers and teachers alike in trying to identify second language learners' errors:

> The determination of errors is clearly a difficult process that depends on the immediate context of the utterance in question as well as on an understanding of the content of the lesson, the intent of the teacher or student, and at times, the prior learning of the students.
> (Chaudron 1986b:69)

Moving on from researchers' difficulties in defining error, we will now consider error in first language acquisition, in conversations between native speakers, and in the process of second language learning.

5.2 'Errors' in first language acquisition

Part of the picture we all have of language errors is experience in witnessing children learning a first language. It is a fascinating process and one which has been studied a great deal in the past thirty years. Before considering second language learners' errors, it will be instructive for us to consider what the research says about the 'mistakes' children make when learning their native language.

We know that when children acquire their native language, their 'caretakers' (the persons responsible for their supervision) interact with them verbally. We also know that the caretaker – whether it be a parent, an older sibling, or someone else – normally attends to the *meaning* of what the children say. That is, the older person (who is also the more competent speaker) typically focuses on whether or not what children say is true and appropriate, rather than on whether or not it is linguistically perfect: factual content and effectiveness are emphasised over form in such interactions.

Often the caretaker expands and elaborates on the child's speech by using the raw material supplied by the child, frequently preserving the word order given in the original utterance. For example, the youngster's comment, 'Daddy coat', may elicit as a response, 'Yes, that's daddy's coat', or, depending on the context and the intonation curve of the child's utterance, 'Daddy will get your coat.' The caretaker's reaction utilises the child's contribution to the discourse and adds words and morphemes (such as the contracted copula verb *is* in *that's* and the possessive -*'s* in the first example cited above) which render a complete and grammatical sentence. This correct model serves as input to the child's developing grammar. It is through this process of interactive discourse that children seem gradually to acquire their first language.

Children's first language development generally progresses through regular stages, including 1) pre-babbling and babbling, when children learn to make the segmental and suprasegmental phonemes; 2) the holophrastic stage, when utterances consist of one word at a time; 3) the two-word stage, which becomes 4) telegraphic speech, in which there are several content words, though many of the function words and grammatical morphemes may be missing. Eventually children's speech is elaborated to the point where it conforms to the adult model. This process includes mastery of a very complex linguistic system: the sounds, morphemes, lexicon, syntax, and discourse rules of the surrounding language.

Children's progress through these developmental stages can be characterised by the ways in which their emerging language differs from the language that surrounds them. Indeed, children's language is different from adult language, in one sense, because of the gaps in their linguistic systems. In other words, we can describe children's speech in terms of the *errors* they make – though it seems strange, of course, to use the term in this context. In part, this concept is odd because people seldom react to children's deviant utterances as errors. In fact, Schmidt and Frota (1986:216) summarise the evidence on error treatment in first language acquisition as follows: 'negative information is not systematically provided [by the caretakers], and when it is provided it does not seem to have much effect [on the learners]'.

It seems clear from observing children acquiring their first language that the process involves gradual accumulation of both data and rules, rather than simply memorising individual sentences or responding to adults' limited corrective reactions. We know this to be so since many of the utterances children produce are never heard in the surrounding environment. For example, children whose first language is English may use the past tense form *went* correctly for months and then suddenly switch to *goed*, a form which is both ungrammatical and unused by adult speakers. This change apparently occurs because the children have learned the rule for forming the regular past tense, and the rule is so powerful a device in the emerging grammar that it is applied too broadly. (This phenomenon is called 'overgeneralisation', and it also occurs in second language learning.) Soon children realise that *to go* is an irregular verb which does not form the past tense by the usual means, and *went* re-enters their speech. When it does (along with several other irregular verb forms), we can say they have acquired the irregular past tense verbs, as well as the restrictions on the use of the regular past tense rule. Progress though the stages of first language acquisition is thus characterised by the disappearance of 'errors' in children's speech. We will see, in section 5.4, that this process is analogous to stages in second language learning.

5.3 'Errors' in native language conversations

While errors are quite apparent in the speech of language learners, it is important to note that they occur even in the speech of adults talking together in their common first language. When such errors do occur, they are often ignored unless they cause some sort of breakdown in communication. For example, in a discussion of anxiety in second language classrooms, one teacher spoke about 'overcoming intuition'. The other people in the conversation were all language teachers and they understood him to have meant 'overcoming inhibition', so no one commented at the time.

This kind of mistake is sometimes called a 'performance error'. It may be explained on the following grounds. *Intuition* and *inhibition* are similarly shaped words: both begin with the prefix *in-* and end with the suffix *-tion*. Both have four syllables with the primary stress on the third syllable. And semantically, both words have to do with internal states or feelings. These parallels suggest that such words may be 'filed' similarly in the psycholinguistic filing system, and that this particular mistake was one of inaccurate retrieval from the system. It is called a performance error because it was only a momentary lapse or 'slip of the tongue'. It does not reflect a gap in the speaker's actual competence. He clearly knew the difference between *inhibition* and *intuition*, and was surprised to learn later that he had substituted one word for the other. But since his meaning had been clear from the context, no one reacted to the error or corrected him: there had been no serious communication breakdown. However, when an error does cause communication difficulties, there are various ways in which the problem can be sorted out, or 'repaired'. Research on conversation has documented the repair patterns that occur in English.

Think about your own experiences in speaking English with native speakers (or with competent adult non-native speakers). Several questions seem to run quickly through the minds of adult native speakers when a serious communication error is perceived. One question has to do with who will verbally note the existence of the error – the speaker or someone else in the conversation. This issue is referred to as 'self-' or 'other-initiation', since someone must get started on fixing the breakdown, by pointing it out – either verbally or nonverbally. The actual fixing of the error is called 'repair', and it too may be accomplished either by the speaker ('self-repair') or by one of the interlocutors ('other-repair').

Thus there are four possible combinations of initiation and repair involving *self* or *other* which occur in ongoing spoken discourse (Schegloff, Jefferson and Sacks 1977):

1 *self-initiated other-repair*, in which speakers note breakdowns and request assistance (for example, in a word search – the familiar tip-of-the-tongue phenomenon when the speakers cannot produce the word they wish to use);
2 *self-initiated self-repair*, in which the speakers themselves both notice and correct the errors;
3 *other-initiated self-repair*, in which the interlocutors note and comment on the errors, but the speakers themselves are able to repair the breakdowns; and
4 *other-initiated other-repair*, in which people other than the speakers both call attention to the errors and provide the corrections.

By way of illustration, we can consider the following example of native speaker discourse, in which overlapping turns are marked with double slashes:

Transcript 4: Single beds'r awfully thin
Lori: But y'know single beds'r awfully thin tuh sleep on.
Sam: What?
Lori: Single beds. / / They're
Ellen: Y'mean narrow?
Lori: They're awfully narrow / / yeah.

This transcript is taken from Gaskill 1980:127, citing Schegloff, Jefferson and Sacks 1977:378.

Here Sam initiates the repair sequence by asking 'What?' in response to Lori's statement that 'single beds'r awfully thin'. Ellen then supplies the repair, substituting the lexical item *narrow* for *thin*. This is an example of other-initiated other-repair.

While such repair strategies have not yet been widely investigated in other languages, research into English conversations has shown a strong propensity for self-initiated self-repair: speakers normally notice and fix breakdowns as they occur (Schegloff *et al.* 1977). At other times, other-initiated self-repair is used, where the listener seeks clarification or repetition, which is then supplied by the original speaker. However, other-initiated other-repair (such as the example given in Transcript 4) is relatively rare in normal conversation among linguistic equals.

How do these patterns of normal conversational repair relate to second language learning and teaching? Using the framework proposed by Schegloff *et al.*, Gaskill (1980) investigated initiation and repair strategies in conversations among native and non-native speakers of English. He found that other-initiated corrections were relatively infrequent. When they did occur, they usually displayed uncertainty, and their delivery was softened somewhat. Thus Gaskill's results largely agree with those of Schegloff *et al.*

Kasper (1985) used the analytic framework devised by Schegloff *et al.* (1977) in her investigation of repair in foreign language teaching. Her analysis was not limited to learners' utterances, however, as she took into account repair of teacher utterances as well. In her work, the concept of 'trouble source' (that is, the problem that provokes the initiation and subsequent repair) is much broader than the concept of error which we are using here. Kasper divided the lessons in her data base into segments with a language-centred phase and those with a content-centred phase. She found that repair in the content-centred phase was similar to that in non-educational discourse among speakers of equal status: 'self-initiated and self-completed repair is preferred by both learners and teacher' (1985:213). In the language-centred phases, trouble sources were identified by the teacher and repaired by the teacher or another learner, rather than the original speaker.

Given the findings from these studies and our experience (as both teachers and learners), we can suggest that one characteristic of language classes that marks them as somehow different from 'real life' is the preponderance of other-initiated other-repair: teachers often tell learners that they have made errors and then tell them what to say instead.

One of the issues language teachers must consider, when faced with learners' errors, is deciding whether or not the learners themselves can employ self-initiated self-repair, or other-initiated self-repair. In the event of a communication breakdown, can they fix whatever has gone wrong? Do they have the linguistic knowledge, the competence, to detect the error and then to self-correct? If not, do they have the 'strategic competence' (Canale and Swain 1980; Tarone 1981) to deal with the problem? (Strategic competence is the ability to overcome linguistic deficiencies by asking for help, using appropriate nonverbal signals, working around an unknown structure or vocabulary item, etc.) We will examine the question of self-correction in more detail below, when we consider the options teachers have in responding to learners' errors.

5.4 Developmental stages in second language learning

Let us consider the case of people adding another language to their existing competence in their first language. Like children learning a first language, people acquiring a second language naturalistically (that is, without formal instruction) are thought to progress along a continuum whose two poles are their first language and the target language. This continuum is marked by a series of fluctuating stages delineated by the types of errors learners make at any given stage. This sequence of stages has been given various labels. 'Interlanguage', a term coined by Selinker (1972), is one widely used name. It stresses the systematic nature of the learner's linguistic development between the two languages.

To take one example, researchers investigating the acquisition of English by six Spanish speakers (two children, two teenagers, and two adults) found that over a period of ten months, most of the learners went through regular stages in learning the negation system, and that these stages could be characterised by the kinds of errors the learners made. The general sequence seemed to have four stages:

1 *no* plus the verb, as in 'I no understand';
2 *don't* plus the verb, as in 'He don't like it';
3 correct negation of the auxiliary verb, as in 'You can't tell her'; and finally
4 the disappearance of the *no*-plus-verb form and the increasingly regular use of analysed *don't*, as in the target language form, 'He doesn't spin'.

(based on Cancino, Rosansky and Schumann 1978:229)

The researchers noted that there was some overlap among these stages. For instance, some learners produced *no*-plus-verb constructions during the same period when they used the *don't*-plus-verb form for negative utterances. The important point here is that the errors the learners made were systematic in nature, and that in most cases they gradually gave way to other forms, which – while often erroneous in and of themselves – were closer to the target language form than utterances in the earlier stages had been.

To emphasise the systematic nature of such developing interlanguage rules, Corder (1967) has drawn a distinction between 'mistakes' and 'errors'. He uses the term *error* to refer to regular patterns in the learner's speech which consistently differ from the target language model. The regularity of such patterns reveals the learner's underlying competence – the system of rules that governs his speech. In contrast, he uses the term *mistake* to refer to memory lapses, slips of the tongue and other instances of performance errors, as the term is used in analysis of first language data. Second language learners can often correct their own *mistakes*, but the *errors* they make, from this perspective, are part of their current system of interlanguage rules and hence are not recognisable (to the learners themselves) as 'wrong'. Thus, their errors are not amenable to self-repair, but their mistakes may well be.

To a large extent, the concept of an interlanguage continuum is useful in the classroom setting as well as in studying naturalistic language acquisition. One way of viewing instruction is that it is the teacher's job to help students move along the interlanguage continuum. Teachers try to help learners, first of all, by teaching them what they need to learn next in the sequence, and second, by pointing out where their production differs from the target language model. In doing so, teachers try to get learners to 'notice the gap' (Schmidt and Frota 1986), so that they can move along to the next interlanguage stage. The 'notice the gap' principle refers to the idea that learners must be aware of differences between their own language use and that of native speakers in order to make changes in their developing rule systems. We will return to this point in section 6.4.

Whether or not teachers know about the concept of interlanguage, they usually do strive to correct the errors that occur in learners' speech, although there is considerable variation among teachers in this respect, as work by Nystrom (1983) and Chaudron (1986b) has shown. There may also be variation among different methods of language teaching. Nowadays, it is certainly true that some of the so-called 'innovative methods' deliberately avoid error treatment, or at least downplay its role in formal instruction. Much classroom research is needed to document the use of error treatment in communicatively oriented language lessons. (This possibility will be addressed in the end-of-chapter activities.)

If we adopt the notion of interlanguage in a discussion of second language learners' errors, we can see that by treating errors, teachers are trying to help students move ahead in their interlanguage development. However, mistimed error treatment may not be helpful, and may even be harmful if it is aimed at structures which are beyond the second language learners in terms of their stage of interlanguage development. We will return to this issue in section 6.4, in considering how teachers decide when to treat oral errors.

At this juncture, in order to complete our picture of the background to teachers' decision making regarding errors, we will consider some ideas about how learners in classrooms move along or get stuck at various points on the interlanguage continuum. Then we will be in a position to examine more closely how teachers respond to oral errors.

5.5 Hypothesis testing and fossilisation

One possible explanation of what happens in the second language learner's mind borrows the metaphor of 'hypothesis testing' from experimental science. (A hypothesis is usually a clearly worded prediction about a correlation between two variables, about significant differences in groups' performance, or about cause and effect relationships.) In scientific experiments, researchers set up testable hypotheses. Then they gather data, analyse the results and either reject or confirm their original hypotheses. Second language learners are thought to do much the same thing (though the process may not be nearly so purposeful or so conscious) in trying to communicate in the target language.

The logic of the metaphor goes like this: second language learners try a new form (that is, they pose and test a hypothesis). This may be a form they have heard or seen or been taught but have not said before, or it could be something they invent. For example, Tarone (1981) has documented the use of 'word coinage' – a communication strategy in which a second language learner makes up a word that sounds as if it could or should be a word in the target language. Afterwards, the learners get feedback in the form of comprehension signals, blank looks, or requests for clarification from their interlocutors. Depending on the feedback, they may then alter the hypothesis and try again or continue with the original idea of how to communicate successfully.

Another metaphor – the concept of 'fossilisation' – is often used in discussions of second language learners' errors. Some learners seem not to make much use of the feedback they receive in terms of altering their output. The speech of many second language learners is characterised by the familiar phenomenon of getting stuck with a fixed system of linguistic forms that do not match the target language model. The idea that a non-native form (an error) can become 'cast in stone' over time, that it seems impervious to correction or input, makes the notion of fossilisation intuitively appealing to teachers who have struggled with the existence of such errors in their students' speech and writing.

Brown (1987:186) has pointed out that 'the internalization of incorrect forms takes place by means of the same learning processes as the internalization of correct forms, but we refer to the latter ... as "learning"' while the former is called fossilisation. In other words, learning correctly consists of internalising appropriate forms of the target language, while fossilisation is the consistent use of recognisably erroneous forms.

While we do not know exactly why fossilisation occurs, some researchers (for example, Brown 1987, and Vigil and Oller 1976) believe it has to do with the type of feedback second language learners receive. Vigil and Oller noted that second language learners get at least two kinds of feedback from their interlocutors. The first is 'cognitive feedback' – information about the language they use. The second is 'affective feedback' – emotional reactions in response to their uttterances and signals as to the interlocutor's desire or willingness to continue communicating.

Vigil and Oller suggest that to prevent fossilisation of erroneous forms, clear cognitive information about the problems in the learners' output should be provided. But to ensure continued communication, such information must be accompanied by positive affective feedback; otherwise the learners may receive such discouraging affective signals that they will stop their efforts to interact in the target language. Conversely, of course, in Vigil and Oller's model, positive affective feedback must not be so encouraging that the learners see no reason to change their erroneous output.

Both types of feedback are simultaneously supplied to language learners by their interlocutors in most communicative settings. As the learners test their hypotheses about how to communicate in the target language, the people they are talking to respond, usually with both cognitive and affective feedback.

5.6 Summary

So far we have considered a great deal of background information related to the phenomenon of error in language learning. We have seen that both first and second language learners make errors, and that these forms differ from the adult or target language model which typically surrounds the learners and serves as input to their developing grammatical systems. We noted that progress in language development, whether in a first or second language, is gauged, in part, by the gradual decline of formal errors. We also saw, however, that some second language learners generate or pick up and then systematically continue to use erroneous forms – that is, their errors fossilise.

We saw too, from the research on first language conversational interaction, that, in English at least, there is a propensity for self-initiated self-repair when speech errors do occur: people normally correct themselves. Furthermore, we suggested that in many language classrooms, when an oral error occurs, the response pattern often involves other-initiated other-repair; that is, teachers typically correct learners' errors. We turn in Chapter 6 to a more detailed consideration of exactly what teachers do in their attempts to correct second language learners' oral errors. Before doing so, however, we will suggest some activities which should illuminate the concepts covered in this chapter.

DISCUSSION STARTERS

1 What are the ways in which you, as a language teacher, can recognise learners' errors? In other words, how do *you* define error? Think about your own teaching. In practice, how do you know, in split-second decision-making terms, that a student has made an error?
2 What are the differences, if any, between formal errors and communicative errors? What are the implications for how we, as teachers, respond to such errors? Do you make a distinction in your classes?
3 How might (or should) a teacher's response to error differ depending on the student's proficiency levels? That is, should we treat beginners' errors differently from those of intermediate or advanced learners? Why or why not? (Think about the stages of interlanguage development.)
4 To what extent does the concept of interlanguage apply to classroom language learning, and in what ways is it a useful idea in understanding naturalistic language acquisition? How can we, as teachers, help learners move along the interlanguage continuum? What examples of interlanguage development have you noticed among learners?
5 Have you ever known a language learner who appeared to have fossilised errors? How can a teacher tell if the learner's interlanguage system has truly fossilised? Or, to put it more positively, how can teachers recognise temporary plateaux in learners' interlanguage development, and subsequently help the learners to move on?
6 Do you see a clear distinction between cognitive and affective feedback? If so, what balance would you look for between the two?
7 Based on your own experience, either as a language learner or in helping and observing language learners, do you have any evidence that hypothesis testing actually takes place? In other words, is hypothesis testing merely a useful metaphor, or does the term have a basis in psychological reality?

SUGGESTIONS FOR FURTHER READING

1 For detailed discussions of speech variation among native speakers, see Wolfram and Fasold (1974) or Trudgill (1974).
2 Some useful background on first language acquisition may be found in Brown (1973), R. Clark (1980), and Gathercole (1988).
3 Two accessible books about communicative language teaching are by Brumfit and Johnson (1979), and Littlewood (1981).
4 Given the background information in this chapter, it would be interesting to see what several different 'innovative methods' have to say about error treatment. Some good sources would be Blair (1982),

Oller and Richard-Amato (1983), Richards and Rodgers (1986), and Larsen-Freeman (1986).

5 Some very early influential work on interlanguage and fossilisation was done by Selinker (1972, reprinted in 1974). It appears in a book about error analysis which was edited by Richards (1974), along with several other articles on related topics. Selinker, Swain and Dumas (1975) have written on interlanguage as it relates to children's learning of a second language.

6 Another useful book on error analysis and interlanguage is by Corder (1981). His earlier work on interlanguage (1967, 1978) was also influential.

7 Repair in language learning has been investigated by Gaskill (1980), Schwartz (1980), Kasper (1985) and van Lier (1988).

8 Bialystok (1983) has written an interesting paper about inferencing, entitled 'Testing the "hypothesis-testing" hypothesis'.

9 For an investigation of developmental stages in language learning in an instructional setting, see Lightbown (1983).

10 Vigil and Oller's (1976) model of cognitive and affective feedback and their role in fossilisation has interesting implications for language teachers. These implications have been discussed by Brown (1987), particularly in his Chapter 9, which deals with interlanguage.

11 James (1980) summarises a great deal of information about the theory and practice of contrastive analysis. Courchêne (1980) has written about contrastive analysis, error analysis, and their relationship to error treatment in language classrooms.

MINI-PROJECT: INITIATION AND REPAIR

This mini-project will give you an opportunity to work with the concepts of initiation and repair (Schegloff *et al.* 1977) in analysing transcript data.

STAGE ONE: GETTING TO KNOW THE CONCEPTS

To begin, it will be useful to prepare a blank chart like this one:

| | | **Initiation** | |
		By self	By others
Repair	By self		
	By others		

Now find a small piece of transcript just to practise on. For example, you could turn back to section 2.3.3 and use Transcript 1 (beginning at the point in the lesson where S8 says, 'They took a branches ... '). Try to identify each example of initiation and repair first, and then classify each example according to the self/other distinction. When you have produced your own analysis, enter it on your chart, with one tally mark for each example.

Next, check your analysis with other people who have worked on the same bit of transcript. If there are instances over which you disagree, discuss the differences and refine your understanding of the concepts of initiation and repair. If you are particularly interested in this topic, it would be worthwhile to read the original Schegloff *et al.* (1977) paper at this point. You could also consult articles by some of the language researchers who have used this framework (for example, Gaskill 1980; Kasper 1985; van Lier 1988), in order to see how other people have utilised these same concepts to analyse transcripts.

STAGE TWO: ANALYSING OUT-OF-CLASS INTERACTION

Record just two people in conversation for at least a few minutes. If possible, record a non-native speaker talking to a native, or a caretaker talking to a small child. Whoever you record, get their permission first, and tell them what you will be doing with the recording. (To avoid triggering the observer's paradox, you should not tell them that you will be analysing initiation and repair of conversational trouble spots; however, you should openly tell them you will listen to their conversation to help you, as a teacher, understand how people interact.) Be sure to promise the speakers that you will not use any parts of their conversation that they would prefer to have kept confidential.

Listen to the recording and make a note of the tape counter number whenever you hear repairs. Use this technique to locate a section of the tape that promises to be a rich source of examples of initiations and repairs. Now transcribe at least a page or two of that part of the interaction, and analyse it as you did in the first stage of this mini-project. If your colleagues have each been making their own recordings and analyses, you can then compare notes and further refine your understanding of the concepts and how to use them operationally.

Finally, keep your recordings, your transcripts, and your analyses. They will be very useful comparison data if you later decide to do a project on the treatment of oral errors in a language class.

6 The treatment of oral errors: what teachers do

Now that we have considered some of the research findings related to error in both first and second language situations, we can turn to a discussion of error in the language classroom. Our chief concern will be to examine the decision-making processes teachers go through when they react to learners' oral errors.

The word 'react' as it is used here has a technical meaning. It is derived from work by Bellack and his colleagues (see, for example, Bellack *et al.* 1966), who have offered a simple description of classroom discourse involving a four-part framework: 1) structure, 2) solicit, 3) respond, and 4) react. The following transcript, taken from an English lesson, will illustrate these four types of moves. (Bellack's categories are given in bold print.)

Transcript 5: What's a conductor?

- T: OK. Now. A conductor. (**Structuring**) Pedro, what's a conductor? (**Soliciting**)
- S: A conductor is the people who is boss in the in the em (inaudible) for example, in music. (**Responding**)
- T: OK. (**Reacting**)

This transcript is reprinted from Long 1980a, reprinted in Seliger and Long 1983:8.

As can be seen from this example, teachers use 'structuring' moves to inform the learners as to the instructional plan before asking a question or setting a task for the learners to do, via a 'solicit'. The learners then perform the task or provide the requested information (the 'response'), at which point teachers offer evaluative comments of some sort (that is, they 'react'). Typically (though not always), such reacting moves are part of the teacher's role, rather than the learners'. Such evaluative feedback on the form of an utterance is not what we expect in normal, non-teaching conversation.

6.1 Treatment versus cure

Perhaps the major finding of research so far on the treatment of error is that it is an infinitely more complex area than we had previously imagined. We have already seen, in the preceding pages, just how complex the background is, conceptually. When we look at error treatment in actual language classrooms we face both conceptual and practical complexities.

The basic conceptual problem is that, as we know from medicine, treatment and cure are not the same. Just because the teacher treats an error in some way, or just because the learner, in response to the treatment, manages immediately to get something right that was previously wrong, does not mean that a permanent cure has been effected. Many teachers have had the uncomfortable experience of getting learners who made repeated errors to use the correct form in the class, only to hear the incorrect form re-emerge in the corridors outside the classroom during the break. No matter how hard a teacher tries to correct errors, in the long run, only the learner can do the learning necessary to improve performance, regardless of how much treatment is provided. It is for this reason that we will generally avoid using the word 'correction' in the rest of this chapter, because it implies a 'cure', whereas studies so far have really only been able to investigate the treatment given to errors and their immediate effect on learner behaviour.

If one of our goals as language teachers is to help our learners move along the interlanguage continuum, getting closer and closer to the target language norm, then, the thinking goes, we must provide them with the feedback they need to modify their hypotheses about the functions and linguistic forms they use. (Notice that there is an assumption here – the assumption that providing feedback will help learners to alter their output in constructive and long-lasting ways.) However, we are often faced with difficult choices about how best to do this without discouraging the learners. We also need to be confident that we treat errors in such a way that the learners will, in fact, alter their output for the better. In this sense, using Vigil and Oller's terms (1976), teachers must provide learners with appropriate cognitive feedback as well as affective support.

6.2 How teachers react to learners' oral errors

The research on teacher treatment of learner error, including studies by Allwright (1975), Chaudron (1977, 1986b, 1987), Fanselow (1977b), Long (1977), and Nystrom (1983), shows that teachers do not treat all the errors that do occur. The findings also reveal that teachers have a wide variety of techniques available for the treatment of errors, but they do not typically make full use of the repertoire of behaviours from which they might choose in providing feedback. These findings are certainly not remarkable. What is remarkable is the complexity of the decisions teachers must make in order to treat learners' errors appropriately.

The following discussion will take as its point of departure a model of the decision-making process a language teacher goes through when an oral error occurs. This model (see Figure 4, opposite), which was proposed by Long in 1977, details the choices the teacher must make between the moment when an oral error occurs and the actual behavioural manifestation of feedback that follows.

The issues depicted in this flow chart can be framed as a series of questions about the teacher's role and the timing of the reacting move following the student's erroneous response. In a recent review of the error treatment research, Chaudron (1987) adopted as a framework the following questions, which were originally posed by Hendrickson (1978):

1 Should learner errors be corrected?
2 If so, when should learner errors be corrected?
3 Which learner errors should be corrected?
4 How should learner errors be corrected?
5 Who should correct learner errors?

In the present discussion, we will follow closely the decision-making process faced by teachers, taking up the sorts of questions raised by Hendrickson and Chaudron. In so doing, we will suggest some slight modifications of Long's (1977) model.

6.3 Deciding whether to treat oral errors

The first question in following the flow chart proposed by Long is whether or not the teacher notices a learner's error as it occurs. If an error is in fact noticed, does the teacher decide to treat it as an error or to let it pass without comment? Many factors influence the decision-making process even at these early steps. For instance, have the learners been exposed to the form or function involving the error before? To many teachers, it may not seem fair, in some basically human sense, to 'penalise' the learner by reacting with negative cognitive feedback to an error which may have been a good guess at a form or function which had not been encountered before.

Teachers who are non-native speakers of the target language may perhaps be expected to have a rather special problem in terms of their ability even to notice learners' errors. They may ask what their own place is on the interlanguage continuum. Non-native teachers cannot be

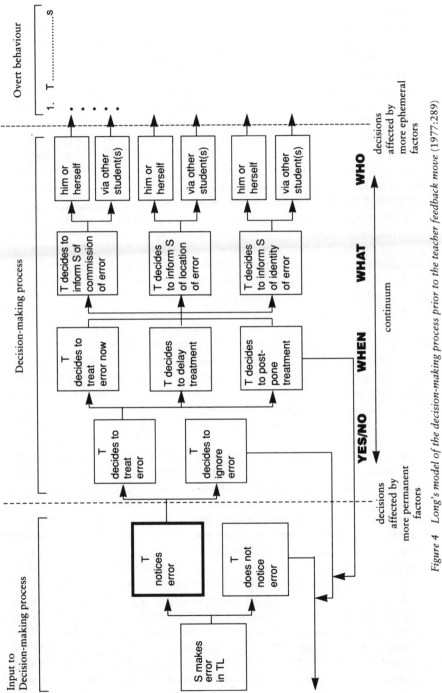

Figure 4 *Long's model of the decision-making process prior to the teacher feedback move* (1977:289)

expected to treat errors that they cannot detect. A non-native speaking teacher's own target language grammar may not include all the phonological, morphological, lexical, syntactic or discourse rules needed to recognise and treat all the errors in the learners' output.

Curiously, however, recent research on 'error gravity' (that is, the perceived seriousness of an error) has shown, first of all, that native speakers who are not teachers are less severe in their reactions to learners' faulty utterances than are language teachers. Furthermore, non-native speaking teachers of the target language are consistently more severe in their reactions to learners' errors than are their native-speaking counterparts. This pattern has been documented in a review (Ludwig 1982) of the error gravity research conducted on several languages, including German, Spanish, French, and English.

Another question which teachers face in deciding whether to treat an error or to ignore it is whether the error is within the learner's grasp in terms of his or her place on the interlanguage continuum. It may do no good at all to try to give learners feedback on a form they are not ready to learn. For example, the 'morpheme studies' (such as Dulay and Burt 1974a,b; Bailey, Madden and Krashen 1974; Larsen-Freeman 1976; J. D. Brown 1983) show that the third-person singular s-marker on present tense English verbs (*he walks, she drives, John dances*) is a consistently late-learned morpheme. This pattern may be due to the fact that if it appears in a sentence with a subject it is a redundant marker which provides no new information, given the obligatory subject slot in English; it is irregular, compared with the unmarked verb conjugations for other persons; and it is not always phonologically salient. Hence, it is simply not as notable as other morphemes (Krashen *et al.* 1977).

The dilemma these findings present to English teachers is the question of whether or not treatment of learners' errors on this morpheme will help speed the acquisition of the correct form, or simply be futile until the learners reach a stage of interlanguage development where they can make use of such feedback to modify their hypotheses about how the present tense is marked. There may be many such instances in which the wisest thing a teacher can do is to ignore an oral error.

A problem arises here, however, since the output of any learner in a classroom may serve as input to any other learner, as well as to the entire class. The auto-input hypothesis, discussed by Schmidt and Frota (1986), suggests that the erroneous form may even serve as further input to the person who uttered it. If a teacher chooses not to treat an error in one learner's utterance, the other learners may assume that the form or function was correct as it stood. This assumption could conceivably lead to some learners incorrectly internalising errors. Teachers also worry that some learners may even modify their existing correct hypotheses to include incorrect forms, in order to conform with their classmates' uncorrected output.

Some research has shown that teachers' and second language learners' perspectives differ on the desirability of error treatment. Cathcart and Olsen (1976) found that learners say they want more correction than is typically offered by their teachers. Chenoweth *et al.* (1983) obtained similar findings when ESL learners reported wanting more correction than they were receiving in conversations with their native English-speaking friends. Of course, they may still react badly if their teachers or friends begin to 'over-correct'. The problem is to find the right balance all the time. Thus, even the first stage of the decision-making process – that is, the question of whether to treat the error or to ignore it – is not a simple matter.

6.4 Deciding when to treat oral errors

The next issue, depicted in the WHEN column of Long's flow chart, is the question of when to treat an error. The teacher may deal with it immediately, or delay treatment somewhat (for example, until the learner finishes with the message she or he was trying to convey), while still treating the error within the boundaries of the same lesson in which it occurred. The problem with immediate error treatment, many teachers feel, is that it often involves interrupting the learner in mid-sentence – a practice which can certainly be disruptive and could eventually inhibit the learner's willingness to speak in class at all. In Vigil and Oller's terms (1976) the affective feedback would be negative.

Alternately, teachers may postpone the treatment for longer periods of time. For instance, oral errors, particularly if they are patterned and are shared by a group of learners, may form the starting point for a future lesson. Unfortunately, as Long points out (1977:290), the psychology research literature shows that feedback becomes less effective as the time between the performance of the skill and the feedback increases. What we, as teachers, must nevertheless somehow decide, is how far to apply the results of psychological experiments to our classroom settings.

The classroom research to date is sparse regarding the relative value of immediate, delayed, or postponed feedback. So as teachers or classroom researchers, we must observe the results of implementing these various strategies in our own classrooms and make our own informed decisions. Fanselow (1977b) has argued that teachers should offer learners the greatest possible variety of treatments, not only because we know of no one way that always works, but also because different people need to be treated differently anyway. Also, teachers need to keep on trying out different possibilities to see what happens.

At this point we might usefully consider in more detail a related principle of language learning which we mentioned briefly in section 5.4. Schmidt and Frota (1986) have articulated this principle as 'notice the gap'. The idea comes from a diary study of Schmidt's acquisition of Portuguese, in both tutored and untutored situations in Brazil. Schmidt and Frota concluded that in order to change an incorrect form, Schmidt needed to become consciously aware of the difference between what he was saying and what other people were saying before he could alter his output. The researchers started with Krashen's concept of 'i + 1', where 'i' stands for the learner's current stage of interlanguage development, and the '+ 1' represents the next level of language to be acquired (1982:20–9). They hypothesised that corrective feedback 'juxtaposes the learner's form "i" with the target language form "i + 1" and the learner is put in an ideal position to notice the gap' (Schmidt and Frota 1986:313). Unfortunately, simply noticing the gap did not mean that Schmidt's errors automatically got corrected. Instead, Schmidt and Frota feel that this conscious awareness of the gap is a necessary first step but not a sufficient condition for improvement.

It would be unwise simply to assume at this point that all learners are like Schmidt in needing to notice the gap. But if this idea is supported by future research and experience, then the teacher's responsibility in treating errors would become, first, to choose the optimum moment for providing feedback when learners are most open to noticing the gap. Finding the 'optimum moment' is no small problem, though. We can expect our learners all to be at different stages in their learning, all ready for quite different things. Pienemann (1984) discusses the concept of 'learnability', suggesting that learners at any one stage will find 'learnable' only those things that are at just the next stage of natural development. It may be possible to accelerate their progress through the stages, according to Pienemann, but not to jump stages altogether.

The next problem is that teachers would have to choose the best type of treatment to provide in order to help the second language learners achieve this needed awareness. (Simple repetition or modelling of the correct form may be useless if the learners cannot perceive the difference between the model and the erroneous forms they produce.) The feedback would have to be appropriately pitched, so that learners are not uselessly being harangued about errors their interlingual developmental stage has not yet prepared them to cope with (for example, premature treatment of characteristically late-learned forms). Finally, the feedback would have to be delivered in such a way as to provide affective support, so the learners will not be demoralised, at the same time as the negative cognitive information is transmitted.

6.5 Deciding what treatment to provide

Once teachers do decide to treat noticed errors, and decide when they will do so, they have a variety of methods at their disposal. Unfortunately, perhaps, such treatment is sometimes ambiguous and not always systematic. Allwright (1975), however, has pointed out that teachers may have an obligation to be inconsistent, in a certain sense, in their use of treatment behaviours, since within any one class, learners' needs and levels may differ widely.

Teachers react to learners' errors in many ways, both verbally and nonverbally. It is beyond the scope of this chapter to go into detail on the repertoire of behaviours available to teachers. Several other papers (such as Allwright 1975; Chaudron 1977; Salica 1981; Nystrom 1983) have dealt with this topic in considerable depth. The most detailed model of teachers' reacting moves comes from Chaudron's (1977:38–9) research on corrective discourse in French immersion instruction in elementary school classes in Canada. Chaudron's model was tested by Salica (1981) in an ESL setting with adult learners. It is reprinted overleaf as Figure 5, to reveal how incredibly complex this facet of oral error treatment really is.

Along with this flow chart, Chaudron produced a catalogue of over thirty types of steps a teacher can take following an oral error. (See Appendix G for his list.) These include 'repeat', 'prompt', 'clue', etc. – all with examples from classroom transcripts. Each of these strategies for error treatment is described in detail in Chaudron's work (1977, 1987). The reader is referred to his publications and to Appendix G for further information. Here we will simply use his model as a depiction of the types of complex decisions teachers make about how to treat errors, over and over again, on a daily basis, the moment that an oral error is made. At this point, we will return to the fifth column of Long's model – the WHAT of teachers' reacting behaviours.

Long notes that teachers have (at least) three choices in deciding what to treat: 1) to inform the learner that an error has been made, 2) to inform the learner of the location of the error, and 3) to inform the learner of the identity of the error, an option which subsumes both 1 and 2. (You will see that Chaudron's model spells out in more detail how each of these steps may be accomplished. For example, 'explanation', in Chaudron's catalogue of correcting behaviours, is one of the ways in which teachers indicate to learners the cause and/or type of error that has occurred.)

Notice that each succeeding box in this column of Long's flow chart (Figure 4) demands less cognitive work of the second language learner. A certain amount of demanding cognitive work may be a very good thing in getting the learners to attend to both form and meaning of the language.

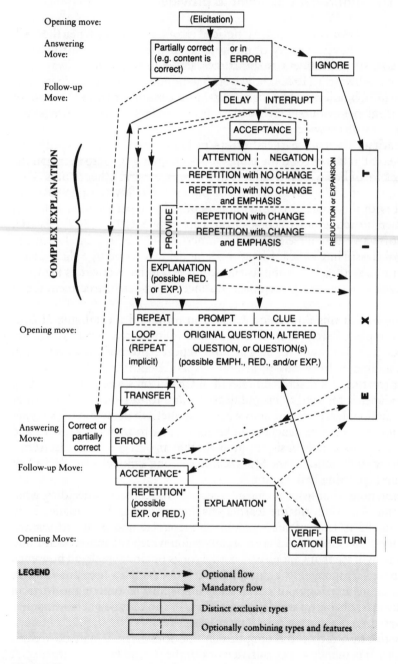

Opening move: (Elicitation)

Answering Move: Partially correct (e.g. content is correct) | or in ERROR | IGNORE

Follow-up Move: DELAY | INTERRUPT

ACCEPTANCE

ATTENTION | NEGATION

REPETITION with NO CHANGE
REPETITION with NO CHANGE and EMPHASIS
REPETITION with CHANGE
REPETITION with CHANGE and EMPHASIS

REDUCTION or EXPANSION

PROVIDE

COMPLEX EXPLANATION

EXPLANATION (possible RED. or EXP.)

Opening move: REPEAT | PROMPT | CLUE

LOOP (REPEAT implicit) | ORIGINAL QUESTION, ALTERED QUESTION, or QUESTION(s) (possible EMPH., RED., and/or EXP.)

TRANSFER

Answering Move: Correct or partially correct | or ERROR

Follow-up Move: ACCEPTANCE*

REPETITION* (possible EXP. or RED.) | EXPLANATION*

Opening Move: VERIFI-CATION | RETURN

T · I · X · E

LEGEND
----------▶ Optional flow
──────▶ Mandatory flow
☐☐ Distinct exclusive types
☐┊☐ Optionally combining types and features

Figure 5
Chaudron's (1977:37) Flow chart model of corrective discourse

This notion leads to the question of who will treat the error, the issue raised in the fifth column of Long's flow chart.

6.6 Deciding who will treat oral errors

The most common source of feedback to language learners in classrooms is treatment provided by the teacher. While this claim is not surprising, we should question whether this type of treatment is the most fruitful in terms of the teacher's and learners' common goals. More actual learning may ensue if the learners accomplish a substantial proportion of the corrective task themselves. If it is not the teacher who treats the error, then it could be either the learner who erred (self-correction) or another member of the class (peer correction).

In Long's flow chart 'him or herself' in the column labelled WHO refers to the teacher informing the student about the commission, location, or identity of the error made. Certainly we could add another box to each option of the WHO column which would capture the possibility that, in all cases, the teacher could offer the learner the opportunity to try to self-correct without any further help from the teacher. As we noted in section 6.1, only the learners are actually capable of making changes in their developing interlanguage systems. This is, of course, our long-term goal: that our students will repair their own communication breakdowns and produce the target language accurately and fluently without guidance from us, and that the correct forms will be internalised.

Ideally, we would hope to 'work ourselves out of a job' by helping our learners become capable of self-correction or – better yet – we would hope that they would not make errors in the first place. This latter condition, of course, is in part how we recognise proficient second or foreign language speakers: the relative absence of errors in their speech. In one interpretation of language acquisition, Krashen (1977) suggests that the 'monitor' (a label for the internalised 'editor' or collection of rules one has learned) can prevent or repair some errors (or rather *mistakes*, in Corder's terms) under some conditions. These conditions include a) a focus on form, rather than on communication of meaning, and b) adequate time for the learner to process the output. So, when possible, we would be pleased to see learners able to apply the rules they had learned to correct their own mistakes. Put another way, we want our learners to be able to make self-initiated self-repairs. We should therefore allow them both time and opportunity in our classrooms for self-repair, whether it is self- or other-initiated.

The concept of 'wait-time' is relevant to the notion of repair (Rowe 1969; Holley and King 1974; Fanselow 1977b). Wait-time is the length of time a teacher (or possibly another interlocutor) will wait after having posed a question or a task to a learner, before prompting, rephrasing, or redirecting the question or task to another student. The phenomenon was studied by Rowe (1969) with native English-speaking children studying science. She found that as teachers increased their wait-time, the quality and quantity of the students' responses increased. In an early study of imitation and correction in foreign language learning, Holley and King (1974) reported on a small-scale intervention in which they asked teachers of German to wait five to ten seconds if a learner erred or hesitated in answering a question. They reported that in over fifty per cent of the cases they videotaped no corrective efforts from the teacher were needed. The learners themselves were able to respond correctly, given this brief additional pause.

Another possibility is that other learners in the classroom could help to provide corrective feedback if it is necessary. In one experimental study related to this issue, Porter (1986) found that second language learners interacting either with native speakers or with other second language learners were able to accurately correct other learners' errors, though they rarely did so. (In this work, 'correcting' means saying what the other speaker should have said. It does not mean trying to teach the other person to say the correct thing in the future. It may therefore be very different from the teacher's treatment of error.) While the learners corrected each other only 1.5 per cent of the time, they miscorrected one another less than three-tenths of a per cent of the time. In other words, they treated each other's errors very infrequently but when they did, they were five times more likely to be right than to miscorrect. The native speakers other-corrected only eight per cent of the errors that occurred in the learners' speech. The differences between the native and non-native speakers' correction rates were not statistically significant, so Porter concludes that teachers should probably not worry, when learners are working together in groups, about students miscorrecting one another.

Since, in any one language class, the learners' developing interlanguage grammars may differ widely, it will be possible for many students to recognise and repair their classmates' errors. But peer correction has been systematically studied in the area of feedback on written work more than in oral classroom discourse. We do not have much solid data on its usefulness, and this is one area that could be profitably studied in classroom research projects.

It seems clear, however, that if peer feedback is encouraged, it will be important for the teacher to establish a tone of mutual support, so that learners are not overwhelmed by corrective input. The manner in which errors are treated – whether by the teacher, the learners themselves, or by their peers – may do much to influence the learners' openness to treatment. If learners are put on the defensive by heavy-handed error treatment, they may not be able to notice the gap or process the incoming cognitive feedback. This issue, the learners' receptivity, will be covered in depth in Chapters 9 and 10. Here we will briefly turn to questions of how teachers' attitudes and behaviour during error treatment may influence learners.

6.7 Error treatment and affective concerns

We have spent considerable time discussing error in second language learning, in general, and teachers' reactions to learners' oral errors in particular. (We have not even attempted to consider the growing body of literature about feedback on learners' written work!) Before we close this chapter, though, we will examine an excerpt of a transcript in order to focus on some of the ways in which error treatment is related to affect. The transcript is taken from an intermediate EFL vocabulary lesson for young adults. ('T' stands for the teacher's verbal turns and 'S' for individual students, indicated by identifying numbers.)

Transcript 6: Carlos's trousers

T: ... OK? Chemical pollution. OK.
S4: (Yawning) O-o-o.
T: Trousers. Alright, Carlos (S4), do you wear trousers?
S4: Alway. All my life.
Ss: (Laughter)
T: Always. You've worn, I have ...
S4: Eh, wear, wear (inaudible)
T: I have ... Well, do you wear trousers?
S5: I wear.
Ss: I wear, I wear.
S4: Yes, I I do.
T: Yes, you do. What's how do you say that word?
S4: Trousers.
T: Trou**sers**.
S4: Trou**sers**.
T: **Trou**sers.
S4: **Trou**sers.
S3: Trousers.
T: Mm-hmm. Have you got trousers on?
S3: Yes, I have.
T: What kind?
S3: Jeans
T: Jeans. Say the word jeans. Jeans.
S3: Jeans.
T: Jeans.
S2: Jeans.
T: Jeans.

E

S1: Jeans.
 T: OK. OK. Huh! Does anyone need an ashtray?

(Excerpt from *Classroom Oriented Research in Second Language Acquisition* by H. W. Seliger and M. H. Long. Copyright © 1983 by Newbury House Publishers, Inc. Reprinted by permission of Harper-Collins Publishers.)

A number of interesting things are going on in this brief vignette of an EFL lesson. To begin with, Carlos (S4) makes a double behavioural error. First he yawns audibly during the vocabulary review. In response, the teacher calls on him with the display question, 'Do you wear trousers?' A 'display question' is used for the purpose of getting students to display their knowledge of the linguistic forms or factual content needed to respond. A subset of display questions is called 'known information questions' – that is, questions to which the teacher already knows the answers, which is clearly the case here. (See Long and Sato 1983, for further discussion.) Carlos's second behavioural error is that he introduces humour into the discussion at a time when the teacher seems to deem it inappropriate: his classmates laugh when he responds, 'Alway. All my life.'

The teacher ignores both the truth value and the humour of this remark and focuses on S4's linguistic error by modelling the correct form and then prompting Carlos to respond with a full sentence: 'Alway*s*. You've worn, I have ....' Carlos, possibly somewhat taken aback, searches for the correct form of the verb: 'eh, wear, wear ...' but his voice fades out. Instead of providing the information Carlos needs to complete the utterance, the teacher repeats both the prompt and the question: 'I have ... well, do you wear trousers?' At this point, S5 and other students in the class begin to coach Carlos, providing the correct form. Carlos opts for the basic affirmative response to the yes/no question, however, and says simply, 'Yes, I I do.' Up to this point in the lesson, Carlos has never uttered the word *trousers*, which was the vocabulary item that led to this exchange. The teacher confirms his affirmative response but prompts him to say the actual word: 'Yes, you do. What's how do you say that word?'

At this point a curious classroom discourse phenomenon occurs. In the next exchange we see an example of 'teacher-induced error' – an error which the student (probably) would not have made except for the 'guidance' he received from the teacher. He responds to the teacher's solicit by correctly pronouncing the word, 'Trousers'. The teacher, perhaps remembering the missing *s* from Carlos's first linguistic error ('alway') repeats the word, but stresses the second syllable: 'Trou*sers*'. Carlos, by now fully cowed, dutifully repeats the teacher's model: 'Trou*sers*'. In so doing, he makes a phonological error of misplaced word stress (the teacher-induced error), which the teacher now deals with by

110

saying, '*Trousers*'. Again, Carlos repeats, thus reiterating his original correct pronunciation: '*Trousers*'.

At this juncture, S3 also repeats the word, and the teacher now turns to this student and asks another known-answer display question: 'Have you got trousers on?' S3 responds with the simple affirmative response, 'Yes, I have', which seems to be the safest thing to say in this class. Again, a display question is posed ('What kind?') and S3's response provides the basis for the next several utterances. From this point the repetitions continue with no errors until the teacher decides the discussion of trousers in general and jeans in particular has gone on long enough.

As language teachers, all of us have known frustrating days and have struggled to keep a lesson on track when the learners do not seem fully thrilled or even very co-operative. Many teachers, of course, feel it is important to maintain control over the learners' behaviour in class. It is not our purpose here to belittle this teacher's strategies or to defend Carlos's *behavioural* errors. Instead, we are trying to illustrate how the teacher's response to Carlos's *linguistic* error (deleting the word-final -*s* on 'alway') and the interactions that follow contribute to a climate of stiff non-communication. Leo van Lier has pointed out (personal communication) that drilling itself may offer teachers too much control: it may be, in part, Carlos's insult to the ritual of the drill which seems offensive to the teacher here.

What were the students likely to learn in this series of exchanges? The learners may have decided that it is important to pronounce /z/, the last phoneme in *always*. They may have learned not to make jokes, or even not to yawn, in class. They may have learned (if they did not already know) that *trousers* is stressed on the first syllable, although there could certainly be some justifiable confusion on this point. It is not clear that anything about the verbal exchanges in this vocabulary lesson explicitly taught them the meaning of *trousers* if they did not already know it – only that Carlos has always worn them and that jeans are the kind which S3 is wearing. While they may have gained little or no linguistic information from this stretch of discourse, the students probably have learned that it does not pay to annoy this teacher: the reaction in this case was swift and severe error treatment, even to the point of leading the student to make an extra error, which was itself then summarily treated.

You will recall Vigil and Oller's (1976) notion that both cognitive and affective feedback are important parts of the message conveyed when teachers or native speakers react to language learners' errors. In this transcript, we see a clear example of a teacher using error treatment (ostensibly a linguistic procedure) to (re)establish classroom control (a social objective). We cannot tell whether Carlos understood the cognitive feedback, since he does not correctly produce the target form *always*. Nor can we tell if he is puzzled about which syllable of *trousers* should actually be stressed. But it appears that the teacher made the affective point very clearly: error correction in this classroom can be used as a form of disciplinary action. We will consider the possible effects of such actions in Chapter 10, when we discuss the concept of self-esteem as it relates to receptivity.

6.8 Summary

Throughout this chapter we have looked at error treatment in terms of the sorts of questions teachers quite reasonably ask about the issue. We would all like to know exactly which errors to treat, exactly when, and exactly how. It is now time, however, to reconsider these questions in the light of all the research that has been done so far.

The most obvious conclusion we can draw from the research we have reviewed is that the treatment of error is, to say the least, an extremely complex business. Researchers who have set out to unravel the processes of decision making which teachers must go through have clearly shown us just how complicated these processes are. Under the circumstances, it seems entirely appropriate to marvel at the everyday achievements of good language teachers the world over, but at the same time it must seem equally appropriate to doubt that our simple questions could ever be given very simple answers. We have to start with the simple questions, of course, just in case there are some simple answers. But we can also use our simple questions as starting points for our explorations, our research investigations, and these may lead quite directly to a much more sophisticated understanding of the issues involved. Then we can at least deal properly with anyone who comes along claiming to know all the answers.

Another point worth making here is that explorations in the area of the treatment of error need not be left to the researchers. This is an area that lends itself particularly well to explorations by teachers themselves, in their own classrooms. At a time when advocates of communicative language teaching are suggesting that teachers should pay much more attention to communication problems and perhaps much less attention to problems of linguistic accuracy, it would be interesting for teachers who wish to follow this advice to study their own behaviour when they treat errors, to make sure they really are managing to change in the way they would like to.

DISCUSSION STARTERS

1 Do you accept the medical analogy used in this chapter to illustrate the distinction between treatment and cure?

2 Teachers may really notice more errors than they treat. If you recognise this possibility, what sorts of errors are you most likely to notice but then ignore, do you think? Do you ignore the same sorts of errors as other people? In other words, is there an agreed upon idea of error gravity – of some errors being more important to treat than others?

3 Learners often seem to want more error treatment than they get. What happens if you try to treat absolutely all their problems though? Have you tried it? If not, what do you *think* would happen?

4 Are you the sort of language learner who depends on 'noticing the gap'? If so, do you recall any particular examples of how a teacher either did or did not find the optimum moment for you to notice the gap? If you are not that sort of learner, what is your alternative strategy?

5 Do error treatment options differ according to the *teacher's* language proficiency? That is, do you think native speaking teachers treat learners' errors differently from non-native speaking teachers? If so, how? Why?

6 Figure 5 provides a model of the correction types Chaudron discovered in his classroom research (1977) on immersion programmes. Further elaboration of these moves is given in Appendix G. Which of these options do you use most often? Which do you think are most effective? Does your answer to the last question differ, depending on whether you are a language teacher or a language learner? Would different options work better with different levels of learners – say, beginning, intermediate and advanced?

7 If our ultimate goal is self-correction, what role do you see for peer-correction? Is it a step along the road, or just a pedagogic trick to enable the teacher to share the work-load a little? Alternatively, is peer-correction more useful to the 'corrector' than to the person being 'corrected'?

8 Teachers may use learners' errors as an opportunity to exercise social control in the classroom. For example, they may try to silence learners who are too talkative by drawing attention to even their smallest errors. In the light of the discussion on cognitive and affective feedback in section 5.5, what is likely to be the effect of such treatment?

SUGGESTIONS FOR FURTHER READING

1 Four classic studies on error treatment are by Allwright (1975), Chaudron (1977), Fanselow (1977b), and Long (1977). These authors influenced one another's thinking. If you read all four papers, you will be able to trace the development that runs through them.

2 For a very good up-to-date review of error treatment, read Chapter 5 of Chaudron (1988a). Chapter 7 of van Lier (1988) takes a different approach to the concept of error treatment, working from the perspective of conversational analysis.

3 Two studies that incorporate the teacher's point of view are by Nystrom (1983) and Chaudron (1986b). Cathcart and Olsen's (1976) research was one of the earliest studies to elicit the learners' point of view about error treatment. This tradition has been continued by Chun *et al.* (1982), and by Chenoweth *et al.* (1983). For a treatment of the respective roles of teachers and learners see Bruton and Samuda (1980).

4 This chapter has dealt exclusively with oral errors. However, much recent research has investigated phenomena associated with errors in language learners' written output. Some of the interesting treatments of this topic include articles by Cardelle and Corno (1981), Chaudron (1984a), Green and Hecht (1985), and Robb, Ross and Shortreed (1986).

5 Read Ludwig's (1982) review article about the error gravity research. Do you agree with her summary of the findings? Do you think the results would differ if different languages were studied? Clearly this type of work is not, strictly speaking, classroom research, but it does have a strong bearing on what we, as language teachers, decide to do about error treatment in our classes.

6 Kasper (1985) discusses repair in foreign language teaching, including the relationship of repair strategies to classroom activity type.

7 For information on error treatment in a foreign language setting, see Yoneyama (1982).

8 Two studies which examine corrective feedback in conversations between native speakers and non-native speakers are by Brock *et al.* (1986) and by Crookes and Rulon (1985).

9 Beretta (1989) has used Chaudron's (1977) catalogue of error treatment moves in his research on error treatment in the Communicational Language Teaching Project in Bangalore, India.

MINI-PROJECT: CODING ERRORS AND BUILDING MODELS

The purpose of this project is to give you an opportunity to try coding transcripts and to test the two models introduced above in the process. To begin, we will be analysing the transcript about Carlos's trousers.

STAGE ONE: USING THE FLOW CHARTS

First, use Long's flow chart (Figure 4). Working with the data in Transcript 6, trace the interaction with the chart, following the route which you think depicts the teacher's decision making, from the point at which Carlos deleted the -s on *alway*.

Next, use Chaudron's flow chart (Figure 5), and the explanatory list of his categories given in Appendix G to analyse the same transcript. That is, try to trace the route of each line in the transcript using Chaudron's model.

These two models depict different aspects of teacher behaviour. Long's deals with decisions regarding the entire process of error treatment, and Chaudron's deals primarily with the specific ways in which teachers deal with errors. In other words, Chaudron's model expands the WHAT column of Long's flow chart by depicting the various things teachers do to treat errors. What sorts of differences and similarities are produced by your use of these two systems?

STAGE TWO: REFINING LONG'S MODEL

Even a cursory glance at Figure 5 shows that Chaudron's model is more complex than Long's (Figure 4). This idea leads to the intriguing possibility that each of Long's other columns (WHETHER, WHEN and WHO) might also be developed into more detailed taxonomies of behaviour. Given the data in the Carlos transcript and your own experience as a teacher and/or learner, try to elaborate on one or more of Long's remaining columns. For instance, when Carlos's classmates coach him by providing the correct form of the verb he is unable to produce (Ss: 'I wear I wear'), they are offering peer correction unsolicited by the teacher. You may recall that in Kasper's (1985) research on repair in foreign language classrooms, the teacher called upon learners to complete other-repair moves.

These observations suggest that the presence or absence of *solicitation* of correction may be another important but as yet unexplored variable to consider. And in cases where treatment is solicited, it may matter who requests it. We could easily hypothesise that language learners may be in a better position to notice the gap, in Schmidt and Frota's terms, if *they* solicit the treatment themselves. Or, alternatively, we might propose that learners only solicit feedback once they have noticed the gap (between their own form 'i' and the native speaker's 'i + 1' utterances), or when they become aware of their own uncertainty. How could these issues be worked into an elaboration of Long's flow chart?

STAGE THREE: TAKING THE LEARNER'S POINT OF VIEW

An equally important issue is the learner's response to corrective feedback. What would a model of the second language learner's decision-making processes look like? Start from the moment of uncertainty when Carlos must realise he has done something wrong. Where does that moment occur? What would Carlos's options have been? Could the interaction have proceeded any differently?

Try to draw a model that represents your thinking on this question of the *learner's* cognitive processes in the face of error treatment. Compare your model with those produced by your classmates or colleagues.

MAJOR PROJECT: ERROR TREATMENT IN CLASSROOMS

The primary purpose of this project is to give you some first-hand experience in recording, transcribing, and analysing language classroom data. We also hope that in the process you will become more familiar with the concepts introduced in Chapters 5 and 6. We think of this project as 'major' because the collection and transcription of classroom data, properly done, is a painstaking process, but highly rewarding in the long run.

STAGE ONE: DATA COLLECTION

Record one of your own lessons, on audiotape. If you do not at the moment have a class, find a teacher or a colleague who is willing to be tape-recorded *and* willing to talk about the lesson afterwards, and who is also potentially interested in getting feedback from you. (It might be particularly interesting to collect error treatment data in the class of someone using a teaching method derived from a communicative approach to language learning.) Since your focus is on teacher treatment of learners' errors, you will need the microphone to be able to pick up both the teacher's and the learners' voices.

STAGE TWO: INITIAL ANALYSIS

Listen to the tape straight through (without stopping or rewinding it) and tally the number of error corrections that occur. This procedure will give you a sense of what it is like to try to code errors and their treatment in 'real time' (as if you were observing and coding during a class lesson). The experience will also show why it is so often important to take the trouble to produce a transcription if we really want to examine interactions in depth.

Try to form an impression of a) the types of errors that occurred, and b) how the teacher reacted to the various errors. What percentage of the errors were treated and which problems were treated most consistently – grammar errors, vocabulary, pronunciation, discourse or content errors, or errors involving the classroom task posed by the teacher? Is there any evidence that the learners solicited correction? Which of the errors (or perhaps mistakes, given Corder's 1967 distinction) did the students self-correct? Which were treated by other learners and which by the teacher?

STAGE THREE: TRANSCRIPTION AND CODING

Next transcribe a small segment of the same classroom lesson – approximately three or four pages of transcription. (Appendix H contains one set of transcription conventions for classroom discourse. You may use these as guidelines in transcribing your own data if you wish.) Often people who try transcription for the first time are very surprised at how time consuming it is. Transcribing conversations among two or three people typically takes four or five times the length of the conversation. Thus a five-minute conversation can take twenty or twenty-five minutes to transcribe, without even doing a close phonetic transcription. And, as we have already mentioned, transcribing an hour of classroom data, where there are often twelve or more speakers, can take up to twenty hours.

Now, working from your transcript, try to tally the types of errors which occurred and the corresponding treatments that followed. For guidance on the meaning of the types of reactions, see Chaudron's categories in Appendix G. As one approach, you could make a grid depicting the types of errors (for example, phonological, morphological, lexical, syntactic, discoursal, content, procedural, etc.) on one axis, and the types of treatments (from Chaudron's list) on the other. You may find, however, that it is sometimes difficult to decide exactly what an error is, so this sort of coding can be tricky.

STAGE FOUR: FURTHER ANALYSES

Compare your impression of the frequency and types of errors from the tape-recorded data (in roughly 'real time') with your actual count of the errors (both treated and untreated) made on the basis of the transcript. How do the tallies differ? Why? Which is more revealing to you about how language lessons proceed and how treatment of error occurs?

Finally, if it was not you who did the teaching, ask the teacher who taught the lesson to listen to the tape with you and to identify the errors that occurred. This procedure was followed by Nystrom (1983) in her study of elementary Spanish–English bilingual classes, and by Chaudron in his work with teachers in French immersion classrooms (1986b). In your own data, you can compare the teacher's identification and categorisation of errors with your own analyses, from both the coding and the transcribed data. What kinds of discrepancies occurred? In what instances did you and the teacher agree? What was the teacher's opinion about which errors were most important to treat? What information would you want to give this particular teacher about his or her error treatment patterns? What did the analysis of the errors and treatments in this classroom suggest to you about your own teaching?

If you were the teacher you taped, are you in any way surprised by the treatment patterns you have uncovered? If so, what lessons, if any, can you draw from the experience?

If you are working with a group of people who completed the same project, it would be useful to have a follow-up discussion in which you share your findings and discuss the pitfalls you encountered. In this way, you could begin to build up a record of suggestions for teachers who are just beginning to conduct their own classroom investigations.

Part IV Input and interaction in language classrooms

As language teachers we are all concerned with how best to use classroom time with our students to promote their efforts to learn the target language. This concern will be addressed in this part of the book, as we look, in the next two chapters, at research on interaction in the language classroom. In Chapter 7, the focus will be on the basic concepts of 'input' and 'interaction', which will lead us to look at research on how talk is distributed in language classrooms, and at the fundamental question of the value of talk as a contribution to language learning. In Chapter 8 we will look at some of the other topics studied as aspects of classroom interaction: teacher talk, learning strategies, groupwork, and forced participation.

7 Input and interaction in language classrooms

In Chapter 2 we saw that input to the learners is the result of unplanned factors as well as the planned implementation of the syllabus. Research, theory, and practical experience all point to the fact that input is crucial to language learning. 'Input' refers to the language which the learners hear (or read) – that is, the language samples to which they are exposed. Since this concept has come to influence much of our thinking about the role (and shortcomings) of classroom instruction, we will briefly summarise some of the key ideas about input here, before moving on to the topic of interaction.

7.1 Comprehensible input

'Comprehensible input' is a term popularised by Krashen. It refers to the fact that not all the target language to which second language learners are exposed is understandable: only some of the language they hear makes sense to them. Krashen hypothesised (1977, 1982, 1985) that target language data which were understandable but with effort – and were slightly more advanced than the second language learner's current level of comfortable understanding – would promote learning. He called this type of input 'i + 1', where the 'i' can represent the learner's current stage of interlanguage development and the '+ 1' designates that the input is challenging but not overwhelming to the learner. In such cases, comprehension is possible, with effort. (We saw in section 6.4 that the concept of 'i + 1' can be related to Schmidt and Frota's 'notice the gap' principle, but we should point out that Krashen feels there is no value in the learner consciously noticing the gap.)

Another way to look at the question of appropriate target language input is to talk about how much of it is available to be used by the learner – that is, how much of it can actually become 'intake'. This distinction was proposed by Corder in 1978, to point out that while second language learners, particularly those living in the target culture, may be exposed to a great deal of language, not all of it can be utilised by their developing internal grammatical systems. Only a portion of the input can serve as 'intake'.

Let us take an illustration. Imagine yourself as a beginning student of

German, trying to understand an engineering textbook written for German college students, or listening to a radio news broadcast in rapid-fire German. How much would you understand? How much of the language would be useful to you, in an instructional sense? Perhaps the graphs and illustrations in the textbook would help provide some context from which you could infer the meaning of some unfamiliar phrases. In other instances, seeing written cognates would help you interpret the German. Other portions of the text would be virtually unintelligible to you without assistance; they would not serve as comprehensible input. However, some portion of what you had puzzled out (the input) might in some way be retained (as intake), and thus be available to be learned.

The German radio broadcast would probably be even more difficult to process since 1) you could not digest the rapid speech at your own pace, as you usually can with written material, and 2) the oral presentation would presumably provide fewer contextual clues to help you interpret the spoken text. Of course, radio broadcasts are a specific kind of speech event. The speaker and the listeners do not have visual contact and they are separated, often by great distances. Most important, they do not truly interact: the communication is unidirectional. Thus the listeners do not have the opportunity to ask questions, to indicate their confusion, or to request clarification or repetition. These are all features of face-to-face interaction.

Krashen's concept of comprehensible input, though intuitively appealing to some, is nevertheless problematic in a variety of ways. First, it is not at all obvious that incomprehensible input is of absolutely no value to the language learner, since there is much to be learned beyond linguistic forms and their meanings (typical intonation and stress patterns, for example). Second, it is not easy to see how mere exposure to input, even if comprehensible, actually promotes language development. One possibility is that it is the effort made by the learner to comprehend the input that fosters development. Where this effort is made in face-to-face interaction, we may suggest that it is the interaction itself which is productive.

7.2 Interaction

Long (1983b:214) has proposed the following model to account for the relationships between negotiated interactions, comprehensible input, and language acquisition.

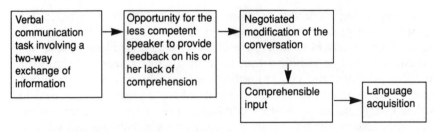

Figure 6   Long's Model of the relationship between type of conversational task and language acquisition (from Long 1983b:214)

This model is different from Krashen's idea of the sequence of events involved in acquisition. Krashen summarised his position as follows:

> Comprehensible *input* is responsible for progress in language acquisition. *Output* is possible as a result of acquired competence. When performers *speak*, they encourage *input* (people speak to them). This is conversation. (Krashen 1982:61)

In contrast, Long's model emphasises the primacy of conversation (interaction) and its role in getting comprehensible input.

Swain (for example, 1985) has offered an interesting hypothesis on the basis of her years of research with French immersion programmes in Canada. She feels that, while comprehensible input may be sufficient for acquiring semantic competence in the target language, 'comprehensible output' is needed in order to gain grammatical competence. That is, language learners must struggle with producing output which is comprehensible to their interlocutors if they are to master the grammatical markers of the language. Such mastery would come about as a result of the negotiations in the process of interacting, depicted in Figure 6.

Long's model, however, does not explicitly spell out the plausible interpretation noted above: that language acquisition can perhaps best be seen, not as the outcome of an encounter with comprehensible input *per se*, but as the direct outcome of the *work involved in* the negotiation process itself. This possibility, which is related to Stevick's (1976) notion of 'investment', is diagrammatically represented in Figure 7, opposite:

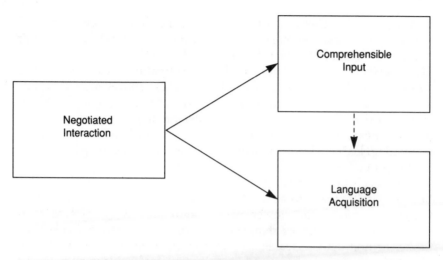

Figure 7   An alternative model of the relationship between negotiated interaction and language acquisition

(The broken line between Comprehensible Input and Language Acquisition represents the possibility that comprehensible input might still make a direct contribution to language acquisition.) The important point here is the implication that it is the work required to negotiate interaction that spurs language acquisition, rather than the intended outcome of the work – comprehensible input.

Further research should help us better understand such possibilities. Meanwhile we can explore in more depth the concept of 'negotiated interaction'. This term refers to those modifications that occur in conversations between native speakers and second language learners (or advanced non-native speakers and less proficient second language learners). These interactional adjustments include a whole range of attempts to understand and be understood. Three of the most important processes are comprehension checks, confirmation checks, and clarification checks (Long 1983b). In the explanations and examples that follow the 'speaker' refers to the teacher, native speaker or more competent speaker, and the 'interlocutor' refers to the second language learner:

1 A 'comprehension check' is the speaker's query of the interlocutors to see if they have understood what was said: 'Do you understand?' or 'Do you get what I'm saying?'
2 A 'confirmation check' is the speaker's query as to whether or not the speaker's (expressed) understanding of the interlocutor's meaning is correct: 'Oh, so are you saying you did live in London?'

123

3 A 'clarification check' is a request for further information or help in
   understanding something the interlocutor has previously said: 'I don't
   understand exactly. What do you mean?'

(The examples and definitions above are paraphrased from Long
1983b:218–19, and Chaudron 1988a:45.) These conversational signals
and strategies provide moments of concentrated focus on contextualised
input tuned to the learner's level of understanding (though sometimes
without awareness on the part of the interlocutor). In the process of
interacting, learners have opportunities to negotiate meaning by seeking
further input.

   The speech that is typically addressed to learners, sometimes called
'foreigner talk', tends to be modified in systematic ways. Among other
things, it tends to be slower paced, more clearly enunciated, and
syntactically less complex than speech addressed to native speakers or
proficient non-native speakers. (It is similar, in many respects, to the
phenomenon of 'caretaker speech' in first language acquisition, discussed
briefly in section 5.2.) Most native or fluent speakers have an apparently
natural ability to roughly tune their speech to language learners in these
ways, in order to facilitate communication and – potentially at least – the
learning process itself.

   But what happens in classrooms? If interaction is thought to be so
important in naturalistic language acquisition, how is it accomplished in
formal instructional settings? We will now examine the findings of some
classroom research to see how learners and teachers interact in language
classrooms.

7.3 Turn distribution and turn taking

How is it that within a single class some learners seem to get much more
than their 'fair share' of the talk turns? Teachers may call upon a
particular learner to talk – a 'direct nomination' or 'personal solicit'.
Alternatively, teachers may throw the turn open to the whole class – a
'general solicit'. Teachers may, of course, call upon some learners more
frequently than they do on others, and some learners may choose to
respond more frequently to general solicits, or even to speak without
waiting for a solicit of any kind. And also, just occasionally, some
learners will steal a turn intended for someone else. Conversely, some
other learners get less than their 'fair share' of talk-time, and this is
another interesting topic for investigation.

   One adult learner of English as a second language was called by the
pseudonym 'Igor' in a pilot study we conducted in Los Angeles (as
reported by Allwright 1980). Igor was observed to get far more turns
than his classmates, even though he did not seem to steal turns. Nor did

he respond more frequently to general solicits. We wondered whether 'Igor' got more turns because he was a better communicator than his fellow students in this lower-intermediate college-level ESL class. But when we examined the transcripts of the lessons, we found that Igor got more turns because he was a relatively poor communicator. Not that his English grammar or pronunciation was necessarily worse than his classmates': on the contrary. But Igor's discourse style was to speak in topically faulty utterances. That is, he made the teacher work extra hard to determine what he was trying to say. She called on him, or, rather, continued conversations with him in an attempt to understand the points he was trying to make, even though such conversations often apparently caused the lesson to go astray.

In the following transcript excerpt, S2 is Igor and T represents turns taken by the teacher. Ss are other students and xx indicates unintelligible speech. An indented line represents overlapping utterances. The reading passage under discussion was about traffic; hence, traffic is what is called the 'carrier topic' for the lesson – that is, the topic which provides the vehicle for discussing or framing the language practice, whether it be grammar, vocabulary, etc. At the point where this excerpt begins, the group was discussing the verb *to claim*.

Transcript 7: 'Just a second, Igor.'

T: Yeah. Or to make an accusation. OK. You say he he did, he killed that man, OK. You claim that, but you, if you can't prove it, it's only a claim. Yeah?

S2: It's to say something louder?

T: No. That would be exclaim. To to make shout, say something loud, it's exclaim.

S2: He claims ...

T: Yeah.

S2: I think they'd better produce electric machine for car to use.

T: For, for to to end the pollution problem?

S2:   Yeah

S2: Yeah

T: Yeah. OK. What does this mean? 'Get to'? Uh.

Ss: xx

T: OK. It says the group has been trying to get the government, the city government, to help uhm draw special lanes, lanes like this (draws on board) on the street. OK. These are for cars. These are for bikes ... (pointing to the blackboard).

S2: You know, in Moscow they reproduce all all cab.

T: Uhm?

S2: They reproduced all cabs xx

T: They produce?

S2: **Re**produce

T: D'you mean uh they they use old cabs, old taxis?

S2: No, no, no, they reproduced all A-L-L cabs.
 T: All the cabs?
S2: Yeah, all the cabs for electric electric, you know electric (points)
 T: Cab. Oh, you mean they made the cabs in down in downtown areas uh uh use electric uh motors?
S2:   Yeah, no downtown, all cabs in Moscow.
 T: Where?
S2: In Moscow.
 T: Oh. And it's successful?
S2: Yeah.
 T: OK. Uhm. Just a second, Igor. Let's what does this mean? If you get someone to do something. Uhm.

Transcript 7 is reprinted from Allwright (1980:180–1).

This transcript is from Allwright's (1980) research (in the naturalistic enquiry mode) on turns, topics and tasks in classroom interaction. That paper provides a detailed numerical analysis of how the participants used their turns to set or avoid tasks, and how different topics are nominated. Here we will simply note a few of the interesting features of the interaction.

First, we see Igor testing his own hypothesis about the meaning of *claim*: 'It's to say something louder?' The teacher responds by differentiating between *claim* and *exclaim* (stressing the first syllable of *exclaim* in her explanation). Then Igor returns to the carrier topic (traffic) by commenting on electric cars. The teacher responds with a question about pollution to make sure she has understood his point but then tries to move along to the next vocabulary item, the phrasal verb *get to*. Igor, however, not to be dissuaded by a mere lesson plan, raises a related topic that interests him: 'You know, in Moscow, they reproduce all all cab'. The teacher responds with a query, 'Uhm?', which Igor interprets as an invitation to repeat. There follows an interesting sequence in which the teacher uses the word *produce*. Igor corrects her by saying '*R*eproduce' (using the same contrastive stress strategy that she had employed to show him the difference between *claim* and *exclaim*). His response leads her to hypothesise that old cabs had been renovated in some way, but Igor corrects her again, repeating and even spelling A-L-L. After further negotiation, the teacher summarises her understanding of Igor's point: 'Oh, you mean they made the cabs in down in downtown areas uh uh use electric uh motors?' This seems to be a reasonable paraphrase of his point, but again he corrects her, having taken exception to her use of *downtown*: 'Yeah, no downtown, all cabs in Moscow.' While he's explaining, the teacher's question, 'Where?' overlaps Igor's speech and he then provides further repetition: 'In Moscow.'

Two turns later the teacher explicitly pulls the topic back to the grammar point *get to* by signalling to Igor that she wants to move on: 'Just a second, Igor. Let's what does this mean? If you get someone to do something. Uhm.' The irony, of course, is that the teacher is having a lot of trouble getting Igor to do something – namely, to proceed with the vocabulary lesson she had planned. However, it is at least plausible that by his apparent digressions, Igor is making the language and the concepts real to himself as he negotiates an understanding with his teacher over a topic that he has nominated and maintained.

In the same classroom there was another learner, whom we called 'Chuck'. When the research team began to analyse the transcripts of the tape-recorded classroom interaction, it appeared that Chuck, like Igor, got a much greater proportion of the speaking turns than did his classmates. But when we asked the teacher for her impression, she told us that Chuck seldom spoke in class. When we showed her the transcripts and played the tape, she was very surprised to hear how much Chuck spoke. When we looked at a map of the classroom drawn by the observer who had taken notes during the recording session, we discovered that Chuck had been seated directly beneath one of the stereo recording microphones suspended from the ceiling for the data collection. The microphone had accurately recorded Chuck's speech, but he had not taken any turns that were loud enough to be noticeable by the teacher. Instead, he took very quiet private turns that went unnoticed except by the microphone. His way of practising the target language in class was through 'egocentric speech' – talk directed at himself and not shared with anyone else. The teacher was very surprised, since she had viewed Chuck as somewhat indifferent and uninterested in participating in the language lessons. In fact, he was working very hard – but not doing so in an easily observable way.

What is participation? How do learners make use of the practice opportunities afforded them by language classrooms? One of the difficulties we have in answering these questions is that classroom research, like many other forms of research, usually deals primarily with observable data. If we adopt a strict stance on this issue in studying classroom interaction, this means we can record, measure, and count only those actions which can be documented by another observer or a recording device. As we noted in Chapter 3, many researchers deal only with observable data, but they may do so at the risk of missing important insights. Figure 8 overleaf is a tree diagram depicting some aspects of classroom participation patterns. It highlights some of the issues (of turn distribution, presence or absence of bidding, types of nomination, verbal and nonverbal behaviour) that classroom researchers must be aware of when they study participation. Note that Figure 8 deals only with issues in turn *giving*: it does not address the complex set of learner behaviours involved in turn *getting*.

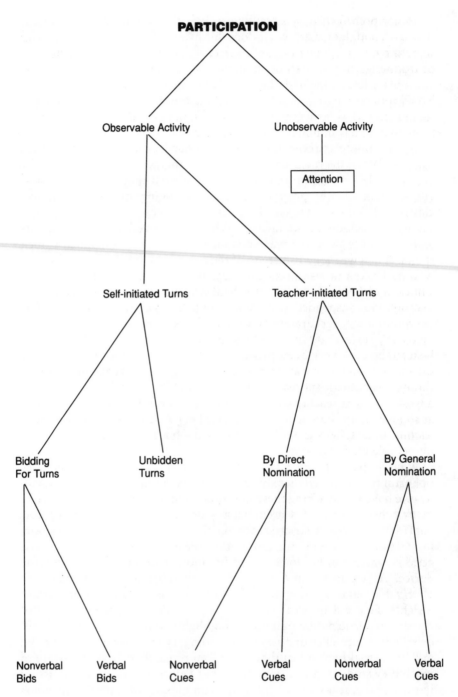

Figure 8   Some factors in observable participation in classrooms

128

There is a direct parallel between the teacher's problem in gauging learners' participation and the researcher's problem in dealing exclusively with observable data. As we saw in Chuck's case, teachers use the observational information available to them (for example, eye contact, raised hands, audible verbal turns, nodding, etc.) to judge the extent of learners' participation, and to draw inferences regarding their involvement, motivation, interest, etc.

But not all forms of participation are observable. Participation, or more specifically, 'engagement' (sometimes called 'involvement' or 'investment') with the language learning task at hand, may in some instances be largely an internal, mental phenomenon. Alternative research techniques (for example, the diary studies and other forms of self-report) are being explored to try to tap into some of the largely unobservable issues related to language learning: cognition, affect, motivation. (Issues like these will be addressed in some detail in Chapters 9 and 10, on 'Receptivity'.)

Some researchers, in an attempt to get at hidden information, have utilised think-aloud protocols and elicited self-report data (Faerch and Kasper 1987). For example, Cohen used these procedures to gain information about the students' level of involvement during actual classroom lessons. With the teachers' permission, he queried learners as to what they were thinking about at various points while the language lesson progressed. While we do not yet know how valid such a directly interventionist technique may be, it represents a bold and ingenious attempt to get at learners' in-class thinking.

Cohen and Hosenfeld (1981) summarised the somewhat disturbing findings of this process as follows:

> Attending to content matter seems to range at any given classroom moment from 25% to 82%, according to the age of the learner and the interest value of the material, among other things. It appears that on the average, 50% of students are attending to the content of a lesson, and most are just repeating the material to themselves.

Cohen and Hosenfeld note that learners become skilful at looking as if they are attending to the lesson even though they may not be – an observation that comes as no surprise to teachers who have sat through years of graduate school or hours of in-service training. Thus not only is engagement at least partly unobservable; identifying learners' 'disengagement' in a language lesson is also a problematic issue for teachers and classroom researchers alike. (We will return to this study in section 10.1.)

7.4 Some quantitative studies of classroom interaction

Is interaction a 'good thing'? This is a primary question for language teachers who seek to find an appropriate balance of activities in their classrooms. Teachers and researchers alike want to know whether classroom interaction does, in fact, lead to enhanced language learning.

In the research that has utilised observable data to document turn taking in classrooms, the terms 'high input generators' and 'low input generators' are sometimes used. These notions originally came from a study by Seliger (1977), in which he documented the participation patterns of these two different types of adult learners in a single ESL classroom in New York City. He tried to relate their participation behaviour to their achievement in English. Seliger described high input generators (HIGs) as learners who, by initiating and sustaining conversations through taking turns, caused other people to use language with them, to provide them with language samples. In other words, their communication strategies presumably generated high levels of input. In contrast, another type of learner seemed to participate minimally – to speak only when called upon and to be generally passive in classroom interaction. These people Seliger called low input generators (LIGs) because they did not actively use language to get more exposure to the target language.

Seliger posed the question, 'Does practice make perfect?' because he wanted to know if the learners' participation patterns were in any way related to their progress in mastering English. To answer this question he observed a small number of learners (three 'HIGs' and three 'LIGs') and then studied their performance on two English language tests. He also gave the subjects a questionnaire, called the 'Language Contact Profile', about their use of English outside class. Thus Seliger's study represents one of the earliest attempts to combine observational language classroom data (documenting *process* variables) with language test results (a *product* or *output* variable) and self-report data generated by the language learners.

Seliger found that the HIGs did, in fact, outperform the LIGs in English achievement. They also reported having more out-of-class contact with native speakers of English. From these patterns, Seliger concluded that 'learners who initiate interaction are better able to turn input into intake' (1983a:257). Notice that he does not claim a linear, causal relationship here: we cannot tell if these learners initiate more interaction because they are more proficient, or if they are more proficient because they initiate more interaction.

Later Seliger conducted another study (again with six subjects) in which he investigated the relationship between errors and participation. He found that HIGs produced more language and, hence, more frequent errors, than did LIGs. Furthermore, a somewhat higher percentage of the LIGs' errors were traceable to first language interference than were HIGs' errors. Seliger concluded that 'the greater willingness of HIGs to make errors while interacting . . . allowed them to test more hypotheses . . . than the more cautious LIGs. In short, more errors do not mean that the learner is learning less' (1983a:261).

Since Seliger's studies both involved only six subjects, they are best considered as 'pilot studies' of classroom interaction patterns, as he points out. One concern, given the small sample size, is that his results may not be reliable or valid. For instance, in his selection of the three top HIGs and the three lowest LIGs, Seliger chose not to examine the performance of the other members of the class (those falling between the two extremes on the continuum of frequency of verbal participation). If their data had been included, there might be no significant differences between, say, one half of the class and the other, if all the students had been evenly divided into HIGs and LIGs. This was indeed what Slimani (1987) found when she attempted to replicate Seliger's study on her data (involving just thirteen learners). Significant differences favouring the HIGs could be found if only the extreme cases were considered, but across the class as a whole, such differences disappeared.

Another problem is that Seliger's findings might not hold true for other students in other settings. This is a matter of some concern because a goal of most experimental research is to obtain findings that are generalisable. You will recall from section 3.3.3 that if a study is generalisable, the results will be true for more than just the (relatively few) learners who are studied as research subjects. For this reason, researchers often take two precautions to help ensure generalisability. The first precaution is that researchers try to select their subjects at random from among all the people they could possibly choose to study. This procedure, called 'random sampling', is thought to maximise the chances that the subjects studied will be representative of the larger population of interest. Another precaution is that researchers usually try to work with as large a number of subjects as possible. (The logic behind many statistical tests for determining significant relationships is predicated upon having a sample size of thirty or more.) This goal of having a large sample or 'large n' (where *number* is abbreviated as 'n' in the research literature) is a result of the influence of experimental psychology on second language research. However, this goal is often extremely difficult to achieve in classroom research, given the complicated kinds of data that such studies generate.

In addition to using random sampling and large sample sizes, researchers working in the tradition of experimental science sometimes replicate studies with different subjects to see if the same results occur. Other researchers have also used Seliger's ideas but tried to improve upon his

131

original design. Day (1984) was intrigued by Seliger's ideas, but he detected some problems in the way the research had been conducted. Day replicated Seliger's study with a larger population of mostly Asian students in Honolulu. (Seliger's subjects had been selected from various nationalities, ethnicities, and first language groups.) In his own study, Day found that there was no observable relationship between the frequency with which these learners participated in class and their achievement on an English test.

Day pointed out (1984) that the HIGs and the LIGs in Seliger's study had originally been identified by how often they spoke in class. In other words, he felt that what Seliger had measured was how often the students' produced *output* rather than their strategies for getting input. (This observation has led to the humorous suggestion that Seliger's research was really about 'HOGs' and 'LOGs' rather than HIGs and LIGs.)

Slimani's (1987) work, mentioned above, has thrown more light on Seliger's and Day's findings. Developing research proposals by Allwright (1984), she used the term 'uptake' for whatever information or skills learners claimed to have got from language lessons. She then looked for relationships between learner participation and learning, as measured both in terms of 'uptake', and in terms of test scores. Building on both Seliger's and Day's work and using their procedures to analyse the data (collected in an Algerian university classroom), Slimani was unable to confirm Seliger's positive findings. Generally, she had to conclude that there seemed to be no satisfactorily strong evidence that interaction should be interpreted as causing progress. However, she was able to conclude that it would nevertheless be well worth continuing to look for a causal relationship, but in the opposite direction. Her work suggested that the more proficient learners in her class did indeed seem to be more willing to interact, but perhaps because they were more proficient and therefore found interaction less stressful.

Anecdotal evidence in support of this possibility can be taken from the case of Igor, which we discussed earlier in section 7.3. Igor was by far the most proficient learner in the class we studied, and the most prolific participant (after the teacher). At the end of the ten-week course he was judged to be so proficient that he was allowed to skip a level. In his new, much more advanced class he found himself among people whose proficiency matched or even exceeded his own, and he settled down to work without showing any more inclination to interact than anyone else. It seems then that his willingness to participate so much in the lower class had not been a learning strategy or a personality trait on his part so much as a simple reaction to his relatively high proficiency in that context. It was easier for him to participate, and so he did. But it may not have been more profitable for him to interact, apparently, since his teacher in that lower class judged him at the end of the course to be the learner who had made the least progress of all.

Slimani also found an intriguingly complex relationship between proficiency, interaction, and uptake. In her study the most proficient learners interacted more frequently than their less proficient classmates, and apparently participation was relatively profitable for them: roughly 50 per cent of what they claimed to have learned was derived from episodes of classroom interaction they had personally taken part in. Basically, for the less proficient learners it appeared that listening to other learners was more profitable than participating verbally themselves. We will return to this possibility in section 10.1 when we consider John Schumann's preference for eavesdropping over active participation in target language conversations (Schumann and Schumann 1977).

In another naturalistic study of classroom participation patterns, Sato (1982) used a quantitative analysis to examine her own learners' turn-getting behaviour. She was curious about the familiar stereotype of Asian learners as being more passive and quiet than other ESL learners. Through the use of videotapes and observations, she determined that her Asian learners did indeed take fewer turns than the others. Furthermore, the Asians took fewer self-selected turns and teachers allocated fewer turns to them. The Asians also had different 'bidding' patterns when compared with the non-Asians. ('Bidding' refers to the behaviours by which students signal to the teacher that they wish to speak – hand-raising, eye contact, an in-breath, etc.) The Asians tended to bid more than the other learners before speaking – that is, they took fewer unbidden turns: they bid before 38 per cent of their speaking turns, while non-Asian learners apparently felt freer simply to speak out, with bidding occurring before only 18 per cent of their spoken turns.

Sato interprets these findings as meaning that Asian learners have more constraints on their notions of permissible classroom participation patterns than do learners from other cultures. Her study raises the interesting issue of the relationship between cultural traits and inter-action patterns. These issues have not been fully explored in classroom research to date, so there is much work in this area that could be done by interested teachers.

In an investigation prompted by Sato's work, Moss and Corneli (1983) tried to replicate her investigation of ethnicity and turn taking in an ESL classroom. But they felt the learners' knowledge (or their perceived knowledge) would influence the extent to which they might respond to general solicits in class. So, with the co-operation of the teacher, they planned an experiment in which the learners sometimes had the oppor-tunity to bid for turns following a general solicit and then respond verbally, and at other times, they were to respond to the teacher's question by writing the answer on a card. In this way, the researchers hoped to determine whether learners' volunteering or bidding behaviour was related to their (perceived) ability to answer the teacher's question.

Moss and Corneli assumed any one of the following four conditions might arise:

1 Learners might know the answer (or think they did) and bid for verbal turns.
2 Learners might not know the answer (or think they did not know it) and still bid for turns.
3 Learners might know the answer (or think they did) but choose not to bid for turns.
4 Learners might not know the answer (or think they did not know it) and therefore not bid for turns.

In fact, in their data analysis, Moss and Corneli found that three of these four situations emerged: only situation 2 did not occur. Moss and Corneli point out, however, that this was a pilot study with only seven learners in the classroom. With a larger number, all four patterns might easily arise. The implication of their findings for classroom research is that we must be very careful in attributing observable turn-taking patterns in response to general solicits to variables such as ethnicity, particularly in the absence of data about the learners' actual or perceived knowledge of the topic under discussion.

These studies would bear replication, and many other research questions about classroom turn taking come to mind. Do males participate significantly more (or less) often than females? Or do participation patterns relate more closely to questions of personality, interest in the lesson, or confidence in one's knowledge of the topic? Research opportunities abound on topics related to turn taking in classrooms.

7.5 Summary

This chapter has considered the important issues of input and interaction as they relate to classroom language learning. Some researchers (for example, Krashen 1982) hypothesise that comprehensible input is the causal variable in language acquisition, while others (notably Long 1981, 1983b) have argued that it is the negotiated interaction leading to comprehensible input that is most important. We have tried to look at this debate from the classroom research point of view and have suggested that it is the interactive work (whether visible or non-observable) learners do in classrooms that should concern us as language teachers. There is a need for more process–product studies in classroom research to help the field document and understand how input and interaction lead to learning, and with what effects.

We know from the observational research and from our own experience as teachers that learners participate verbally in language classrooms to very different extents. Some are verbally reticent, while others tend to dominate the interaction. Some of these behaviours seem to be related to cultural origins – and, as Sato's exploratory study has indicated, there is a tendency towards cultural stereotyping of turn-taking behaviour in heterogeneous classes.

As teachers we can investigate our own turn distribution patterns and the ways in which the learners in our classrooms get (or avoid) turns. We can alter our behaviour, following the action research paradigm, in an attempt to observe what changes ensue in the learners' subsequent interaction. By systematically speaking less, waiting longer after posing a question, or calling on learners we might have previously ignored, we may see different patterns of behaviour emerge. We can be aware of how our own participation in negotiated discourse influences the type of practice and learning opportunities that result. Finally, we can and should be sensitive to learners' preferred interaction patterns and realise that apparent passivity in classrooms can mask a great deal of active attention.

DISCUSSION STARTERS

1 In your experience, both as a teacher and as a second language learner, you will have no doubt noted that some learners participate more actively than others in classroom language lessons. What observable differences have you noticed? What factors may account for these differences?

2 In terms of your own classroom style as a language learner, would you consider yourself a high input generator or a low input generator? Are these two distinct categories, or simply two poles of a continuum? As a teacher, do you prefer one of these types of learners over the other? Why?

3 What, in your experience, makes learners' participation patterns vary from lesson to lesson, or even from moment to moment? Draw up a list of factors to discuss with your colleagues.

4 In the sorts of lessons you are familiar with, does the teacher typically respond positively or negatively to learners' attempts to initiate topics? On what does the teacher's reaction depend, in your experience? Make a list of factors to compare with those of other people.

5 What, if anything, should teachers do about learners who seem to get more than their fair share of classroom interaction? Have you ever had an 'Igor' in your class? To what extent is it the teacher's responsibility

to monitor the turn-taking patterns and make sure that the quiet learners also get verbal turns?

6 Compare Figure 6 (Long's model) and Figure 7 as representations of the role of interaction in language learning. Are the distinctions important to you? Does either model more closely depict your idea of the language learning process? If not, could you sketch out an alternative model which conveys your idea?

7 To what extent do you feel differing classroom participation patterns can be explained by cultural norms? Have you observed intra-cultural variation (that is, among learners from the same culture) in language classroom participation?

8 As a learner, what can you learn by *listening* to the target language, without interacting? In your experience are there some things that can only be learned through active verbal participation? Try to think of some clear examples and compare your ideas with those of your colleagues.

SUGGESTIONS FOR FURTHER READING

1 Chapter 3 of Krashen's (1982) book deals specifically with the relationship of input and acquisition. A later book (1985) focuses entirely on the input hypothesis. Krashen's ideas on this topic have been influential in sparking debate, pedagogical change, and further research.

2 Long's (1983b) article, from which Figure 6 is derived, looks at conversations between native speakers and non-native speakers of English. His work on input and interaction is particularly interesting for classroom researchers because he has investigated language learning both in the formal instructional setting of the classroom and in more naturalistic settings. His 1985 paper deals with input and second language acquisition theory.

3 Up-to-date reviews of interaction in language classrooms can be found in Chapter 5 of Chaudron (1988a). Chapters 5 and 6 of van Lier (1988) deal with turn taking and the structure of classroom participation, specifically as the latter relates to topic and activity.

4 Sato's (1982) study of ethnicity and turn taking represents one teacher's attempt to study the interaction patterns she had detected in her own classroom.

5 Several articles in Gass and Madden's book *Input in second language acquisition* (1985) deal with the issues presented in this chapter. Likewise, some articles in Day's book, *Talking to learn* (1986), are pertinent as well. The article by Cathcart in Day's book is directly related to the issues raised in this chapter.

6 Several researchers have tried to model the role of input in language learning. An interesting article which integrates several different researchers' models is by Tollefson, Jacobs and Selipsky (1983). Chaudron (1985) has devised a model for examining the relationship between input and intake.

7 *Classroom interaction*, by Malamah-Thomas (1987) gives both a great deal of information and over 150 possible tasks for language teachers who wish to explore this topic further. For another viewpoint on how to promote interaction in the classroom, see Richard-Amato (1988).

8 It may be interesting to read and compare Allwright's (1980) study of turn taking with Seliger's (1977, 1983a) work on the same topic. These two authors choose very different approaches to data collection and analysis. Day's (1984) follow-up of Seliger's work is an interesting example of how researchers try to push ahead our knowledge of classroom processes by building on earlier work.

9 Enright (1984) wrote an interesting paper about the organisation of interaction in bilingual kindergarten classrooms. Enright used the concepts of emic and etic units of analysis, and included the teachers' points of view in his report.

10 Ellis's work (see especially 1980, 1985) is a good source of information on the role of interaction in language learning.

MINI-PROJECT: USING ANALYTIC CATEGORIES

INTRODUCTION

Other people's analytic categories may look very clearly defined or very problematic, but you can never be sure until you have actually tried using them on some authentic data. This mini-project will enable you to test your first impressions of the different observation instruments introduced in the mini-project of Chapter 1. Here are the suggested procedures:

1 Find two other people to work with. Select the set of categories (from among the Appendices) that interests the three of you the most, for whatever reasons. Find the original reference and study the author's definitions of the categories.

2 Each of you should now select a piece of transcription to work on. This time, agree with the other two people to take up different pieces of transcription.

3 Try out the chosen set of categories on your piece of transcription. Rotate the transcriptions as soon as you are ready, so that all three of you try out the categories on all three pieces of data.

4 As a group, go back to the original authors' paper(s) about the instrument you are using. Examine their category definitions and consider how adequately they are stated in the light of your attempts to use them. If necessary, propose your own refinements of the definitions. These may be extremely useful in your later work. Discuss the proposed refinements with the other members of your group.

Of course, you could also individually follow the steps outlined above if you are not working with a group. If you are working on your own, you might consider trying to use the same set of analytic categories on a few different transcripts, to see if the instrument is amenable to coding various sorts of classroom data.

8 Wider perspectives on classroom interaction

It would be quite wrong to give the impression that language classroom interaction studies have focused exclusively on the issues raised in Chapter 7. Many other aspects of classroom talk have been studied in considerable detail, as we saw in the two chapters dealing with the treatment of oral errors. In this chapter, we will have room to cover just a few more such topics. We hope that the increased breadth of coverage will compensate for the relative lack of depth it entails. Our topics for Chapter 8 include teacher talk, learning strategies, forced participation, and group work. They are four distinct and independent topics, but we will draw attention to their interconnections as appropriate.

8.1 Teacher talk

Observations of many different classes, both in content area subjects and in language instruction, consistently show that teachers typically do between one half and three quarters of the talking done in classrooms. (This finding is partially explained by the observation that of Bellack's four classroom discourse moves, discussed in the opening paragraphs of Chapter 6, three are usually restricted to the teacher: *structuring*, *soliciting*, and *reacting*. Only one, *responding*, is typically the students' prerogative.) Talk is one of the major ways that teachers convey information to learners, and it is also one of the primary means of controlling learner behaviour. Since we, as teachers, do so much talking, it will be useful to ask what our talk is like. What regularities can be observed, and how does teacher talk relate to learners' gradual progress in the target language?

One of the curious things about language teachers talking with students is that we seem to be very skilled at judging the learners' level of competence and pitching the complexity of our own speech so that they can understand. For example, Gaies (1977) tape-recorded a group of teachers-in-training talking in two different situations: 1) with their peers (the baseline data), and 2) with their own students in practice teaching assignments. These teachers-in-training included both native speakers and non-native speakers of English. Gaies found that in classroom speech with learners the teachers modified their speech considerably. With every measure he used in the analysis, syntactic complexity was low in the teachers' speech in beginning level classes, and increased in regular increments with each subsequent level of instruction. It was even more pronounced in the teachers' speech to their peers (the baseline data).

Gaies' observation of the increasing complexity of the teachers' speech relative to their learners' proficiency levels can be related to Krashen's idea of 'i + 1' – the notion that optimal input is just slightly more advanced than the learner's current level of interlanguage development (see section 6.4). Gaies' research shows that syntactically, at least, some ESL teachers, even during their training, can already tailor their speech so that they provide increasingly complex input in speaking to learners of increasing proficiency. In this way they could be maintaining (whether knowingly or not) a degree of syntactic complexity at the 'i + 1' level. However, in practice the i + 1 concept is not operationalisable (that is, we cannot define with confidence what i + 1 consists of) and therefore we cannot know whether or not these teachers were typically operating at some other level of complexity. A further complication is that we must not assume that all learners are at precisely the same stage in their development in any case, and therefore what is 'i + 1' for some learners may be 'i − 3' or 'i + 5' for yet others. It would nevertheless be useful to see replications of Gaies' study carried out under other circumstances (for example, with younger learners, other target languages, in a foreign language setting rather than a second language setting, etc.). Gaies' initial findings certainly suggest that language teachers' ability to adjust the complexity of their speech to suit the learners would repay further study.

As we have looked closer at classroom discourse, however, we have come to question the usefulness of some characteristics of teacher talk. A number of studies have revealed, and quite convincingly so, that the language to which second language learners are exposed in the classroom is often *unlike* the language they will encounter in talking to native speakers outside the classroom.

In one such study, Long and Sato (1983) analysed transcripts of six elementary adult ESL classes with an average of twenty students per class. The data were audiotaped in Honolulu, Los Angeles, and Philadelphia. The researchers compared the teachers' speech to the learners with baseline data collected in an experimental (non-classroom) study of native speakers and non-native speakers interacting in pairs called 'dyads' (Long 1980b). One point of focus in this research was on teachers' use of display and referential questions. (We saw in the transcript about Carlos's trousers that display questions are asked by teachers to get learners to display their knowledge. In contrast, referential questions, or 'true information questions', are those which refer to actual information sought by the questioner.) The study also compared the teachers' and the native speakers' use of comprehension checks, clarification checks, and confirmation checks.

A number of striking statistically significant differences emerged in Long and Sato's study, among which the following are most relevant to this discussion:

1 ESL teachers used significantly more display than referential questions in the classroom. They also used significantly more display questions and significantly fewer referential questions than did the native speakers in the dyads. (In other words, following Long, there was less genuine communication going on in the classrooms than in the experimental native-speaker/non-native-speaker pairs.)
2 The teachers used significantly more imperatives, more statements and fewer questions than the native speakers did in the dyads.
3 The teachers' speech was significantly more oriented to the 'here and now' than was the native speakers' speech in the informal dyads.
4 The teachers used a significantly greater number of comprehension checks (to see if the learners had understood them) than did the native speakers in the dyads. However, they used significantly fewer clarification requests and confirmation checks when compared with the native speakers in the dyads.

(These findings are summarised from a lengthier list found in Long 1983b:217.) These results may be interpreted as follows:

> Insofar as (the findings) are representative of at least elementary level ESL instruction, the second language classroom offers very little opportunity to the learner to communicate in the target language or to hear it used for communicative purposes by others.
> (Long 1983b:219)

Of course, we can point out that talk between two people will naturally differ somewhat from talk among several people, and that talk in classrooms is structured differently from other kinds of talk because of the very nature of instruction. However, Long rightly points out that the picture revealed by these data is one of a transmission model of education – the idea that the teacher's task as the knower is to transmit information to the learners. This approach to education leaves the learners little opportunity to practise genuine communicative uses of language in a full range of functional moves or to negotiate for meaning.

8.2 Learning strategies

Recently some classroom research in language learning and teaching has focused on what action learners take to try to master the target language.

F

Their efforts in this direction are typically called 'learning strategies'. This topic is related to classroom interaction in the sense that some types of turns learners take in classrooms may be direct evidence of their own private efforts to learn. For example, Chuck's egocentric speech (in section 7.3) can be seen as an instance of a learning strategy of talking to oneself, in which the learner chooses to 'practise in the target language by engaging in verbal behaviour directed to him/herself' (Chesterfield and Chesterfield 1985:49), as opposed to (or in addition to) practising out loud with other members of the class.

Learning strategies have been well documented in recent studies (for example, Chamot 1984; the work of O'Malley and his colleagues 1985a, 1985b; Oxford-Carpenter 1985; Wenden 1985; Reid 1987; Ehrman and Oxford 1989), but it is beyond the scope of this discussion to review them all. Instead, we will focus on a taxonomy of verbal learning strategies developed by the Chesterfields in their observational research on children in bilingual classes. The categories related to classroom participation include the following:

1 *Repetition*: echo/imitation of a word modelled by another, or incorporation of a word or structure used previously into an utterance.
2 *Use of formulaic expressions*: words or phrases which function as unanalysed automatic speech units for the speaker, often serving the function of initiating or continuing a conversation and giving the impression of command of the target language.
3 *Verbal attention getter*: any means by which the speaker attracts the attention of another to him/herself so as to initiate interaction.
4 *Answer in unison*: response by providing the answer aloud together with others.
5 *Elaboration*: providing information beyond that which is necessary to carry on the interaction.
6 *Anticipatory answer*: guessing from context to provide a response for an anticipated question, or prematurely filling in a word or phrase in another's statement.
7 *Appeal for assistance*: spontaneously asking another for the correct term or structure, or for help in solving a problem.
8 *Request for clarification*: attempt to broaden understanding or knowledge of the target language by asking the speaker to explain or repeat a previous statement.
9 *Role play*: spontaneous practice of the target language in interaction with another by taking on the role of another in fantasy play.
(Adapted from Chesterfield and Chesterfield 1985: 49–50)
All of these learning strategies, and many more which may or may not have been identified yet, are means that learners seem to employ to help themselves improve their target language proficiency.

In the following excerpt from a transcript, one learner's use of the strategy called 'Appeal for assistance' triggers an interesting interaction in which all the learners participate verbally with the teacher – all, that is, except Maria, the one who asked the original question that prompted the explanation. The excerpt is from a vocabulary lesson with a small group of lower intermediate adult ESL learners, all of whom were native speakers of Spanish. The carrier topic for the vocabulary lesson was a report of hazardous road conditions. (As before, indented turns indicate overlapping utterances. The observer's contextual comments are given in parentheses. S1's pseudonym is Maria.)

Transcript 8: Things get muddy

T: Mud.
S1: What you mean?
T: Oh, OK. OK. You know what dirt is.
S2: Mmhmm (affirmative).
S3:   Dirt.
T: OK. When it rains, the dirt turns into mud.
S2: Lodo.
T: Wet.
S3: Yeah.
S2: Lodo.
S4: Lodo.
T: Lodo?
S3: Yeah.
S4:   Lodo.
T: And things get muddy. We say things get muddy. (Takes the microphone and speaks directly into it.)
S4: (Laughs)
T: MUDDY (in a deep voice). M-U-D-D-Y. MUDDY. (Everyone laughs a lot.) DIRTY. D-I-R-T-Y. DIRTY. (Everyone laughs.) This is the FBI (he laughs). OK, that's what mud is. How do you say it, lodo?
S4: Lodo.
T: Lodo.
S3: Lodo.
T: Loco lodo. OK. What is a camper, Maria?
S1: Like a van with bed, kitchen and bathroom

These data were collected and transcribed by Mandy Deal.

Let us analyse the instructional interaction revealed in this excerpt of classroom discourse. Note that the teacher responds to the content of Maria's question ('What you mean?') and not to the formal error it involves. He assesses what the learners already know ('You know what dirt is') and then builds on that knowledge ('When it rains, the dirt turns into mud'). Another learner, S2, offers the Spanish translation, *lodo*, and the teacher supplies the English word *wet* to explain further the idea of mud. The Spanish equivalent, *lodo*, is repeated by S4, at which point the teacher attends to S4's comment and asks, 'Lodo?' with rising intonation. S3 confirms the teacher's query, and the Spanish word is also repeated by S4. Next the teacher employs the strategy of elaboration as he uses an English phrase to provide and contextualise the adjective form of the new lexical item: 'We say things get muddy.' There follows a clear example of reactivity, in which the presence of the observer's recording microphone stimulates some general amusement about the classroom researcher being like the FBI (Federal Bureau of Investigations) recording people's conversations. The teacher begins to conclude the discussion of mud ('OK, that's what mud is'), but then checks his own recall by asking the students about the Spanish word once more: 'How do you say it, "lodo"?' S4 repeats with confirmatory intonation. (These two confirmations from the students, like the corrections Igor made above, provide relatively rare examples of learners using Bellack's evaluative *reacting* move.) After this, the teacher, in one further moment of silliness, says 'loco lodo' ('crazy mud'). He then signals the beginning of a new discussion topic by asking S1 (via a direct nomination) about the next vocabulary item ('What is a camper, Maria?'). Maria, who asked the original question and had been listening quietly to all the foregoing explanation, responds to his question correctly, both in terms of grammar and of content, and the lesson proceeds.

This sequence of classroom interaction illustrates how one learner, via her appeal for assistance, influenced the course of the lesson. The example is hardly dramatic, but we do not yet know the importance of such 'diversions'. Slimani's work (1987) suggests that they may have more influence on what gets learned than episodes where only the teacher introduces new material. We need more investigations to look into the power of learner-introduced material. Meanwhile, Transcript 8 reveals an interesting possibility: in the process of the teacher and S1's classmates jointly explaining *mud* to S1, the students may have taught the teacher the Spanish word *lodo*. At several points in the transcript we see the teacher-turned-language-learner use the strategy of repetition, and once the strategy of request for clarification. (In fact, several days later, when the teacher was asked – out of context – if he knew the Spanish word for *mud*, he responded, 'I think it's *dolo* or something like that.')

8.3 Forced participation

One thing for teachers to keep in mind is that pupils' learning strategies may not always parallel teachers' teaching strategies, and sometimes they may even be at odds with each other. Some learners, for example, may wish to be quiet and listen in order to learn, while their teachers believe they will learn by speaking. Such a discrepancy was documented in a diary study by John Schumann, who found he strongly preferred 'eavesdropping' rather than speaking as a learning strategy (Schumann and Schumann 1977:247). While he could employ his preferred strategy in Iran when he was studying Farsi independently, he found he could not do so while enrolled in an Arabic class in Tunisia, where the teacher had expectations about how the class members should participate. (See also section 1.2.)

Thus we see that some learners' level of observable verbal interaction in classrooms may be related to their own opinions about how they learn best (whether or not such opinions are well articulated, or even accurate). In some cases, learners may wish to speak out but feel inhibited in doing so. Thus in turn distribution, as in error treatment, teachers are faced with highly complex decision making, and it must be said that this area is even less well charted for them as yet. All we can say with confidence is that it is a dangerous oversimplification to suggest that verbal interaction in the classroom is just a case of 'the more the merrier'. This topic would bear much more exploration and is certainly an area where language learners could be profitably involved in the research enterprise.

In fact, there may be times when teachers' desires to get students to interact verbally can be counter-productive. Felix conducted a study in Germany, in which he and his colleagues observed a first-year secondary school class consisting of thirty-four ten- and eleven-year-olds studying English as a foreign language via a 'liberal audiolingual approach' (1981:90). During the eight-month investigation period, all class hours (forty-five minutes per day, five days per week) were tape-recorded and three observers took notes. Transcripts of classroom interactions were used to analyse instances of learners' attempts at four target language phenomena: negation, interrogation, sentence types, and pronouns. (Thus this study provides an example of the linguistic, rather than the sociological, focus in classroom research.)

Felix's work is complex and will repay further study, particularly since relatively little classroom research has been done in foreign language contexts. We will only summarise his main points here, however, without going into detail about the linguistic structures he investigated.

Felix notes that with beginning learners in particular, it may be useless to teach structures which occur late in the processes of naturalistic interlanguage development. Under such circumstances, his data suggest that learners use two means of coping with the pressures to participate in classrooms prematurely. Either they select a response at random from among the structures studied, or they fall back on the internal (and possibly universal) principles of natural language acquisition. Felix makes a point which is important to consider in any discussion of classroom interaction:

> Whereas the untutored L2 learners are free to ignore those structures which they do not feel ready for, the high school students are consistently forced to produce utterances even if they have not mastered the structural features of the sentences involved.
> (Felix 1981:109)

Thus, the powerful classroom interaction rule, 'Thou shalt answer thy teacher's questions', forces students who are called upon to speak – sometimes before they are ready. The responses that are generated, while they may or may not be syntactically correct in and of themselves, are sometimes nonsensical and incoherent. For instance, Felix recorded these (and many other) instances of random responses in question and answer drills:

T: Is it a dog?
S: Yes, it isn't.

T: Can you see a sofa in Peter's room?
S: No, I can.

T: Who is this girl?
S: Yes, it is.

T: Are you a girl?
S: No, I am Kiel (name of a city).

T: Is it a blue flag?
S: No, I can't.

T: Are you a girl?
S: No, he is.

T: Am I your teacher?
S: Yes, I am your teacher.

Such bizarre responses occurred across all the linguistic structures investigated in this study. These sorts of utterances may cause serious communication difficulties or contribute to fossilisation if the notion of auto-input is correct. The auto-input hypothesis, as summarised by Schmidt and Frota (1986:316), is the idea that the learner's own output 'is a very significant part of his or her input, which affects the course of language learning'.

Felix's results suggest that we, as teachers, need to be aware of the linguistic demands our classroom tasks impose upon learners and to match such demands with the learners' current stages of interlanguage development $(i + 1)$, to the extent that we can. (We have already acknowledged the difficulty of identifying such stages and the probability that, in any given classroom, the learners are likely to be at several different stages of interlanguage development, especially considering their mastery of various linguistic structures or communicative skills.)

VanPatten (1987) has looked at Krashen's input hypothesis and the whole concept of 'i + 1' as it relates to *foreign* language teaching. One feature of Krashen's philosophy is that learners should not be forced to speak in the target language – that they will speak when they are ready and that learners, rather than teachers, should make the decision. VanPatten has suggested that the emphasis on whether or not learners should be expected to interact verbally in language classes is largely a matter of their interlanguage development, with different expectations for participation placed on learners at differing levels of development.

8.4 Classrooms and group work

A closely related issue that has been investigated in classroom research has to do with the relationship of group size to learner's oral participation. The question is, when learners interact in relatively small groups, is their participation different from the interaction patterns they experience in larger groups? Specifically, can their participation be enhanced in some way by manipulating group or class size? Another question is whether the teacher's presence or absence alters the learners' interaction patterns. All of these questions are related to a point made in Chapter 2 – namely that the learning opportunities that do arise in language lessons result from both the planned methods in use and other variables not entirely under the teacher's control. A number of studies have addressed these issues.

In an early study of college students learning English as a foreign language in Mexico, Long *et al.* (1976) compared the amount and types of the target language the learners used when they worked in pairs (called 'dyads') and when they interacted with the teacher and the rest of their classmates (called the 'lockstep' condition). 'Lockstep lessons' are segments of classroom interaction in which all the learners and the teacher interact together, such that all the learners must mentally 'march in step' at the same tempo, dealing with the same topic, etc. In the lockstep condition, learners have less freedom to negotiate input than they do in smaller, less formally structured groups. Also, unless the teacher is using choral repetition, typically only one learner at a time can speak, and the others are supposed to listen to what is being said.

Using the Embryonic Category System (Appendix D), these researchers found some striking quantitative and qualitative differences in the amount and types of the target language used by the learners in dyads, compared with the lockstep class (which provided the baseline data). Not only did the learners in pairs get more turns (which is to be expected since there are fewer people among whom the 'talk-time' must be divided), but they also performed a wider range of communicative functions with the language. That is, many of the moves which were normally the teacher's

147

responsibility in lockstep lessons (such as asking clarifying questions) were taken over by one or the other of the learners in the dyads.

Building on the ideas proposed by Long and his colleagues, Doughty and Pica (1986) did a study in Pennsylvania with college students of English as a second language. These researchers wanted to know which of two types of group-work activities – small groups and dyads – would produce more modified interaction, compared with lockstep, teacher-fronted teaching. The task consisted of placing cloth flowers on a felt-board 'garden' to duplicate a 'master plot' which was not seen by any of the participants. However, each person had one bit of information needed by the others to complete the task. This condition forced a two-way information exchange: everyone had to give and receive information for the task to be done properly.

While the researchers found no differences between the verbal interaction of the small groups and the dyads, both of these conditions resulted in significantly more modified interaction, more negotiation for meaning, than did the same task in the teacher-fronted condition. Doughty and Pica analysed transcripts of the interaction for Long's categories of confirmation checks, comprehension checks, and requests for clarification. (You will recall from section 7.2 that Long's research has suggested that such discourse modifications may be associated with second language acquisition, as depicted in Figure 6.) The results of this study showed that there was a significantly greater occurrence of negotiation for meaning in the small group and dyad activities than in the lockstep activity – in fact, nearly four times greater. To the extent that Long's model in Figure 6 has predictive power, this finding suggests that perhaps we should be doing more group work and fewer teacher-fronted lessons. However, since Doughty and Pica's research did not include any language test data as outcome measures, we cannot say conclusively that learners who actively negotiated for meaning actually achieved more, linguistically speaking, than those who did not. (The study was not designed to test this prediction from Long's model.)

8.5 Summary

In this chapter we have seen that teacher talk serves as a valuable source of input to language learners, and that teacher talk, like the language addressed to young children acquiring their mother tongue, is modified in interesting and potentially important ways. We also know, from the available classroom research, that learners experience a different quantity and quality of interaction in small groups or dyads than they do in large-group lockstep activities. Other research has focused on the differences that emerge in interaction patterns depending on the type of task the learners face. All of these issues point to the importance of the teacher's decision making in setting up activities and participant structures that will provide opportunities for the learners to interact and negotiate for meaning, with one another and the teacher, in the target language.

It is important to remember, however, that while teachers have a certain amount of power in the classroom, learners also clearly influence the pace and direction of the interaction. As we saw in the transcripts entitled 'Things get muddy' (in section 8.2) and 'Just a second, Igor' (section 7.3), learners utilise their own learning strategies, and these sometimes run contrary to the teacher's plans.

In this chapter, we have looked at how the interaction that occurs in classrooms is important, because it determines what learning opportunities the learners get. We have seen how teachers and learners together manage the classroom interaction and at the same time manage these learning opportunities. In the process, lesson plans give way to reality. Learners do not learn directly from the syllabus. They learn, partly, from whatever becomes of the syllabus in the classroom. Our concern with interaction is related to our three outcomes for learning: the input provided for learning, the practice opportunities that emerge, and the effects of all that happens on the receptivity of the learners. Receptivity, our next major topic, is a relatively broad issue which may have considerable bearing on both error treatment and interaction.

The major question, though, the one that cuts across everything else in this part of the book, is whether or not active observable participation is a 'good' thing. Is it psycholinguistically right, and therefore presumably universally right, since we are all humans with the same basic cognitive equipment, for teachers to encourage all their learners to be active contributors to classroom language lessons? This is the major question we have been addressing in this chapter, and quite clearly researchers do not yet know how or to what extent learners' observable participation is related to their success in mastering the target language. As we have seen, the research results so far are very mixed. There are theoretical and practical reasons for expecting learner participation to be productive, but no really compelling evidence that it actually is. We can also hypothesise, along with VanPatten, that the learners' level of interlanguage development should determine, in part, the extent to which they should be expected to participate verbally in classrooms. It may well be that 'invisible' participation, Schumann's 'eavesdropping' perhaps, is just as valuable, at least for some people, as are the observable strategies and behaviours which have been studied more often. If so, of course, then we will need to develop further our rather embryonic classroom research tools for dealing with unobservable behaviour. Meanwhile, the major point to take from the research is that perhaps we should not be too determined to make sure that all of our learners are equally and fully active contributors to our lessons, because there are likely to be some who think they will learn best by simply paying attention to what other people are saying, rather than by saying very much themselves. This position is countered by Swain's (1985) argument about comprehensible output: learners must try to make themselves understood if they are to gain grammatical mastery of the target language.

It seems clear then that making learners actively participate as much as possible cannot be universally right, if only because not all learners learn best in the same way. What all learners do need, universally, is an environment in which they can settle down to productive work, each in their various subtly different ways. This brings us to the topic for the next chapter, since learners pushed to behave in ways which they do not find helpful or congenial are very unlikely to be receptive. Receptivity is a wide issue, however, related to much more than just a learner's willingness to participate actively in lessons. Receptivity is also an issue that cannot be studied simply by observing behaviour. As we shall see, researchers investigating receptivity have had to develop a range of techniques to handle unobservable aspects of language learner behaviour. In so doing, they may well have developed the sorts of tools called for above, which will enable us eventually to make significant progress on the unobservable facets of classroom participation in particular and to study better the role of interaction in general.

DISCUSSION STARTERS

1 What is the difference in the risk involved in speaking in a small group, compared with speaking in front of the entire class? Could a small group pose a greater risk sometimes? What effect might this element of risk have on learners' verbal participation?
2 As a teacher, do you prefer lockstep classes or group work? What about when you are in the position of being a language learner?
3 What is your philosophy as a teacher – do you think learners' classroom participation should be regulated by the teacher, or should language learners only have to speak when they volunteer? Is your opinion the same or different when you are in the position of being a language learner?
4 What is the role of display and referential questions in language classrooms? You will recall Politzer's (1970) 'principle of economics' from section 1.5. (This was the idea that an activity is neither good nor bad in and of itself, but rather its value depends on the teacher's choosing well among several options.) Given this stance, do you feel that either display or referential questions should be used to the

exclusion of the other? If you opt for a balance, how will you decide on that balance? Does your answer depend, in part, on the learners' proficiency level?

5 Section 8.2 listed some of the learning strategies documented by the Chesterfields in their classroom research on young children in bilingual classes. Try using the Chesterfields' categories of verbal learning strategies to classify the behaviour of learners you are currently working with. (If you have no learners to think about, consider your own experience as a language learner.) Add new categories as necessary, and refine the Chesterfields' categories if you find them unsatisfactory in any way. Are all the strategies you have identified of equal value? If not, try ranking them in order of importance. Then compare your ranking with those of your colleagues.

6 In section 8.3 we listed some examples of learners' utterances from Felix's (1981) research. Are these just bizarre anomalies or are they typical of low-level learners' responses when classroom participation is forced?

7 You have now seen three different transcripts taken from segments of language lessons reviewing vocabulary: the transcript about Carlos's trousers in Chapter 6, 'Just a second, Igor' in Chapter 7, and 'Things get muddy' in this chapter. Based on the data from the transcripts only, what would you say are the similarities among the three teachers' classroom behaviours? What are the differences? Do you have a preference as to which teacher you would rather have if you were a language learner? Why or why not? How closely is your preference, if you have one, related to the teachers' interaction patterns?

SUGGESTIONS FOR FURTHER READING

1 Hatch (1983:154–65) and Long (1983c) both provide clear reviews of the research on language addressed to learners, as does Chaudron (1988a) – especially in Chapter 3.

2 An excellent synthesis on the learning strategy research can be found in Chapter 4 of Chaudron's book (1988a). Other articles on learning strategies can be found in the reference list at the end of this book. See, for example, the citations to papers by Chamot (1984), the Chesterfields (1985), Ehrman and Oxford (1989), O'Malley and his colleagues (1985a, b), Reid (1987), Wenden (1985), Wenden and Rubin (1987) and Oxford-Carpenter (1985).

3 A good review of the research on group work can be found in an article by Long and Porter in the *TESOL Quarterly* (1985).

4 An article that deals specifically with the learners' point of view is

Cohen's paper (1985) entitled, 'What can we learn from the language learner?' Other work that has explored this topic is by Rubin (1975) and Stern (1975).

5 Some interesting papers on teacher talk are by Chaudron (1983), Schinke-Llano (1983, 1986), Ellis (1985), Kleifgen (1985), Wesche and Ready (1985), Wong-Fillmore (1985), and Strong (1986). Pica and Long (1986) have compared experienced and inexperienced teachers in this regard. Chaudron (1988a) provides a very good overview of this area of research.

6 Several researchers have begun exploring the role of task type and situation in interaction patterns among language learners. Some of the more accessible articles include those by Gass and Varonis (1985), Pica and Doughty (1985), Sato (1985), Cathcart (1986), Duff (1986), Porter (1986), and Rulon and McCreary (1986).

7 Beebe has written an article about risk taking among language learners (1983). Her speculations about the risk-taking behaviour of HIGs and LIGs are especially interesting in terms of the topics we have been discussing.

8 VanPatten's (1987) article about Krashen's input hypothesis in foreign language teaching provides a well written discussion of the decisions teachers must make regarding classroom activities and the importance of input and interaction. His comments are relevant to the forced participation issue raised here.

9 Brock (1986) has written an interesting paper about referential questions in ESL classroom discourse.

10 A collection of papers edited by Candlin and Murphy (1987) on language learning tasks includes articles about learners' contributions to task designs, task-centred writing, tasks for slow learners, and the relationship of instructional tasks and discourse outcomes in second language classrooms.

MINI-PROJECT: ANALYSING INTERACTION IN TRANSCRIPTS

You have now been introduced to a number of different topics in language classroom research. You have also seen three different transcripts derived from vocabulary lessons for adult learners of English: 'Carlos's trousers' in Chapter 6, 'Just a second, Igor', (Chapter 7), and 'Things get muddy' in this chapter. These data form the basis of this project, which is designed to familiarise you with two means of analysing interaction.

STAGE ONE: CODING FOR INTERACTIONAL MOVES

Choose one of the three transcripts and try to analyse the interaction, using Long's three categories of interactional moves: comprehension checks, confirmation checks and requests for clarification. (See section 7.2 for examples.)

STAGE TWO: COMPARING YOUR RESULTS

Now compare your coding with that of a classmate or colleague. Do you basically agree? In cases of disagreement, why did your analyses diverge? For instance, is there any one particular category that generated disagreement?

STAGE THREE: ANOTHER ROUND

After your discussion, try using the same system with one of the other transcripts. Then compare your results with those of your colleague once more. Is your percentage of agreement higher this time? Usually researchers try to achieve at least eighty-five per cent inter-coder agreement before they analyse a large corpus of data. Were your results that similar? When you feel entirely confident that you and your colleague are using the coding categories reliably, code the third transcript and compare your results.

STAGE FOUR: USING THE EMBRYONIC CATEGORY SYSTEM

Now you might try coding the same two transcripts with the Embryonic Category System (Appendix D). If you do this, you can compare the results of your first analysis with those of your second analysis using the same data. Of course, you can also repeat the steps to determine the inter-coder agreement levels.

Both of these category systems were developed by Long, or Long and his colleagues, but at different periods of time and for different purposes. What similarities, if any, can you detect? What are the differences? What research questions could you reasonably approach, using one system or the other?

MAJOR PROJECT: RECORDING CLASSROOM INTERACTION

This project is intended to give you some further experience with collecting and analysing original data. The project can be done in conjunction with a friend or with a group of people working as a team. Such an approach would permit you to establish your level of inter-observer agreement.

STAGE ONE: DATA COLLECTION

Tape-record an hour-long lesson while you observe the class. Draw a seating plan of the participants, on which you indicate the learners' names, if you know them, and their physical positions relative to the teacher and to one another. Give each student an identification number.

During the lesson, make a simple tally of how often each learner speaks. You might set up a worksheet with columns like this:

Learner-initiated turns	*Teacher-initiated turns*
S1	
S2	
S3	
S4	
S5	
.	
.	
.	

STAGE TWO: NUMERICAL ANALYSES

After the lesson, use your worksheet to determine what percentage of the turns were self-initiated and what percentage were teacher-initiated (based on your 'real-time' coding). Later, repeat this coding using the tape-recorded data. This time you may stop the tape to make your tallies. Fill out the chart again. Then compare the results of your real-time coding with the assessment of the tape-recording. Can you tell for certain from the tape which moves are teacher-initiated and which ones are student-initiated?

STAGE THREE: TRANSCRIBING THE DATA

Transcribe at least a brief portion of the lesson and then use the transcript to determine teacher-initiated and learner-initiated turns once more. Using the tape counter numbers, see if there are differences in your analysis when you work directly from the audio-recording and when you analyse the interaction in the transcripts.

Based on your analyses, determine who are the HIGs and who are the LIGs. What differences (other than the sheer frequency of turn-taking behaviour) are exhibited by these two types of learners? For example, do the HIGs take longer turns, in addition to taking more frequent turns? Do various topics or activities promote more turn taking than others? Are there clearly two groups or is there a range of interactive styles?

STAGE FOUR: A RETURN VISIT

Return to the same class on another day and repeat the observation and recording processes. Based on the second set of data, determine whether the same people are identified as HIGs and LIGs as in the first observation. If not, how different were the individuals' verbal behaviours in the second observation? Were the interaction patterns discernibly related to the task at hand? Do your findings parallel Sato's – that some learners regularly bid for turns while others typically speak out without bidding?

For both sets of data, determine what percentage of the turns were distributed by the teacher's direct nomination of individual students by name. Is there any evidence that the teacher tried to distribute the turns evenly among the learners?

STAGE FIVE: TRIANGULATING WITH THE TEACHER

Ask the teacher if he or she has a philosophy and/or a practical stance on turn distribution in classes, and whether there is a deliberate attempt to ensure equal talk-time for all the participants. Next have the teacher listen to the tape and comment on the interaction patterns that were recorded. What information would you like to share with the teacher, given the results of your data analysis? You will recall that Chuck's teacher was surprised at his level of private verbal activity, when he had appeared to be a passive participant. Are there any similar surprises in your data?

STAGE SIX: REFLECTION

This project has taken a naturalistic enquiry approach, in that you did not implement a treatment (the intervention), nor did you exercise much control (for example, of the type of lesson, the learners selected as subjects, etc.). What have the results and the procedures of this observational project suggested to you about your own teaching style?

You could also do a variation of this project as an action research study if you are recording a class in which you are the teacher. Start by audio-recording a 'typical' class in which you do not try to distribute the turns in any particular way. Using the recording, complete the tally of teacher-initiated and learner-initiated turns, perhaps with the help of a chart like the one above. Summarise your results. Are they what you expected? What you hoped for?

Next try a small-scale intervention of some sort in a similar subsequent lesson. For example, you could avoid making any direct nominations, or you could try avoiding general solicits altogether and use direct nominations exclusively. As an alternative, you could write each learner's name on a card and work through the cards in sequence, to ensure numerically equal turn distribution among the learners.

Regardless of the intervention you choose, audio-record this lesson and analyse the interaction as before. What happens to the participation patterns? Are the data notably different from those collected in the first lesson? Repeat the process in another lesson, using a different intervention if you like. (This is the iterative part of the action research cycle.)

Finally, you could involve the learners in the project by asking them what turn distribution patterns they prefer. It might be helpful in the long run for you to write a brief prose summary after each intervention experience, so that you can document your reactions and the learners', either for reflection or for sharing with your colleagues.

Part V Receptivity in language classrooms

'Receptivity' is not a common term in classroom research, nor in language pedagogy. We are using it here, however, because we find it a useful cover term for a variety of concerns that we believe can be helpfully brought together. By 'receptivity' we mean a state of mind, whether permanent or temporary, that is open to the experience of becoming a speaker of another language, somebody else's language. (Clearly this is a heuristic description rather than an operational definition.) The opposite of receptivity would be 'defensiveness', the state of mind of feeling threatened by the experience and therefore needing to set up defences against it.

In our use of the terms, both receptivity and defensiveness can be active, rather than merely passive states of mind. That is to say, you can be actively receptive, and therefore be working actively to promote the learning experience, or actively defensive, taking definite steps to avoid it. We can see the phenomenon in action in state school systems, as in England, for example, where children may start a foreign language actively eager to learn, but become resentful and unco-operative towards language learning later on in their school careers (Burstall 1970; Burstall et al. 1974).

9 Receptivity: the issues involved

In this chapter we shall be looking at classroom language learning and outlining the various aspects of it that might engage either receptivity or defensiveness on the part of the learners. In the next chapter, we will then turn to the relevant research to see how what we are calling 'receptivity' has been studied, and with what results so far.

Here we shall briefly review a number of such background issues to language learning receptivity, before going into detail on eight more issues of particular importance from the perspectives of classroom research.

9.1 Openness to what?

If receptivity means openness, for our purposes, then the next question must be: openness to what? 'Openness to the new language' is the obvious answer, but the situation is not quite that simple. For instance, learning a new language implies learning about another culture, another way of life. If that new way of life is itself attractive to you in some way, then it may be easier to cope with the moments when language learning seems impossibly slow, or impossibly demanding of concentrated effort. This issue is related to studies on 'integrative motivation' – the desire of the language learner to affiliate in some way with the speakers of the target language (see, for example, Gardner and Lambert 1972; Gardner 1979).

For this reason, receptivity to the target language itself is our first background issue – whether you find the language you are supposed to be learning attractive or ugly to listen to, for example. Along the same lines, some people may find a language elegantly systematic, while others are put off by what they see only as complicated rules.

Another background issue, mentioned above, is receptivity to the people and culture a new language represents. We know that people feel they can judge others by the way they speak, and that this principle holds true across languages, so that if there are prejudices between groups these can quite easily be demonstrated. To take but one example, in a Canadian study (Lambert *et al.* 1960), speakers of English revealed their stereotypes of French-speaking Canadians by judging the personality behind tape-recorded voices speaking either English or French. The French voices got rated as less intelligent, less trustworthy, and so on, than the English ones, although the French and English recordings were made by the same bilingual speakers using the two different languages. (This procedure is called the 'matched guise technique' and has been widely used in sociolinguistic research.) Since the same person was heard, though speaking two different languages, any differences in judgement would have to be attributed to the language being used and its associations in the minds of the people who judged the recordings. The associations are interesting, of course, because they may be far more important than the aesthetic aspects of languages. It is not that French, in itself, sounds less 'intelligent', but that the English-speaking Canadians in the study associated French with people they regarded as less intelligent, and generalised this impression to other speakers of Canadian French. This same sort of pattern has been found in a wide variety of studies encompassing several countries and language groups. (See for example, Lambert, Anisfeld, and Yeni-Komshian 1965; Williams 1973a, 1973b; Galvan, Pierce and Underwood 1976; Ryan and Giles 1982.)

This question of language attitudes as a background issue has major implications for language teaching policy. Should English, for example, be given a major place on a curriculum because of its importance as a world language, even where it is remembered as the language of colonial oppression? The issue also has implications for materials design: can materials be designed in a 'culturally neutral' way, or so that they reflect the native culture of the learners, rather than that of the target language's native speakers? This is not an issue that has been raised by classroom research, and is probably not one that is best investigated by the standard classroom research procedures, but it does have an impact on learners' receptivity to the target language.

Another such background issue is receptivity to the idea of being associated with the other non-native speakers of the new language – your own compatriots perhaps. In many places the association is likely to be positive, where, for example, learners may wish to learn English because it will give them a better chance of joining their compatriots who have interesting and lucrative careers in government. In others it may be negative, where compatriots who have learned the language in question are seen as in some sense disloyal, perhaps even as supporters of an alternative form of government.

As teachers, we sometimes tend to think that our learners really have nothing better to do with their lives than to be our students. And yet we all know that sometimes learners find concentrating difficult, not because there is something drastically wrong with what is happening in the lesson, but because their attention is drawn by other priorities. They are not receptive to what we, as teachers, are offering because they have other, more pressing things on their minds. This problem is probably familiar to anyone who has taught survival language skills to otherwise highly motivated immigrant adults in classes scheduled after their regular working day. Perhaps the learners have only just arrived in the area and are still having major accommodation problems. They may be worried about their health, or their financial security. Perhaps they do not have adequate childcare and must either bring their children to class or stay at home. For whatever reasons, their receptivity may be affected by factors that in themselves have little or nothing to do with whatever happens in the language classroom.

Having briefly introduced some background issues, we can now move on to those aspects of receptivity that are most directly related to classroom experiences. Our discussion throughout the rest of this chapter is more speculative than research-based, but we hope the issues raised will be thought-provoking in terms of how they may relate to language teaching and learning, and how they might be explored through the various approaches to classroom research.

9.2 Receptivity to the teacher as a person

If you ask people about the languages they have learned, then you are likely to arouse memories of particular teachers – perhaps of the teacher who first captured their enthusiasm, or of the teacher who effectively killed it off. Even young children seem to identify school subjects strongly with the teachers who teach them, and sometimes find it very difficult to like a subject if they do not like the person who teaches the class. It would seem important and helpful, to most people, to be able to get on well with their teacher, to be open to the sort of person that he or she is. Although some teachers may infect practically all their learners with their own enthusiasm, other teachers may succeed in ruining the experience for practically all theirs. The situation is further complicated by the possibility that learners may disagree about their teacher, even within a given class, so that some learners feel unable to get on with a teacher who is clearly very well liked by other learners in the same class.

9.3 Receptivity to fellow learners

Yet another background issue, on a much more modest scale perhaps, concerns receptivity to the notion of being associated with your fellow learners. Do you want to be seen as someone who is interested in learning foreign languages, and who likes the company of people who like learning foreign languages? Among English school children, this question can be a gender issue, with languages typically seen as girls' subjects. In the United States the study of certain languages (such as French) has at times been perceived as a girls' subject, thus sometimes making it difficult for boys to allow themselves to look interested. This is a problem well worth the attention of classroom researchers, who might investigate how such prejudices are maintained, or observe the effect of a positive attempt to fight the prejudices using the action research paradigm.

The question of receptivity to one's fellow learners has immediate pedagogical implications for classroom interaction, particularly in teachers' efforts to structure group-work tasks. Some learners may just not be open at all to the experience of working with other members of the same class. This is likely to be especially important in language work wherever the emphasis is on learning by interacting in small groups, with other learners and without the teacher's constant attention. Beyond the very real possibility of simple personality clashes, however, there may also be all sorts of inter-ethnic or political prejudices that threaten learners' receptivity to each other as people.

There is also the further possibility that learners may not wish to work with each other because, for example, the more proficient may feel they have nothing to gain from interacting with the less proficient, or the less proficient may feel demoralised by the superior performance of the others. In such cases a lot may depend on just how the teacher manages the class – our next point.

A related concern has to do with the impact of other learners themselves. Put negatively, this amounts to the potentially influential role of peer pressure in classroom language learning. Gardner (1979) conducted a survey in which teachers of Native American children were asked about their learners' motivation levels. The teachers judged the children's motivation to speak English as starting high in the first and second grades, and then dropping precipitously in subsequent years until it hit a low point in fifth to seventh grade. At the same time, negative peer pressure (not to use English) was judged the lowest in the early grades with a sharp increase in the fifth to the seventh grades. In other words, Gardner feels there is a relationship between peer pressure to avoid using the target language and the learners' motivation levels (as perceived by the teachers).

9.4 Receptivity to the teacher's way of teaching

Receptivity to the teacher's way of teaching (including the teaching method, of course, but that is too narrow a term here) is probably more important than receptivity to fellow learners' ways of learning. At least we suspect this is the case in many of the world's language classrooms,

161

where the teacher is such a dominant figure and the learners rarely get much of a chance to develop an individual approach. (However, the extent to which learners in such classes do remain individuals should not be underestimated.) A teacher may be liked as a person, and well respected as a professional, and yet not teach in a way that suits everybody in the class, to the extent that some learners may find that teacher quite useless to them.

9.5 Receptivity to course content

Language courses are not only about language. Quite apart from the cultural content we have already mentioned, there has to be something to talk about, even in the most mechanical of sentence pattern practices. Very often this carrier topic is not intrinsically interesting to learners. (The term 'carrier topic' is used, as we noted in section 7.3, because the topic carries the language items being practised.) There comes a point when the learners no longer wish to talk about the fictitious Robinson family that lives nowhere in particular, with a stupid dog and two boring children.

More worrisome, courses whose content has been specially designed to be relevant to learners' academic, social, or occupational needs may not lead learners to feel receptive because 'relevance' itself is not necessarily compelling. If learners have just had a week of biology as university students, they may not want their English lessons to carry on with yet more of the same, however relevant it is, and however useful it ought to be in helping them cope with the next week's work in biology. So even the most well-intentioned attempt at ensuring receptivity, through matching content to learners' ostensible needs, may backfire.

Many teachers have also experienced the difficulties that arise when their approach to organising course content does not match with the learners' expectations as to what a language course should involve. For instance, learners from traditional educational systems sometimes react negatively to attempts to teach communicatively, or to organise a situational or functional syllabus, if they feel that grammar is the proper focus for a language course and everything else is just wasting time or, perhaps more positively, having fun.

9.6 Receptivity to teaching materials

Sometimes, even if everything else seems favourable, learners can 'switch off' because they do not like the way the content of their course is presented in the teaching materials. The textbook may perhaps be dull to look at, with crowded pages and very few illustrations to catch the eye. Or learners may be offended by the illustrative style used in textbooks. In an experimental study, for example, Pearson (1983) found that learners from various cultures reacted very differently when faced with different cartoon styles illustrating ESL materials.

Another possibility, quite closely related to the way of teaching, is that the materials will present activities and some bits of the language for learners to work with, but include nothing that explains anything to the learners. This pattern seems particularly likely to occur with some modern communicative textbooks, which can be quite useless to learners as reference materials, and so of no help to them if, for instance, they are trying to study independently, or to catch up on a lesson they have missed. Learners may come to see such materials as generally unhelpful, and as a reason for feeling that they are never going to succeed as learners.

In other cases, learners may disagree with, or be offended by, much of the content of reading passages and dialogues. Such materials may represent a distinct gender bias, for example, or may involve subjects that are culturally taboo (perhaps for religious reasons). Such materials may merely lose credibility, or they may even be rejected altogether as totally unusable.

9.7 Receptivity to being a successful language learner

Put negatively this may sound like a rather odd issue: how could anyone not be open to the idea of being successful? But let us start with the positive side. Many school children, apparently, like the thought of taking a foreign language because it offers the chance of success, a chance not offered by other subjects which they see as being more 'academic'. They can imagine themselves being successful and they are open to the possibility of success, at least for the first year or so, but after that many seem to decide that success in language learning is not for them. Perhaps part of the problem is that such disenchanted, disillusioned learners have really closed themselves to the possibility of being successful. Such a decision may be quite realistic, given the learners' experiences. (We shall see later how the 'graded objectives' movement in Britain has sought to restore faith in the possibility of continued success for a majority of learners.)

In quite different learning circumstances, it is possible to imagine a learner being afraid of success with reason, because of what success might bring. To take but one example, a Japanese woman married to an American businessman might be apparently highly motivated to learn English for the sake of communicating with her husband, and yet fear the consequences for her life-style as a Japanese person if success in learning English would mean playing a much more active role in helping her husband entertain business guests. Learners do need to feel confident that success will bring positive rewards that at least outweigh the likely extra burdens which that success may also bring.

In some circumstances, learners may also need to be receptive to the idea that complete success is neither possible nor necessary for them. One of the possible causes of drop-out from foreign language classes is the mismatch between high initial hopes of quickly becoming very proficient, and the reality of the large amount of hard work necessary for even a quite modest level of attainment.

9.8 Receptivity to the idea of communicating with others

Many people do not actually enjoy communicating, or attempting to communicate, with others, especially with people from other cultures. Such people are unlikely to enjoy interactive methods of language learning, or the prospect of using whatever they have learned inside the classroom outside in the 'real world'. Such people, it could be said, are not receptive to the whole idea of face-to-face communication. It may be because they lack the self-confidence and self-esteem to deal well with social encounters in general. This area, the topic of 'communication apprehension', has been widely investigated in first-language situations in the field of speech communication (McCroskey 1977; Friedman 1980; Daly and McCroskey 1984).

For many people, communication apprehension may be even more severe when they are speaking in a second or foreign language (Foss and Reitzel 1988). Clearly the lack of target language mastery contributes to this problem, but there are also cultural differences in the handling of social talk, in terms of frequency, duration, topics, participants, etc. Of course, within any given culture there is a great deal of interpersonal variability on this point: some people simply enjoy communicating more than others.

9.9 Summary

We have now considered eight specific issues related to learner receptivity: receptivity to 1) the target language and culture, 2) the teacher as a person, 3) other learners, 4) the teacher's way of teaching, 5) course content, 6) the materials, 7) the idea of being a successful language learner, and 8) the idea of communicating with other people. Although research has not yet clearly demonstrated the importance of these issues to language learning, there are some studies which lead us to believe they are worth pursuing.

In the next chapter we will be reviewing some findings of existing research on topics which we have grouped together under the rubric of receptivity. Our coverage of these concerns here represents an initial attempt to map the territory. We have listed them as possible areas that you might wish to pursue, as a reader and classroom researcher, and the next chapter will illustrate just some of the possibilities. Meanwhile, the *Discussion starters, Suggestions for further reading*, and project ideas should enable you to explore in greater depth this whole complex area we have labelled 'receptivity'.

DISCUSSION STARTERS

1 Have you ever been in a situation where you had to learn a language that did not appeal to you? Or where you did not feel an affinity for the people and the culture represented by the target language? Have you, as a teacher, met learners in this situation? If so, what was the outcome?

2 Have you, as a language learner, ever been in a class where your initial enthusiasm to learn diminished, either quickly or gradually? If so, what factors influenced your attitude?

3 Have you ever been in a language class in which something about the teacher's behaviour, attitudes or teaching method affected your receptivity to the target language, either negatively or positively? What steps can you take, as a teacher or future teacher, to make sure that your influence on learners' receptivity is positive?

4 As a language learner, have you ever experienced a strong reaction, whether positive or negative, to the content of a language course, or to the teaching materials used? If you have experience as a teacher, have the learners in your classes ever reacted negatively to a course you prepared or to a set of materials you used? What did you do? In retrospect, what could you have done?

5 Have you ever known a learner who was afraid of success for some reason? If so, what was the reason and how was the whole thing dealt with?

6 Have you ever known a good language learner who was a poor communicator, someone who found it very difficult to get along with other people socially? If not, does that mean teachers should be trying to help poor learners with their social skills?

7 In general, in what ways is the teacher responsible for the learners' receptivity, and what responsibility rests with the learners themselves?

How do these potentially different areas of responsibility translate into classroom behaviour, for both teachers and learners?

8 In your experience, either as a teacher or a learner, what is the role of peer pressure in language classrooms? Can peer pressure be a positive as well as a negative influence in language learning?

SUGGESTIONS FOR FURTHER READING

1 This chapter owes much to Stevick, and in particular to his 1976 volume, *Memory, meaning and method*, which includes a section entitled 'Learning: defensive or receptive' (pages 109–16).

2 For a description of the introduction, in England and Wales, of French as a primary school subject, and an account of its impact on secondary school language teaching, see Burstall (1970) and Burstall *et al.* (1974).

3 A comprehensive review of language and social attitudes can be found in Giles and St. Clair (1979). Their focus is not on language pedagogy but their material is clearly relevant to many of the issues involved in our field. Other accessible references on language attitudes are by Lambert, Anisfeld, and Yeni-Komshian (1965), Williams (1973a, 1973b); Galvan, Pierce and Underwood (1976); and Ryan and Giles (1982).

4 Communication apprehension in second and foreign language learning has been discussed by McCoy (1979), Lucas (1984), Horwitz, Horwitz and Cope (1986), and Foss and Reitzel (1988).

5 For a report of research on gender bias in ESL materials, see Porreca (1984).

6 Gardner (1979) has conducted survey research in which teachers reported their views of American Indian children's motivation to speak English (see section 9.3). His graphs depicting the teachers' ideas about peer pressure are relevant to the points raised here.

7 Bailey's (1980) analysis of her French class diary documented an initially high motivation followed by a sharp drop in motivation as the class progressed. The same pattern emerged in a diary study by Jones (1977) in her learning of Indonesian.

8 There is some evidence to suggest that learners do better in language classes where the way of teaching matches their own learning style preferences. This literature is reviewed in Chapter 12 of Hatch (1983).

MINI-PROJECT: TYPES OF RECEPTIVITY

1 Thinking of your own language learning experience, how important are each of the eight aspects of receptivity discussed in Chapter 9? Using

the list below, rate each of the eight, individually, on a five-point scale of importance (where 5 = very important and 1 = unimportant).

a)	receptivity to the target language and culture	5	4	3	2	1
b)	receptivity to the teacher as a person	5	4	3	2	1
c)	receptivity to fellow learners	5	4	3	2	1
d)	receptivity to the teacher's way of teaching	5	4	3	2	1
e)	receptivity to course content	5	4	3	2	1
f)	receptivity to teaching materials	5	4	3	2	1
g)	receptivity to the idea of being a successful language learner	5	4	3	2	1
h)	receptivity to the idea of communicating with others	5	4	3	2	1

2 After you have completed your individual ratings of these categories you can then rank order the items in terms of their importance as you assessed them. That is, you can list these items from most to least important, indicating any tied ranks.

3 If you are working with a group, you could also compare your ratings with those of your colleagues as a way of starting a discussion with them. Is your rank ordering similar to theirs? If you compute the average ratings for each item on the above list, what is the group's ranking of the items' importance?

4 In the process of rating, ranking and discussing these items, you may find that the list does not include some types of receptivity which you or your colleagues consider to be important in language learning. If so, add these ideas to the list. If you wish, you may reconsider the rating and ranking of the items on this expanded list.

5 Look back at the transcripts you have worked with in earlier mini-projects in this book. Is there evidence of either receptivity or defensiveness among the learners in any of these transcripts? If you were to observe an actual language class in progress, what behaviour would you accept as evidence of receptiveness, or of defensiveness? Either on your own or with a group, make a list of observable features of classroom interaction which would constitute evidence of either state.

6 Finally, observe a language class (or tape-record one that you are teaching) and try to find such evidence in the record. What does this process suggest to you about our original list or about your list of potential evidence?

MAJOR PROJECT: AUTOBIOGRAPHY OF A LANGUAGE LEARNER

It is a truism that 'we teach as we have been taught'. Given this principle, many language teachers have found it useful to look back on their own experiences as language learners and to reflect on the influence of their language learning experiences on their development as teachers. Our suggestion for this major project, then, is that you write your own retrospective autobiography as a language learner, particularly with the idea of receptivity as a possible organising theme. Depending on the experiences you have had, and the depth with which you choose to record your history, this project could be very substantial.

We suggest that you begin with a time line, organising your experiences in chronological order. Write what you can remember, thinking about the eight topics on our list of issues related to receptivity. Finally, try to see how each experience has influenced you as a teacher (or may influence you, if you are a pre-service teacher). If you are working with a group, it may be useful to share your autobiography with your colleagues, to look for similarities and differences. Does your autobiography suggest any research topics which you could explore, either through naturalistic enquiry, experimental studies, or action research?

10 Receptivity – some relevant research

Chapter 9 introduced the term receptivity and offered brief accounts of eight issues that link receptivity to classroom language learning and teaching. In this way we hoped to bring together a number of topics that are clearly related, but that are normally treated under quite separate headings. Now, in Chapter 10, we will be looking at examples of research studies that similarly might not otherwise be brought together. We see them all as related, however, to the general notion of receptivity introduced in Chapter 9.

We start with research that does not use the term receptivity, but which can easily be related to several of our eight issues in Chapter 9.

10.1 Receptivity as attention

A receptive learner is an attentive learner, presumably, so it makes sense to look at how attention in language classes has been studied. We have reasons to feel that attention is an important factor in classroom language learning even though Krashen has suggested (for example, 1982) that language acquisition which occurs outside of conscious awareness is more effective than conscious learning. Newmark (1972) once argued that language teaching is above all a matter of getting and of keeping learners' attention. We noted in Figure 8 (section 7.3) that attention is one of the unobservable factors in classroom participation. And van Lier has suggested (personal communication) that the learners' attention is the key component which converts input into intake.

Although we know we learn a great deal in our everyday lives without having to be taught (learning to recognise other people's faces, for example), it is still surely reasonable to believe that attending to what a teacher is trying to teach will be more helpful than not attending to it. If our learners' attention wanders away from the task at hand and they start thinking about, say, how long it is to lunchtime, then surely there is very little chance of their learning anything more until their attention is once more attracted somehow. But if we accept attention as a potentially interesting way of looking at receptivity in the language classroom, how are we going to measure attention, for research purposes? Certainly teachers develop their own ways of identifying learners who are not attending, and they probably rely on things like posture and eye movements, but learners also develop their own ways of looking as if they are attending even when they really are thinking about something else entirely. It becomes impossible to measure attention validly or reliably just by observing learners in the classroom.

It may seem equally invalid to simply ask the learners directly what they are thinking about, in the middle of a lesson, but one researcher has done just that, with intriguing results. You will recall from our discussion of participation in section 7.3 that Cohen (as reported in Cohen and Hosenfeld 1981) got permission from a number of teachers at different levels and in different settings (all in Israel) to stop their classes at some point. He then asked the learners to write down, at the moment they were stopped, what was in the forefront of their consciousness. By this simple measure the 'best' attention estimate he obtained was one of eighty-two per cent, in one class, for the proportion of learners who wrote down the topic of the lesson as what was on their mind. The average over a number of classes was about fifty per cent, suggesting that we might expect only about half of any class to be paying attention at any one time.

Cohen's figures may not be entirely valid, of course, because learners might be reluctant to paint too unfavourable a picture of themselves. But if that is the case, the true picture would be even less encouraging for the language teaching profession. Cohen's data may also not be representative, however, of other teaching situations (the generalisability issue). We should certainly not take his rather depressing figures for granted, but rather think of his work as an ingenious opening up of yet another possible step that teachers might take to find out something more about what is going on in their classrooms.

However interesting it may be to have some idea about how many learners are attending at any one time, it would be even more interesting to know why those who are not attending have, if only for the moment, switched off. Some ideas can be obtained by looking at the answers of those learners who wrote down something other than the lesson topic. But if they write, as some do, something to do with food, that only tells us that hunger, at that point, was winning the battle for their attention. There might have been other equally hungry learners who were nevertheless still attending to the lesson. What we need to know is *why* the thought of food prevailed for some, and why others were still concentrating on the lesson. Which of the eight aspects of receptivity outlined above were involved? Were the materials dull, fellow learners insufferable, or was hunger itself really the key factor? These are all questions that could be addressed in action research projects. Certainly they have a local and practical perspective, rather than a global and theoretical one.

10.2 Insights from language learners

One approach, although it was not originally intended to illuminate the issue of receptivity, has in fact offered us some clues that are worth mentioning here. We are referring to the diary studies (Bailey 1983a; Bailey and Ochsner 1983; Matsumoto 1987). A diary study is a first-person account of a language learning or teaching experience in which the researcher/author is also typically the subject. For example, two experienced teachers and researchers, John and Francine Schumann (1977), started investigating their own experiences as language learners by keeping detailed diaries, following Progoff's (1975) 'journal-keeping' procedures. In their reports of learning Farsi in Los Angeles and Iran, and Tunisian Arabic in Tunisia, they identified from their diary entries what seemed to them to be the key factors that either helped or hindered their learning.

To their surprise they found that they were not at all receptive to the teaching method used with them (section 9.4), causing total withdrawal from the class in one case (an option, we should note, that is not normally open to school children). Francine Schumann also found herself unreceptive to the teaching materials available for self-instruction, partly on account of the boring nature of their carrier content (section 9.5) and partly because of their physical appearance (section 9.6). Luckily she tried using illustrated books for children, and found them both very attractive and above all very useful, in spite of their being genuine illustrated story books for native speakers of Farsi (authentic materials), and not language teaching materials at all.

In relation to content, again, John Schumann found himself unreceptive to the course he was attending because he found he had a 'personal agenda' for his language learning, an agenda that was being frustrated by the course syllabus. He also found himself unreceptive to the teaching method (section 9.4 again) because it required active participation of him, when all he wanted to do was to learn by what he called 'eavesdropping' on what was going on in the classroom (section 9.8). And they both had problems external to the classroom that made it difficult to concentrate on their language learning, in addition to everything else (section 9.1). John wrote about what he called 'transition anxiety' – a delibitating sort of anxiety he associated with moving from country to country, or simply with moving from one house to another. Francine wrote about something similar – her inability to concentrate on her language learning until she had properly settled into her new surroundings. She wrote of her 'nesting patterns' – her problems with living out of suitcases and being unable to create a satisfactory living environment under such circumstances. Both John's transition anxiety and Francine's nesting patterns are presage variables – factors which the learners experienced external to the classroom, but which influenced their classroom language learning nonetheless.

Thus the Schumanns' paper, which was one of the earliest published diary studies, highlighted five of the eight aspects of receptivity outlined at the start of the chapter. Later Bailey's (1980) initial analysis of her experience studying French as a foreign language dealt with two more: the idea of being a successful language learner (9.7), and problems in relating to other learners (9.3). She found that, given the pressures exerted by various affective considerations in the classroom, her initially high level of motivation to learn French declined sharply during the second week of the course. It took several weeks for her enthusiasm to climb back gradually to its earlier high levels. In the meantime, she continually reassessed her self-awareness about what it means to be a successful language learner. Her ideas on this point were directly related to her attitudes about the other learners (point 9.3).

Later diary studies have led to a stronger emphasis on the issue of anxiety as a factor in classroom language learning. Before looking at any more studies, however, we should first look at the notion of anxiety itself.

10.3 Anxiety in language learning

The first thing to say about anxiety is that, despite the unpleasant associations we may have with it, it is not necessarily a bad thing in itself. Researchers distinguish between 'debilitating anxiety', which gets in the way, and 'facilitating anxiety', which actually helps people do better than they might otherwise (Kleinmann 1977; Scovel 1978). The idea is not really so very paradoxical, because we all know that sometimes we find it difficult to produce our best (whether it is at learning, or teaching, or playing tennis) if we know that success is virtually guaranteed, if there is no reason to be at all anxious about the possibility of failure. Knowing that success is not guaranteed, but that making a real effort might make all the difference between success and failure, we may do better precisely because our anxiety has spurred us on. If, on the other hand, we would really like to succeed but feel that, no matter how hard we try, we are most likely to fail, then our anxiety is likely to make it even more difficult for us to produce our best. Some aspects of receptivity, then, are not dependent upon just *removing* anxiety, but upon minimising the sources of debilitating anxiety, and optimising the sources of facilitating anxiety so that learners can work with what we might call 'relaxed concentration'.

But is anxiety, for good or ill, a major factor anyway? We do know, in part due to work in North America, that we can expect a relationship between anxiety and speech skills in foreign language learning. (See, for example, a report by Gardner *et al.* 1976, of a survey involving over one thousand Canadian high school students of French.) As one might expect, the more anxious learners are, the less likely they are to do well at speech skills. Furthermore, the older they are and the further they get in the compulsory school system, the stronger this relationship will probably become. Unfortunately it is impossible to say whether it is the increasing anxiety that gets in the way of developing good speech skills, or whether, as may seem at least equally likely, it is the poor speech skills that themselves create the anxiety, as it becomes increasingly embarrassing to have been studying a language but not to have become good at speaking it. Perhaps even more likely is the possibility that the two problems feed off each other.

Another point to keep in mind is the distinction between 'trait anxiety' (a relatively permanent personality feature) and the less stable 'state anxiety' (Scovel 1978). State anxiety – stage fright, for example – is evoked by a particular set of temporary circumstances. As a result of their massive survey of Canadian learners of French, Gardner *et al.* decided that the phenomenon of language classroom anxiety was so widespread as to be an identifiable type of state anxiety.

So anxiety, especially state anxiety, is an acknowledged feature of language learning, whether as cause, effect, or both. But why should anxiety be a special problem for *language* learners? Certainly some school children spend a great deal of their time anxious about most, if not all, of their school subjects, so why should language learning be any different? One possibility, at least wherever methods are used that rely on banishing the learners' first language from the classroom (but perhaps whenever language learners are required to perform in the target language), is that language teaching deprives learners of their normal means of communication and so of the ability to behave fully as normal people. It takes something away from their humanness. Certainly learners report that one of their major worries is that when forced to use the language they are learning they constantly feel that they are representing themselves badly, showing only some of their real personality, only some of their real intelligence. Anecdotal evidence suggests that this sort of deprivation seems apt to breed anxiety about communicating with others (section 9.8) and just the sort of anxiety that will get in the way of doing well both in class and out of it, since it could inhibit the learners' use of the target language and thus deprive them of the potential profit to be obtained from practising what has been learned. In other instances, the teaching method itself (for example, the rapid drills of the audiolingual method or the teacher's silence in the Silent Way) may lead to learner anxiety.

The problem is conceivably even worse for learners who have just arrived in the country whose language they are learning, because, unless they find a community of compatriots to live with (and that in itself will

G

probably cause other problems), they will be misrepresenting themselves not just in the classroom but in everything they do, beginning with a task as simple as getting on a bus. This feeling of 'language shock' has been likened to schizophrenia, where the learners have a self that is perfectly capable of behaving normally in the right linguistic and cultural setting, but are forced by the circumstances to display a self that is fundamentally incompetent in all those things that everybody else around takes completely for granted (Schumann 1975).

Language learning is therefore especially likely to provoke anxiety because it deprives learners of the means of behaving normally. But its aim is precisely to provide them with the means of behaving normally, eventually, and being fully themselves, with people of another language and probably of another culture. This brings in another possible source of debilitating anxiety. In a sense, learning someone else's language means acquiring a way of looking at things from a different angle, getting a new world view. This itself can be seen as threatening rather than exciting, because it means having two, perhaps somewhat contradictory, ways of looking at everything. And it also means being associated, in some way, with that alternative world view. This relates to the background issues introduced at the beginning of Chapter 9, and is often discussed in the literature under the heading of 'anomie' – the feeling of being caught between two cultural groups, and not belonging to either of them (Schumann 1975).

In these ways language learning can represent a threat to a learner's sense of identity. This may sound rather far-fetched in relation to foreign language teaching in compulsory school systems, where typically the levels of success are probably so modest that no one's identity is likely to be at all threatened. But even in such circumstances language learning still seems to be an anxiety-breeding business, because, as we have seen, the way we set about teaching foreign languages in the classroom often temporarily deprives learners of their mother tongue – the very means of communication they might otherwise use in other lessons to help them overcome their problems. Also, to account for anxiety in language classes where the use of the mother tongue is allowed, which may be the majority of classes around the world, we can point to the problem that performing in a foreign language class is in itself potentially somehow more stressful than performing in other subject classes. In mathematics, for example, you may get the answer wrong, but at least you can be reasonably sure of saying the numbers correctly. In language work, by contrast, even if in a sense you get the answer right (you find the correct form of the verb, say, in a blank-filling item) you may still make an almost infinite number of mistakes in what you say – for example with imperfect pronunciation of individual sounds, wrong word stress, wrong sentence stress, and so on. For this reason, the probability of being wrong in some way or other is vastly greater in language learning than in other subjects. And being 'wrong', given many language teachers' views on how important it is to correct errors, is, at best, an open invitation to a more or less mild form of public humiliation (as we saw in the transcript about Carlos's trousers). In short, the risk of making a fool of yourself in a language class is very high, and you need to be a singularly robust character to avoid being affected adversely by feelings of anxiety in such a setting.

The following entries from Cherchalli's diary and interview research with Algerian secondary school learners illustrate these points:

1 'When the teacher is giving explanations my heart beats strongly and I keep saying to myself: "It's going to be my turn now".'
2 'Today the teacher has insisted a lot on tenses. I had beads of sweat! Me and English tenses have never agreed!'
3 'Today we had a quiz. It was very easy but I was so anxious about the second exercise that I couldn't work.'
4 'I'll never forget today and the shame I felt. Everything started when the English teacher asked me to read a few sentences on the blackboard ....'
(Cherchalli 1988)

These comments were taken from language learners' diaries. The learners' discomfort might or might not have been apparent to the teacher or to an outside observer.

Ironically, some learners (the most competent ones) get anxious because they know they could avoid making most of the mistakes other people are making, but, if they do so, they also know that they will stand out from the crowd and perhaps be actively resented for their relative success (a classroom form of the 'fear of success' that was introduced in section 9.7). If they deliberately make some of the (for them avoidable) mistakes other people are making, they will appear 'normal' to the rest of the class. Unfortunately, they will perhaps be regarded as lazy by the teacher (if he or she knows how competent they really are) or even as actually less competent than they really are. Such learners sometimes try to resolve the issue by withdrawing from class interaction, which carries the new risk that they will now be branded as somewhat unco-operative.

There are good reasons, then, why language learning is likely to be anxiety breeding. As Cherchalli's work has shown, if we go back to the learners' diaries we find very considerable evidence of anxiety related to the points just made about possible reasons why language learners have good reason to be anxious.

10.4 Competitiveness in classroom language learning

Bailey's work (1983a) surveying a dozen diary studies brought in another factor which deserves mention here. She noticed that there appeared to be a consistent relationship between anxiety and competitiveness. Quite simply, a surprising number of the diarists revealed themselves to be rather strongly competitive in their language classes, and this itself appeared to be a major source of anxiety for them. Some seemed preoccupied with the strain of wanting to be the 'best', others with the strain of being among the 'worst'. In either case the anxiety was often debilitating rather than helpful. Francine Schumann wrote about it quite explicitly, reporting that she felt guilty when her husband was studying and she was not:

> This guilt was a result of my competitive feeling that if I didn't work as much as he did, he would get further ahead .... Instead of causing me to work harder, this competitiveness resulted in my feeling frustrated and led to a reduced effort.
> (Schumann 1980:53)

While there are problems associated with this sort of self-report (specifically with taking self-evaluation as a true indicator of motives), we cannot disregard the learner's analysis of her feelings.

Influenced by Francine Schumann's work, Bailey reviewed the diary studies that were available at the time, looking for evidence of competitiveness. Where learners did comment on their competitive tendencies (for example, by talking about racing with their classmates, or by comparing their mastery and/or grades with others'), such entries often also included comments on their anxiety levels. Figure 9 opposite reflects Bailey's attempt to depict the interrelations between these two affective phenomena.

Here we have another example of classroom research (this time via the data collection procedure of keeping a diary) generating a pictorial scheme or model of behaviour. Such models, as we saw with Long's and Chaudron's models of error treatment behaviour, are open to empirical testing by other researchers. They may also suggest insights for teachers, who can observe their own behaviour, or that of their learners, and compare it with the model. Such comparisons allow us to perceive patterns, to detect systematicity (where it exists) across different learners in various classroom settings.

We must be careful of making too much of these early diary studies, however, if only because most of them were written by experienced teachers whose egos might have been more threatened in classrooms than those of 'ordinary' learners would have been. Teaching is recognised as an anxiety-breeding profession, and when teachers put themselves in the

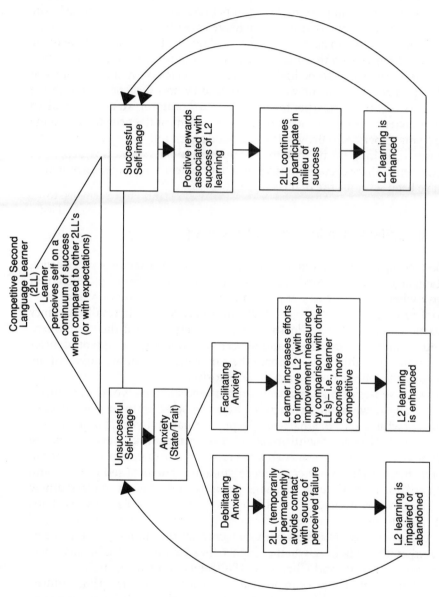

Figure 9 A model of competitiveness and anxiety in the second language learner (Bailey 1983a:97)

role of learner we might expect them to be extra nervous about their classroom performance, feeling that somehow they should, as teachers, be superior to their fellow learners. But the diary studies have alerted us to the potential importance of competitiveness, and in particular its possible role in contributing to language classroom anxiety.

Other caveats can also be raised regarding the diary studies. Like other forms of self-report, they may be subject to a self-flattery factor (see Oller 1979). They may also be highly selective in terms of the event-sampling that gets reported in the final papers (Bailey and Ochsner 1983) if the diarists edit their excerpts too heavily. Furthermore, we are not sure to what extent the very process of keeping a diary influences the language learning experience (Brown 1985a). While such influence can, in fact, be positive, it may mean that the resulting summary does not depict an experience that is representative of what the learner's experience would have been without the diary-keeping process.

10.5 Self-esteem in language learning

Both competitiveness and anxiety relate to a further factor – self-esteem. Language learning poses a threat to a person's self-esteem, as would any task where success was not guaranteed and the probability of making a fool of oneself was (so) very high. In a classroom where all the other learners might be better learners than you (especially if they are people you do not already know and so cannot eliminate as potential competition), they might, to preserve their own self-esteem, be quite willing to give you public proof of their superiority.

But is self-esteem known to be important? Heyde's work suggests so, especially if we make distinctions between self-esteem in general, self-esteem with regard to a particular type of situation (work, home, school, etc.), and self-esteem with regard to a particular task. Heyde found all three types of self-esteem correlated positively with oral performance in French for some American college students, but that self-esteem with regard to the particular language learning task was the most strongly related to performance. (See Heyde 1977, and Heyde-Parsons 1983, for further details.)

Unfortunately, as always with such correlation studies, it is impossible to say with confidence whether high self-esteem is a cause of success or the product of it (and Chaudron 1984b has pointed out that there are problems with Heyde-Parson's use of statistics in her 1983 study). Common sense would suggest, as we noted earlier for anxiety, that they feed on each other, so that, for example, if learners do succeed in a task, their self-esteem is reinforced. This means they approach the next task with more confidence, which itself means a smaller likelihood of experiencing debilitating anxiety about it (as Figure 9 suggests), and so success is more likely because they can concentrate better, and so on.

Heyde's work would have been incomplete without some attempt to study the sorts of classroom behaviour patterns that appear either to enhance or depress self-esteem. Although no causal connections can be established, she was able to point to differences in the behaviour patterns of learners with high self-esteem and learners with low self-esteem. As we might have expected, learners with high self-esteem hesitated less, corrected themselves more, did not need prompting, and so on. Of much greater interest were the findings relating to the way their teachers interacted with them and to what happened to their self-esteem scores after they had completed a speaking task in class.

Learners who started off with quite low self-esteem scores had sharply lower scores afterwards 1) if, for example, their teacher put pressure on them to monitor their own speech and correct themselves as they went along. The same sharp drop in scores occurred 2) if their teacher constantly interrupted to correct students, and 3) if their teacher simply repeated the question in its original wording when students failed to respond. (In this study Heyde used short-term measures of self-esteem: no longitudinal measurement was made.)

The first two interactions mentioned above are easy to understand in terms of anxiety and self-esteem, but the third may need a few words of comment. If you ask someone a question and that person does not understand what you are trying to say, the natural thing is to assume there was something wrong with the question and try to find a different way of asking it. Simply repeating the question the way it was phrased the first time amounts to suggesting that there was something wrong with the other person, not with the question itself. So a straight repeat becomes a challenge to the other person's competence – a put-down, a blow to the other person's self-esteem. (This, in fact, is what the teacher does to Carlos in the transcript excerpt printed in section 6.7.) No put-down may be intended of course, and in language classes it may be important to give a learner a second chance to hear the original wording of a question, but the effect may be the same psychologically, especially if, as Heyde noted, the teacher does not adopt a generally positive and encouraging tone. Perhaps we should also note here that when Gaies (1983b) looked at the way language teachers responded to learners' indications that they needed help he found that straight repeats were second only to some form of extended repeat in terms of frequency. That is to say, one of their most common reactions was a potentially challenging put-down. Gaies found no evidence that the teachers were adapting appropriately depending on the nature of the problems indicated by their learners.

Heyde also presents some interesting anecdotal information related to cases where students performed quite badly and yet subsequently raised their self-esteem scores. In such cases, the teacher tended to give very little feedback or guidance of any kind, and tended to make somewhat ambiguous noises when students made direct or indirect requests for approval. Heyde suggests that students might legitimately have interpreted such noises and the general lack of feedback as wholly positive, indicating that everything was fine. One can imagine, however, that getting low marks when you have been led to expect good ones in this way must be even more demoralising, even more of a blow to one's self-esteem in the long run, than getting low marks when you have not been led to expect anything better.

Heyde's work does help us build up a general picture of receptivity in relation to language classroom interaction. The picture is of a situation fraught with risks, a situation more delicate than most in education, and one that calls for special attention. Such a thought may remind the reader of Chapter 4, where we were discussing (in what may have appeared at that point to be rather unduly dramatic terms) the potential risks involved for teachers and learners if they find themselves involved in a research project. After Heyde's work it is perhaps easier to appreciate that such problems can be very real ones, with real consequences for learners' progress.

10.6 Parent/child/adult roles in language classrooms

We should also consider how the problems of receptivity tie in with patterns of language classroom interaction discussed in Chapters 7 and 8. A procedure for examining this relationship has been pioneered by Hines in New York. She used Fanselow's (1977a) FOCUS system (see Appendix C) and the categories of Transactional Analysis (Harris 1967) to investigate relationships between aspects of teachers' behaviour and learner participation.

Transactional Analysis (Harris 1967) includes the psychological concept that within any individual there are (at least) three possible sources of emotional information which result in three different roles that an individual may take. These roles and the information associated with them are listed below:

1 the 'parent' – those memories, rules and values learned in one's childhood and associated with authority figures;
2 the 'child' – the memories and feelings associated with childhood dependency; and
3 the 'adult' – the functioning individual who is able to make decisions and act independently.

Hines used the categories of Transactional Analysis to categorise teacher behaviour (using extremely high-inference categories) as representative of the teacher as either a) a Parent being 'nurturing', b) a Parent being 'critical', c) an Adult being 'neutral', or d) a Child being 'playful'. Hines found that language students made the most errors after teacher behaviour she classified as that of a 'Critical Parent', as if the critical tone set by the teacher (recall Heyde's findings related to teachers' tone) actually frightened the learners into making more mistakes than they might have otherwise. In cases where there was generally little opportunity for students to talk spontaneously she nevertheless found that spontaneous talk happened most frequently, by far, when the teacher was classified as a 'Neutral Adult', and least often, also by far, with the 'Critical Parent' sort of teacher behaviour (Hines 1983).

While comparing the teacher with the Adult or the Parent, and the adult learner with the Child of Transactional Analysis may seem far-fetched, this analogy has also appeared, independently of Hines' work, in some of the language learning diaries. Jones (1977), Leichman (1977), and Plummer (1976) have all likened themselves (as learners) to children and the teacher to a parent, utilising these terms with the specialised meanings they have in Transactional Analysis. In Plummer's case, having this child's role reportedly allowed her to adopt some childlike behaviours which she felt were useful to her language learning. For instance, Plummer had a 'language learning buddy' in her Indonesian class, with whom she would engage in language play. (Language play is a phenomenon which involves using the language not primarily for its referential meaning, but rather for fun. Characteristics of language play include loudness, exaggerated pitch, lilting intonation, the incorporation of singing into the speech, rhyming sounds, phonological mimicry, altered tempo, and made-up words.) In child language acquisition, language play is thought to provide practice opportunities in an intense affective climate. But while language play is well documented in first language acquisition (Garvey 1977) and child second language acquisition (Peck 1980), it is a less prevalent mode of behaviour in adult second language learning. Yet Plummer's diary provides evidence of adults participating in language play, and documents her perception that doing so helped her learn Indonesian.

We must, of course, be wary of over-interpreting such results, limited as they are in scope and limited as they also are by the impossibility of demonstrating causal relationships. But Hines' work and that of the diarists does help us have more confidence in our contention that receptivity is important, that we are not just being 'soft' to imagine that receptivity matters. Hines has demonstrated how the learning opportunities that are available to learners can be directly affected by the teacher's attitude and behaviour. This relationship is clearly a matter of the learners' receptivity rather than of simply the teaching method.

10.7 Motivation, reinforcement and receptivity

Of interest in this connection is research on motivation. It seems entirely reasonable to suggest that motivation matters in classrooms, that the most motivated learners are likely to be the most receptive ones, at least as long as the teaching meets their needs. But *how* does motivation help? Is it by some hidden process that we can only guess at, or can we see motivation in action in the classroom?

Work in Canada has shown that learners with different types of motivation may display different patterns of interaction in the language classroom and different study habits generally (Gardner *et al.* 1976). As one would expect, in their study strongly motivated students tended to spend more time working outside class (doing homework, for example) and to participate more actively in class as well. Less obviously, the extent of learners' participation in class seems to depend also on the type of motivation, and not just its strength or intensity. Learners with an 'integrative motivation', who wished to learn in order to relate better to, and integrate with, the speakers of the target language, tended to be much more active in class, volunteering more, making more correct responses, etc. In so doing they received more positive reinforcement or encouragement than the 'instrumentally motivated' learners (learners who just wanted academic success or perhaps to get a job for which there is a language requirement). So once again we have a situation where a certain pattern of receptivity (in this case in the form of integrative motivation – receptivity to the people represented by the language being learned, one of our background issues) appears to make an important difference in classroom interaction. Positive reinforcement will enhance self-esteem, and that will probably lead to better performance on future tasks (perhaps because any anxiety is more likely to be of the facilitating rather than the debilitating variety) and better performance is likely to be rewarded with yet more positive reinforcement, and so on. Of course, this is not to say that instrumentally motivated learners cannot be receptive to learning. In fact, the findings in the research literature on the advantages of being integratively or instrumentally motivated are quite mixed (see Oller 1979).

These relationships between reinforcement and receptivity have been extensively explored in modern language teaching in Britain, in the research associated with the Graded Objectives movement (J. Clark 1980, 1987; Page 1985). Teachers within this movement have exchanged their traditional syllabuses for specifications of functional objectives. These objectives are coupled with assessment schemes which directly test the practical achievement of these objectives and are criterion-referenced so that anyone who reaches seventy-five per cent, say, is awarded a certificate that specifies the competencies achieved. In this way many more children are getting much more positive reinforcement – because they are being faced with meaningful classroom tasks that are incrementally arranged so as to be achievable. Learners who were previously quite recalcitrant have been showing great determination in their efforts to win certificates, much to the surprise and delight of their teachers and their parents. Even more significant, in national and 'theoretical' terms, is the fact that there is strong evidence that involvement in graded objectives work so improves learner receptivity to the whole idea of being a language learner that more children are opting to carry on learning a foreign language when it is no longer compulsory. Previously there had been a major problem of learners dropping out of language classes, especially among boys, but the Graded Objectives movement has been so successful in some cases that it seems there might be a problem of coping with the numbers of children who now wish to continue their language studies. It all seems too good to be true, perhaps, but the movement is well documented and carefully researched (see, for example, Page 1985). If the above interpretation is correct, as seems most likely, then we now have a clear demonstration of how receptivity can be enhanced through classroom procedures that bring about positive reinforcement.

10.8 Summary

This chapter has used the general and probably unfamiliar term 'receptivity' to unite a number of topics more commonly dealt with as completely separate categories – especially attention, anxiety, competitiveness, self-esteem, and motivation. It has shown how these factors relate to some major threats to learners' receptivity, and so to their probable learning effectiveness. Other related issues which we have not explored include language learners' investment and self-determination. These topics are just beginning to be investigated by classroom researchers (such as Allwright 1988b).

Even more strongly than elsewhere in this volume, however, we have to emphasise that the findings to date are far from definite. In many cases we have been dealing with relatively unvalidated research procedures, however novel and ingenious, and of course with relatively few studies. Statistical forms of generalisation are generally not possible, therefore, and appeal has to be made instead to more human judgement. Certainly the research procedures themselves stand in need of development, and many replication studies are also indicated, if we are to make more confident claims about the relationships we are beginning to see.

A good number of the issues we have raised under the heading of receptivity, however, would lend themselves to action research projects.

Such projects, if well enough carried out and documented, could make a considerable contribution to our general understanding of this complex area. The *Discussion starters* and suggestions for practical activities that follow have been designed with this goal in mind, to encourage teachers to become more actively involved in this important work.

DISCUSSION STARTERS

1 Receptivity, as presented in the chapter, seems very closely linked to attention, as if you could only learn what you had consciously attended to. But language pedagogy (that is, language teaching theory) often stresses the value of incidental learning, learning out of awareness, when you are actively concentrating on doing something else (like having a conversation). Is there a real paradox here, or can we happily talk about subconscious receptivity?

2 Do you find it easy to believe Cohen's figure of only about 50 per cent of learners attending to a lesson at any given moment? Does it mesh with your recollections of your own attention patterns in language classes? Should teachers be concerned about the issue of attention? If so, what can teachers do to promote greater attention among second language learners? Is attending or not attending to a lesson an either/or proposition, or are there degrees of attention in learners' involvement with their language lessons?

3 From your own experience as a teacher and/or a language learner, does it seem reasonable to suggest that language learning is more anxiety-provoking, more prone to engender competitiveness, and more threatening to one's self-esteem, than other subjects on the curriculum? Why, or why not?

4 Research suggests that motivation both produces and is produced by positive achievement. Does this ring true from your own experience? Do you accept the idea that improving learner motivation is part of the teacher's responsibility? If so, what are some ways that a teacher can enhance second language learners' motivation? To what extent is the learners' motivation beyond the teacher's sphere of influence?

5 If you were to write a diary of your experiences as a language teacher, what sorts of things do you think you would find yourself writing about most often?

6 If your own learners kept diaries of their language learning, what sorts of things do you think they would write about most often? Would you *like* to know what they were writing, or would you rather they kept it to themselves?

7 Does Bailey's model of competitiveness and anxiety in Figure 9 make sense to you as a language learner? Have you ever been in a language

learning situation where you had either a successful or an unsuccessful self-image? If so, do your experiences fit the model? As a teacher, have you ever been aware of learners who seemed to be anxious or competitive in class? What was the outcome?

8 How would you define 'self-esteem'? Would you agree that it can be parcelled out into the categories of general, situational and task-specific self-esteem? Do you have examples from your own experience?

SUGGESTIONS FOR FURTHER READING

1 Scovel (1978) wrote an excellent review of the literature on language learning and anxiety. Kleinmann (1977) ties anxiety to specific linguistic behaviour in terms of what structures second language learners avoid. Horwitz, Horwitz and Cope (1986) developed a questionnaire called the Foreign Language Classroom Anxiety Scale, which yielded high reliability indices. The items from the scale are reprinted in their article. More recently, Young and Horwitz (in press) have assembled an entire volume on this topic.

2 Work on self-esteem in language learning is rather limited at this point in time. Two accessible reports on different aspects of the same study are by Heyde (1977; Heyde-Parsons 1983), who adapted constructs from psychology research in her investigation. Heyde's work has been criticised by Chaudron (1984b), and his brief review is also well worth reading. While self-esteem is a fascinating topic and one which appeals to us, as both teachers and learners, its investigation is fraught with research problems. Some of these problems are associated particularly with the use of self-report data (Oller 1979, 1981), which is an issue in many studies related to the cover-all concept of receptivity.

3 Beebe (1983) has written an interesting paper about risk taking and how it may relate to language learning. For instance, she speculates on the risk-taking tendencies of Seliger's HIGs and LIGs (1977, 1983a).

4 For a general discussion of personality factors in language learning, see Brown (1987). Chapter 6, in particular, covers issues such as self-esteem, anxiety, empathy, introversion and extroversion.

5 Some researchers have studied other learners' diaries. As mentioned above, Bailey (1983a) analysed what eleven learners' diaries revealed about their competitiveness and anxiety. Asher (1983) studied the language learning diaries of several American adolescents whom she supervised on a trip to Europe. C. Brown (1983, 1985a, 1985b) used the diary study approach, along with participant observation, to investigate differences between older and younger language learners – specifically their requests for input (1985b). Grandcolas and Soulé-

Susbielles (1986) utilised diary entries written by future teachers of French as a foreign language, along with other sources of data. (This possibility of using several learners' diaries as a data base will come up again in the practical activities for this chapter.)

6 Bailey and Ochsner (1983) and Matsumoto (1987) have written critical overviews of the diary studies as language research tools.

7 Faerch and Kasper (1987) edited an interesting volume about the use of introspection in second language research. Many of the articles in that book are related to the methodological issues raised here.

8 Cohen and Hosenfeld (1981) wrote an article about the use of what they call 'mentalistic data' in second language research. Seliger (1983b) has written an article critical of such procedures. Reading both articles could lead to an interesting discussion on what can count as evidence.

9 Recently language teachers have experimented with variations on the journal-keeping procedure as pedagogic tools. For an interesting treatment of this topic, see Staton *et al.* (1988).

MINI-PROJECT: ATTENTION

This project is suitable for individual work over one week, but it can also easily be extended as a group project and/or a longitudinal study. The aim is to find out how learners talk about the mechanics of attention in their own classroom experience. Fairly detailed guidelines will be offered because attention is not readily observable and the proposal involves the delicate business of working directly with learners.

This mini-project involves recording a lesson and then playing selected episodes back to the learners and asking them to comment on what factors helped or hindered their attentiveness during the lesson in question. (You could even use some of the recordings made for projects described earlier in this book, provided you still have access to the learners and the events are still fresh in their minds.) As a mini-project, this activity could best be done by an individual, but a group of people could usefully plan the details of all the procedures in common, and then each work with a different class. The project could be completed in just a few days if only one visit was made to each class, or it could easily be extended into a full-scale longitudinal study, as a major project for any one person or group of people. As a longitudinal study it is probably best seen as 'action research', which means that the consciousness-raising effects of the project's procedures can be turned to practical advantage, as input to the improvement of teaching and, one hopes, of learning. The procedures are listed below:

1 You will need permission to record (at least audio-record) a language lesson, and permission to meet the class very soon afterwards for at least as much time as the lesson itself took. A small class will be easier to manage, but as an alternative, you may try to get permission to withdraw just a handful of learners from a large class for the after-lesson discussion session.

2 While the lesson itself is in progress make a note of episodes where attention seems particularly high, or particularly low. (Keeping a note of the tape counter numbers is the simplest way, and very useful later on, but it means you have to be physically near the recorder in the classroom, to be able to see the counter numbers.)

3 If time allows, you might also note which learners seem particularly attentive or inattentive during the different episodes. If your presence in the classroom is likely, in itself, to affect attentiveness radically, then you will need to stay out of the classroom and enlist the teacher's or a learner's help to listen to the recording with you and identify the 'high' and 'low' episodes. While this step would be time-consuming, it has the benefit of providing a form of investigator triangulation.

4 The next step is to play back the tape to the class (or to a representative group from the class), preferably very soon after the lesson in question (that is, at least the same day), and preferably in the same classroom (to assist the memory). Playing back the whole tape would be very time-consuming, so you might wind ahead on fast forward and play only those episodes you have already identified as being interesting, and perhaps only the beginnings of them (just enough to jog the learners' memories). (In selecting episodes in this way, you will of course have biased your sample – a procedure not acceptable in a full-scale project.) For this replay session, you will need an accurate note of the counter numbers, and some confidence in handling your machine efficiently. It may be worth noting that although videotape would probably be a better 'memory-jogger', it is generally considered to be a more obtrusive data collection device. It is also likely to be much more awkward to manage efficiently during the playback session unless you are thoroughly familiar with the equipment. In addition, the learners may well want to see more, and consequently talk less.

5 For the playback session you will also need to have prepared some questions to make sure the discussion is focused. It will help if you develop a routine of asking exactly the same questions for each episode you play back. (Such a procedure is called an 'interview schedule'. See Spradley 1979, for useful ideas on how to structure an interview and analyse the resulting data.) You will need to phrase your questions carefully to suit the particular learners you are working with. (You will clearly need to be especially careful if you are asking them to use the

language they are still learning). Just two questions might be enough. For example:

a) At the time of the episode in question would you rate your attention as 'very high', 'high', 'medium', 'low', or 'very low'?

b) Why?

If they say very little in reaction to 'Why?' you may need to prompt them by suggesting some possibilities – such as the content of the lesson at the time, the difficulty level of whatever they were doing, the teaching method being used, the general atmosphere in the class, and so on. Prepare your prompts in advance and use them systematically.

A word of warning is in order here. The whole project may be threatening to the teacher involved, especially if he or she feels that some 'outsider' is going to be sitting in judgement rather than just providing an objective report. It will help if the teacher can be given guarantees of confidentiality, but it will help even more if the whole investigation can be offered as a genuine service to the teacher, as a way of helping the teacher secure yet more attentiveness from the class.

Of course, if you are teaching a language class yourself, you could use your own classroom as the research setting. In this case, you could draw on your own memories of the lesson as well as those of the students. As an alternative, you could team up with a colleague who would act as a non-participant observer while you teach.

Unfortunately, the whole project might also be seen as threatening by the learners, if they fear that anything they say will be immediately relayed to the teacher. Again, guarantees of confidentiality will be important, but if the teacher is in fact to be helped, then he or she will need to know, in general terms at least, what the learners have to say about their attention, and what helps or hinders them in attending to lessons. The learners, in turn, will need to know that their teacher will be given a general report (which preserves their anonymity), and to know why this is necessary and sensible. It should be clear by now that you will need to find, if you possibly can, a class where a good atmosphere of trust and mutual respect already exists between teacher and learners. If you go into a class that is already defensive, your project may do more harm than good. Ideally, you could observe a class taught by a colleague or a classmate, who could then, in turn, observe a class which you teach.

You will probably need to record the playback session as well, so that you don't have to take copious notes under such restricted circumstances. (Indeed, the second language learners may feel more like talking to you about attention if they feel you are attending to them, rather than writing as they talk.) Then it is a matter of working out what factors the learners have mentioned. The easiest thing is to make lists of all the different factors mentioned, then sort them into sets (such as content factors, method factors, and so on). You can then calculate the frequency of mention of each of the sets, and find out which set is the most important (at least in numerical terms). Probably some things will not be mentioned very often, but will be given very strong emphasis whenever they are. They will need to be reported separately.

A tidier, but probably less productive, way of running the playback session would be to ask the learners to answer your questions in writing, on a very brief questionnaire sheet, for each episode. This would make the later analysis easier, and eliminate the need for recording the playback session itself, but the learners will probably write much less than they would have said, especially if they are trying to write in the language they are learning. You should also recall, from the discussion in Chapter 4, that questionnaires and interview schedules provide structure, but they can also limit the type of information you may get. The face-to-face interview may allow for more spontaneity on the language learners' part and will certainly give you, as the researcher, opportunities to query and pursue points raised by the learners. Of course, the two techniques, of group discussion and individual questionnaires, could be combined. This procedure would be helpful, but you would then have even more data to analyse afterwards. This combined approach to data collection is probably best seen as a way of extending the project, rather than as a simple alternative procedure.

In addition to the extension just mentioned, there are others that would certainly turn the project into something much more substantial:
1 The scope of the mini-project could easily be extended if various observers went into different classes at the same time, so that a broader picture could emerge of different types of learners in different circumstances. (Different times would also work, but your results might then be confounded by the possibility that time of day influences attentiveness, via fatigue factors.) It would certainly be interesting to know if the same factors seem equally important in a variety of situations, or if different factors emerge, as one might expect. The age of the learners might be important, of course, and the culture they come from, as well as their proficiency levels.
2 Another way of extending the mini-project into a major one would be to follow a class (or classes) over a period of several weeks, again to see if different factors emerge or if results are generally stable. Turning the project into a longitudinal study in this way would again convert it into an action research project – one where the emphasis would change from the descriptive focus of finding out what learners think to that of seeing how consciousness-raising could be harnessed to improve levels of attention in the classroom. This latter idea would need the full co-operation of the teacher, of course, since the teacher would be expected to try to adjust his or her teaching activities to take

account of the learners' emerging views, to see if the expected benefits could in fact be obtained.

3 A quite different sort of extension could be achieved if the procedures described above were used to look at somewhat different issues. In particular, anxiety and competitiveness could be explored in this way, but both of them would no doubt need even more delicate handling than would the topic of attention, given the extra degree of defensiveness likely to be involved in talking about such matters. Perhaps a class already used to talking about attention could later be approached on the topics of anxiety and competitiveness. They are tricky concepts to handle, however, and it would be necessary to take seriously the problems of definition involved. There are less direct ways of getting at these topics, as can be seen in the next suggested practical activity.

MAJOR PROJECT: DIARY STUDY

This project is suitable for individual work over a period of several weeks. A number of individual projects could very usefully be combined in a collective project. The project aim is to explore learners' reactions to classroom language learning in order to discover what they think is important about what happens in the classroom.

This diary study is presented as a major project because it requires extensive data collection over a period of weeks (unless the data are obtained in an intensive course or during a trip to a place where the target language is spoken). It also requires an unusual degree of co-operation from learners in that it hinges on the possibility of persuading a group of learners to keep diaries of their classroom experiences, and allow those diaries to be analysed to see what emerges. Anyone seriously contemplating adapting the diary study as a full-scale project would be advised to begin with a pilot project along the lines of one of the simpler alternative projects outlined below.

GETTING STARTED

You will need to find a group of learners who can be expected to keep fairly detailed diaries for you. It will help enormously if the learners are able to write their diaries in their own first language. If you have to ask them to write in the language they are learning, then you will need intermediate to advanced learners to start with. Notice that in such circumstances they may want the written work of their diaries to be corrected for them, and you will need to decide whether or not this is a service you can and should, in fact, provide. We believe that the correction of diaries is best avoided if at all possible, since it may lead to learners writing about only what they can write about accurately, and take the focus away from the real issue of getting all their thoughts and memories down, however imperfectly. The dilemma is, of course, that the promise of correction may help motivate the learners to write diaries in the first place, while if they use their first language it may be technically better (because you can expect the learners to express their thoughts much better in their mother tongue), but it may be much more difficult to motivate them to bother to write anything at all. On balance, however, it is advisable to try to persuade the learners to accept that their diaries will not be corrected. It may help if you can instead promise that the views they express in their diaries will, with appropriate protection of confidentiality, be passed on so that they can be used in subsequent course planning. The learners will no doubt ask you what you want them to write about, and the answer is whatever comes into their heads. The whole point of the diary study is to get at what is on *their* minds. If you do not have access to a group of learners who will keep diaries for you, you could keep a journal of your own experiences as a language teacher or language learner.

You should make sure that the learners know what is going to happen to their diary entries, once they have been handed in to you. You need to be able to guarantee confidentiality, for example, but you will also need to make it clear that you may want to use direct quotations from their diaries for illustrative purposes. You can promise to change all names, of course, but that will not guarantee that they will not be identifiable. One further point is that they deserve to know if your final report is going to be in any sense publicly available, and if they will get a chance to see it, preferably before it is made available, in case they would wish it to be edited in any way.

Some tips for keeping a diary (that is, for the data collection phase of the research) are listed below. These suggestions are based on the experiences of several teachers who have kept diaries or have had their classes keep diaries.

1 Set aside a regular time and place each day in which to write in your diary.
2 Plan on allowing an amount of time for writing which is at least equal to the period of time spent in the language classroom.
3 Keep your diary in a safe, secure place so you will feel free to write whatever you wish.
4 Do not worry about your style, grammar, or organisation, especially if you are writing in your second language.
5 Carry a small pocket notebook with you so you can make notes about your language learning (or teaching) experience whenever you wish.
6 Support your insights with examples. When you write something down, ask yourself, 'Why do I feel that is important?'

7 At the end of each diary entry, note any additional thoughts or questions that have occurred to you. You can consider these in more detail later.

COLLECTING THE DIARIES

Several decisions are necessary here. First, should you ask to see the diary entries as they are produced (daily, perhaps) or should you wait until the end of the whole diary-writing project to call for them to be handed in?

Frequent review may not be helpful, because it is likely to loom too large in the learners' minds. A periodic review may be advisable, at which point you could photocopy the entries and begin your analysis. Waiting until the end of the entire period means running the risk of not getting anything at all, but this risk can be lessened by asking learners to fill in a weekly report sheet guaranteeing that they have indeed been keeping their diaries.

Another possibility is to arrange for weekly course discussion sessions, at which the learners are invited to raise as topics anything in their diary entries that they are willing to make public. In this way, they may get to learn that their diary-keeping work is indeed valued as a contribution to course evaluation. That may 'contaminate the data', however, in the sense that they will get to know something of each other's preoccupations and may adjust their own diary entries accordingly. The risk is probably slight, but worth noting as a possibility at the data interpretation stage.

Here is an example of instructions given to language learners keeping diaries for a research project:

> This journal has two purposes. The first is to help you with your language learning. As you write about what you think and feel as a language learner, you will understand yourself and your experience better.
>
> The second purpose is to increase the overall knowledge about language learning so that learning can be increased. You will be asked to leave your language learning journal when you leave (the school). However, your journal will not be read by teachers at (the school). It will be read by researchers interested in language learning.
>
> Your identity and the identity of others you may write about will be unknown (unless you wish it otherwise) to anyone except the researchers. You will be given fifteen minutes a day to write. Please write as if this were your personal journal about your language learning experience.
> (Brown 1985b:280–1)

In this case the journal writers kept their diaries until the end of the training session.

DATA ANALYSIS

The main task is to discover what the learners think is important about what happens in language lessons. In looking at the diary entries, then, this issue will be your main guide. If you think in terms of being able to report, finally, on a ranked list of topics, with the most important at the top, then clearly you need a way of determining priority. Several considerations need to be taken into account:

a) frequency of mention: the number of times a given topic is identified in the diary entries;
b) distribution of mention: the number of different people who mention a given topic;
c) saliency: the strength of the expression with which a topic is recorded.

Only the first two of these are directly quantifiable. The third could be quantified if different verbal expressions could be given numbered ratings as to their strength (with the strongest expressions numbered 5 and the weakest 1 for example) but such judgements would be wholly subjective. This subjectivity could perhaps be reduced if you could persuade other people to assist you with the analysis, by reaching an acceptable level of inter-rater agreement on the rating of the verbal expressions. It may be preferable, however, simply to report your data principally in terms of the quantifiable measures, leaving the saliency aspect as a relatively informal additional dimension, used for illustrative purposes.

MAKING YOUR REPORT

Once you have analysed the diary entries and identified your learners' priorities, you will already have the substance of your report. In writing it up, however, you will need to pay careful attention, especially when selecting illustrative quotations, to respect the confidentiality of the original diary writers.

Further information on keeping and using diaries as language learning research tools can be found in Bailey and Ochsner (1983) and in Matsumoto (1987). Much of the advice in Spradley's (1980) book, *Participant observation*, would also be helpful in terms of analytic procedures to use with qualitative data.

Part VI Epilogue

11 Towards exploratory teaching

11.1 The story so far

In our Preface we stated three main aims for this book: 1) to bring language classroom research to the attention of teachers to speakers of other languages, as well as to teachers of languages other than English; 2) to explore the implications of classroom research findings and procedures for the actual practice of language teaching, whatever the language involved, and 3) to encourage and help teachers to become 'explorers' themselves, in their own classrooms, partly (as we said in the Preface) for the sake of increasing our overall understanding of classroom language learning, throughout the profession, but mostly for the sake of improving their learners' chances of making good progress.

Our overall goal was 'to help bridge the gap between research and teaching, and more particularly between researchers and teachers'. And to begin the bridging process we pointed to existing signs of a reconciliation and to what we saw in any case as a fundamental 'unity of purpose behind classroom research and language teaching'. Being a good classroom teacher, we said, means being alive to what goes on in the classroom, and being alive to the problem of sorting out what matters from what does not matter, among all the great variety of things that happen in the classroom moment by moment. And that is what being a classroom researcher is also all about, we suggested.

To serve our very first aim we devoted the first two Parts of the book to a substantial review of classroom research as a distinct approach to pedagogic research in general, emphasising its historical development in our field in Chapter 1, and arguing for the crucial nature of classroom interaction in Chapter 2. In Chapter 3 we looked at the variety of forms classroom research can take, and at the major research design concepts involved, before taking up the extremely important data collection and interpretation issues in Chapter 4.

These first four chapters served, we hope, the important twin functions of introducing the reader to classroom research as we understand it, and of whetting the reader's appetite for Parts III, IV and V of our book, where in six chapters we summarised issues, findings and procedures in three main areas of professional and practical interest.

The first of these three areas was the treatment of oral error, a familiar and everlasting problem for all language teachers everywhere. In Chapter 5 we reviewed the general picture on errors, before looking at the relevant research in Chapter 6. At the end of that chapter we concluded that our original straightforward questions about the treatment of oral error, though apparently sensible enough in themselves, could not possibly be given straightforward answers. This was because research had revealed just how complex classroom interaction was. This complexity, we suggested, should enhance our respect for what good teachers routinely manage to achieve in their classrooms. And this in turn, we also suggested, could encourage us to think about how effectively teachers themselves might be able to investigate their own treatment of oral error, in their own classrooms. That suggestion then led to a proposal for a mini-project on the topic of errors at the end of Chapter 6.

The second area was classroom input and interaction, an area that has been a strong focus of attention among theorists as well as among practitioners. Chapter 7 started with Krashen's views on the unique value of maximising 'comprehensible input' and finished by concluding that, once again, the extraordinary complexity of what happens in language classrooms makes it impossible to come to any simple straightforward conclusions – except the familiar conclusion that more research is clearly necessary, and the less familiar but increasingly compelling conclusion that teachers should be encouraged to undertake their own classroom investigations into the topic. Chapter 8 ranged more widely, and in so doing lent more strength to the point that classroom interaction is an almost infinitely complex topic. It stressed the role of learners in influencing, for good or ill, whatever happens in the classroom, and thus whatever learning opportunities get created in the process. The major question in Chapter 8, however, was the apparently straightforward issue of the desirability of overt active participation from learners. Even here we had to conclude that no straight answer was possible, nor would conceivably be possible in the foreseeable future. What we did conclude, positively, was that each learner needed a classroom environment in which to settle down to productive work, and that led to a suggestion for a major project on recording classroom interaction, which itself ended with a move to get learners more actively involved in the research enterprise.

It also led quite directly to our third and final area of major professional and practical interest – receptivity. Chapter 9 introduced eight specific issues involved in this probably familiar area with, in this book, a rather unfamiliar label. This was a speculative survey, with no very firm foundation in research as yet, and that survey led us on to a major project to develop an 'autobiography of a language learner'. This was seen as a possible way of discovering research topics of real personal interest. It also led us to Chapter 10, which set out the relevant research on receptivity so far. This chapter, even more strongly than any of the previous ones, had to conclude with a plea for more research, and for more attention to the development of appropriate research procedures. An expandable mini-project on attention was then followed by a major project suggestion for a relatively ambitious diary study involving learners in making a major contribution to the collection of relevant data on receptivity.

These last six chapters were intended to serve our second aim as well as our first: to explore the implications of classroom research findings and procedures for the actual practice of language teaching. They were also intended, throughout, to serve our third aim, that of encouraging language teachers to begin thinking in an exploratory manner about their own research situations, and to begin to consider ways in which their own classrooms could become the subject of investigations that they themselves, with their learners, could conduct.

11.2 Helping teachers cope with immediate classroom problems

Readers will no doubt have noticed that we have been careful not to promise short cuts to more effective language teaching. Indeed, we did not write this book in the expectation that it would help make language teaching easier. Being an effective language teacher is not, never was, and never will be easy. Our ambition was different – to help language teachers *understand* better their own, and their learners', classroom lives.

We did not expect, however, that this increased understanding could come simply from reading the pages. We did hope that reading them would help, of course, but only as a first step. We also hoped, very strongly, that working through the end-of-chapter sections would help, but again only as one step towards the overall goal of increasing our understanding of classroom language learning and teaching.

Such increased understanding will, we must all hope, make it possible for us eventually to be more effective, both individually and collectively as a profession. But becoming more effective cannot be a simple linear matter. We cannot expect to reach understanding one day, and then simply be more effective the next. We have to work continually for increased understanding, and to work simultaneously for enhanced effectiveness, in a constant cycle with no one starting point and certainly no single and triumphant finishing point.

11.3 The concept of 'exploratory teaching'

What we are describing is our concept of the 'exploratory language teacher'. It is not a new concept of course, but it is becoming an increasingly compelling one, as we learn more about classroom language teaching and learning, and as we develop new ways to make exploratory teaching a practical reality for more and more teachers.

This book has had three basic points to make throughout the preceding chapters. First, that there is a great deal to be learned from the results of the research that has been done so far. Second, that there is even more to learn from the procedures of classroom research. And, third, that teachers, researchers, and learners have a lot in common and therefore can learn a great deal from each other.

The importance of exploratory teaching is the fourth point to be made, and it follows directly from putting the first three together. This fourth point emphasises the central importance of the teacher. The teacher is the researcher's link with learners, and also the learners' link with research. The teacher is contracted to help learners learn, but can do so better by knowing about previous research and by using the procedures of classroom research to understand better what is happening in his or her own classroom. In this way the exploratory teacher will not only improve achievement but will also contribute to our general research knowledge about how language classrooms work. This is what we mean by 'exploratory teaching' – teaching that not only tries out new ideas but that also tries to learn as much as possible from doing so. In fact, you do not even have to try out 'new' ideas to be an exploratory teacher. Any good experienced teacher will no doubt spend a lot of class time on ideas that are tried and trusted. Turning that 'good' teaching into 'exploratory teaching' is a matter of trying to find out what makes the tried and trusted ideas successful. Because in the long run it is not enough to know that ideas do work; we need also to know why and how they work. Until we can throw more light on those issues, successful teaching will remain a mystery.

An example may help here. Not long ago a group of expatriate teachers at a private, after-school English course was asked what, if anything, puzzled them about what was happening in their language classes. After a very long pause one of the teachers came up with this productive question: why is it that our students accept what we do in class, and seem to learn successfully from it? Not a problem, then, but certainly a puzzle, because the teachers had been told that the students had had a very traditional sort of English teaching at school, and would surely expect more of the same in their expensive out-of-school English classes. The teachers, however, felt they were teaching in a thoroughly modern and innovative way. Now if we could understand what was going right in that situation, we might be able to help teachers whose attempts to be innovative are not so well received by their learners.

It will not really be enough for those teachers simply to explore their own teaching situation, though, and leave it at that. If anyone else is going to benefit, then we will need a report of their explorations, a report that helps us understand what might be special to their situation and what might be more universally applicable. Fortunately, this is just the sort of article the major teachers' journals in our field are continually looking for – something that speaks directly from classroom experience, and from experience that has been thoroughly thought through, not just enthusiastically recollected.

We see exploratory teaching, then, as the most promising way of working towards more effective teaching, both for the individual and for the profession. To get started as an exploratory teacher, you do not need a new teaching idea to try out, nor a teaching problem to solve. All you need is a 'local puzzle' – something already going on that simply intrigues you enough to prompt you to want to understand it better.

11.4 The role of the professional researcher

Where would a professional researcher fit into this picture? It may seem fanciful to suggest it, but ideally it would be best to have researchers act as local consultants in school systems, just as educational psychologists already do. Classroom teachers could then turn to such a consultant for expert advice in exploring anything that intrigued them about the learners in their classrooms. This would neatly reverse the present unsatisfactory pattern whereby it is typically the researchers who invent their own research projects and then come to teachers for help in carrying them out.

Professional researchers are in a sense already available through their writings, of course, and we fervently hope this book will have helped make their experience and their expertise much more readily available to you. Although we do not claim to have reviewed all the classroom research studies of the past two decades, we hope the *Suggestions for further reading* have provided you with access routes into the professional literature on the issues we have raised.

Meanwhile, it would help enormously if teachers themselves took the initiative and called upon the research expertise available in colleges and universities (for example) to help them explore their teaching. There is no point in suggesting that such collaboration is always going to be easy, but in the long run it must surely make sense at least to try. Already there are some universities making their own attempt to be of service in this way.

For example, researchers at the Center for Ethnography in Education at the University of Pennsylvania have for several years actively sought to collaborate with classroom teachers on projects of interest to both groups. Other teacher–researcher teams (for example, Florio and Walsh 1981; Wallat *et al.* 1981; Watson-Gegeo and Ulichny 1988) have written about their experiences in this regard, to guide and encourage others.

11.5 The role of fellow teachers

Alternatively, of course, teachers could start by collaborating with each other. Most teachers are so busy that even this is often not going to be at all easy, but again, it must surely be worth working towards. Perhaps some of the energy teachers around the world currently put into collaborating on producing new syllabuses and new teaching materials, in some institutions at least, could be rechannelled into longer-term but hopefully more ultimately productive collaborative work on classroom research.

Following the action research paradigm (see section 3.2.3), groups of teachers could share the initial task of identifying worthwhile issues to investigate by getting together to talk about the things that puzzle them about their classes. They could parcel out the crucial but time-consuming task of reading through the literature to find out about what has already been done, and found out, by other people. They could come together again to design their investigation, and to decide how it is to be implemented and monitored in their different classrooms. This team approach could also be effective in analysing and interpreting the resulting data. And finally, they could share the exacting but vitally important task of producing a succinct yet informative report for a conference presentation or for publication in a professional journal. And of course teachers working collaboratively as a group could expect to be in a much stronger position both to know what they need and to get what they need from professional researchers.

11.6 The role of the learners

Where does this leave the learners? So far we do not appear to have given them a very active role in the exploratory enterprise, although throughout the book we have emphasised just how much they typically contribute to whatever happens in their classrooms. But why should learners not also be interested in understanding how classroom language learning works? Studies have already shown (see especially Cherchalli 1988) just how insightful high school learners can be with their own comments about language classrooms, and just how puzzled they can be about what goes on too.

Perhaps we could most usefully start with the learners, by bringing them properly in at the start of our explorations, and getting them to share their puzzles with us. They might then be willing to help us with the explorations themselves, by keeping diaries to document their classroom lives and out-of-class learning experiences, by recording and transcribing some of their own group-work sessions, and so on. It could all be very useful language work as well, if the target language is used throughout, so they would have no reason at all to feel that they were sacrificing valuable lesson time for the sake of some irrelevant and time-consuming research project dreamed up by outsiders.

11.7 Making exploratory teaching a reality

What will it take to make exploratory teaching a reality? Are we dreaming of utopia? We think not. Such things have happened in some places already, as we have shown through this book. But bringing about fruitful collaboration between researchers, teachers, and learners is a long-term project, and one that calls for very considerable sensitivity as well as determination. Sensitivity is needed, in part, because educational research in general has something of an unfortunate reputation as a parasitic enterprise. Researchers need to show great sensitivity in their relationships with classroom teachers, therefore. But educational administrators will also need to be handled sensitively, if the necessary resources are going to be made available. They need to understand that classroom research can play a major role in teacher development, in giving teachers a renewed sense of purpose and direction. And last, but crucially, our learners need to be handled sensitively so that they can play their part fully and not come to feel that research is being done *on* them, rather than *for* them and *with* them.

Exploratory teaching also calls for people who know what they are doing, people who are familiar with the research so far, both with its findings and with its procedures. We hope that this book will have provided you with just such a background, and that you will be one of those teachers quietly (but publicly) determined to collaborate with your fellow teachers, with your learners, and with any researchers you can find, so that we can all gradually contribute to unravelling yet more of the mysteries of language classrooms, and to becoming more effective in the process.

Appendix A Interaction analysis

TEACHER TALK	INDIRECT INFLUENCE	1.* ACCEPTS FEELING: accepts and clarifies the feeling tone of the students in a non-threatening manner. Feelings may be positive or negative. Predicting or recalling feelings are included. 2.* PRAISES OR ENCOURAGES: praises or encourages student action or behavior. Jokes that release tension, not at the expense of another individual, nodding head or saying, "um hm?" or "go on" are included. 3.* ACCEPTS OR USES IDEAS OF STUDENT: clarifying, building, or developing ideas suggested by a student. As a teacher brings more of his own ideas into play, shift to category five. 4.* ASKS QUESTIONS: asking a question about content or procedure with the intent that a student answer.
	DIRECT INFLUENCE	5.* LECTURING: giving facts or opinions about content or procedure: expressing his own ideas, asking rhetorical questions. 6.* GIVING DIRECTIONS: directions, commands, or orders to which a student is expected to comply. 7.* CRITICIZING OR JUSTIFYING AUTHORITY: statements intended to change student behavior from non-acceptable to acceptable pattern; bawling someone out; stating why the teacher is doing what he is doing; extreme self-reference.
		8.* STUDENT TALK–RESPONSE: a student makes a predictable response to teacher. Teacher initiates the contact or solicits student statement and sets limits to what the student says. 9.* STUDENT TALK–INITIATION: talk by students which they initiate. Unpredictable statements in response to teacher. Shift from 8 to 9 as student introduces own ideas.
		10.* SILENCE OR CONFUSION: pauses, short periods of silence, and periods of confusion in which communication cannot be understood by the observer.

* There is *no* scale implied by these numbers. Each number is classificatory; it designates a particular kind of communication event. To write these numbers down during observation is to enumerate, not to judge a position on a scale

To obtain a complete descriptive picture of what behaviors are used during a lesson, a trained observer tallies every time a different category is used and when the same category is repeated for a consecutive period of time, he records this category every three seconds. The tallies are entered into a ten by ten matrix, resulting in a graphic picture of the lesson. The matrix preserves the general time sequence of the interaction by illustrating which behaviors immediately preceded or followed others. By studying the matrix, teaching patterns can be discovered and analyzed.

The following is an example of how an observation is tallied and entered into a matrix:

The teacher begins by saying, "Open your books to page 160 and answer the first question, Bill" (category 6). Three seconds pass while the students get out their books and open them (category 10). Bill responds to the teacher's direction: "Spain and Portugal form the Iberian Peninsula" (category 8). The teacher reacts with, "Very good, Bill" (category 2). "Who has the answer to the next question?" (category 4). A pupil raises his hand and says, "I don't know where we are" (category 9). The teacher remarks, "We are on page 160, the second question under Exercise I (category 5), and if you had been paying attention, you would have known where we are" (category 7). "Martha, continue by reading your answer to the second question and be very careful to watch your pronunciation as you read" (The observer records two 6's in a row because the length of the statement is longer than 3 seconds). But Martha asks the teacher a question instead: "They don't pronounce the 'h' in Spanish or in French, do they?" (category 9), and the teacher responds, "That's right, Martha (category 2), 'h' is a silent letter in both of those languages" (category 3).

Observations automatically begin and end with category 10. An observer, therefore, would have tallied the above interaction in a column in the following way:10-6-10-8-2-4-9-5-7-6-6-9-2-3-10.

Every number except the first and last 10 is then entered into the matrix twice, which is how the sequence of events is preserved. Each of the 100 cells in the matrix contains an event and what happened directly afterwards. If the behaviors just described are entered into a matrix, they would be paired in this way first:

> 1st pair (^{10}
> ^{6}) 2nd pair
> 3rd pair (^{10}
> ^{8}) 4th pair
> 5th pair (^{2}
> ^{4}) 6th pair
> 7th pair (^{9}
> ^{5}) etc.
> $_7$

The rows in the matrix designate the first event; the columns are the second event. A tally is placed for each pair of numbers in the corresponding cell at the intersection of the appropriate column and row. The first pair above to be entered will go in the 10–6 (read "ten-six") cell. The second will be placed in the 6–10 cell; the third, in the 10–8 cell; the fourth in the 8–2 cell; and so on. When all of the tallies for an observation are entered into the matrix the columns and the rows are each totaled. The totals for the columns and the rows are identical, i.e., the total for column 1 will be the same as the total for row 1. Figure 2 illustrates where the above tallies will be placed on a matrix; the totals for the columns and the rows are also indicated.

When the matrix is complete, percentages for each category are calculated as well as the percentages of teacher talk, student talk, and silence or confusion. Ratios of the amount of indirect to direct behaviors the teacher used are also determined. There are nine of these ratios, which are referred to as I.D. ratios, each focusing on a different relationship.

From the matrix a teacher may find out many specific things about his teaching. A few of these are:

1. What percentage of the class time does the teacher talk?
2. What percentage of the class time do the pupils talk?
3. Does the teacher use more indirect or direct influence during a lesson?
4. Is the teacher more indirect or direct in the way he motivates and controls the class?
5. What kind of immediate feedback does the teacher give to pupils after they respond?
6. To what extent do pupils participate for extended periods of time?
7. What behaviors does the teacher use to elicit pupil response in the class?
8. To what extent are pupil responses which are called for by the teacher narrow, predictable ones and to what extent are pupils given the opportunity to bring in their own ideas?
9. What behaviors does the teacher use more extensively in communicating?

Figure 2.
Sample Matrix for Recording Interaction Analysis

		Second Event									
	1	2	3	4	5	6	7	8	9	10	Total
1											0
2			1	1							2
3									1		1
4									1		1
First 5						1					1
Event 6						1			1	1	3
7						1					1
8		1									1
9		1			1						2
10						1		1			2
Total	0	2	1	1	1	3	1	1	2	2	14

(Moskowitz 1968:219–22, quoting Flanders 1960)

Appendix B Foreign Language interaction analysis (FLint) system

TEACHER TALK	INDIRECT INFLUENCE	1. DEALS WITH FEELINGS: In a non-threatening way, accepting, discussing, referring to, or communicating understanding of past, present, or future feelings of students. 2. PRAISES OR ENCOURAGES: Praising, complimenting, telling students why what they have said or done is valued. Encouraging students to continue, trying to give them confidence. Confirming answers are correct. 2a. JOKES: Intentional joking, kidding, making puns, attempting to be humorous, providing the joking is not at anyone's expense. Unintentional humor is not included in this category. 3. USES IDEAS OF STUDENTS: Clarifying, using, interpreting, summarizing the ideas of students. The ideas must be rephrased by the teacher but still recognized as being student contributions. 3a. REPEATS STUDENT RESPONSE VERBATIM: Repeating the exact words of students after they participate. 4. ASKS QUESTIONS: Asking questions to which an answer is anticipated. Rhetorical questions are not included in this category.
	DIRECT INFLUENCE	5. GIVES INFORMATION: Giving information, facts, own opinion or ideas, lecturing, or asking rhetorical questions. 5a. CORRECTS WITHOUT REJECTION: Telling students who have made a mistake the correct response without using words or intonations which communicate criticism. 6. GIVES DIRECTIONS: Giving directions, requests, or commands which students are expected to follow. 6a. DIRECTS PATTERN DRILLS: Giving statements which students are expected to repeat exactly, to make substitutions in (i.e., substitution drills), or to change from one form to another (i.e., transformation drills). 7. CRITICIZES STUDENT BEHAVIOR: Rejecting the behavior of students; trying to change the non-acceptable behavior; communicating anger, displeasure, annoyance, dissatisfaction with what students are doing. 7a. CRITICIZES STUDENT RESPONSE: Telling the student his response is not correct or acceptable and communicating by words or intonation criticism, displeasure, annoyance, rejection.
STUDENT TALK		8. STUDENT RESPONSE, SPECIFIC: Responding to the teacher within a specific and limited range of available or previously shaped answers. Reading aloud. 8a. STUDENT RESPONSE, CHORAL: Choral response by the total class or part of the class. 9. STUDENT RESPONSE, OPEN-ENDED OR STUDENT-INITIATED: Responding to the teacher with students' own ideas, opinions, reactions, feelings. Giving one from among many possible answers which have been previously shaped but from which students must now make a selection. Initiating the participation.
		10. SILENCE: Pauses in the interaction. Periods of quiet during which there is no verbal interaction. 10a. SILENCE-AV: Silence in the interaction during which a piece of audio-visual equipment, e.g., a tape recorder, filmstrip projector, record player, etc., is being used to communicate. 11. CONFUSION, WORK-ORIENTED: More than one person at a time talking, so the interaction cannot be recorded. Students calling out excitedly, eager to participate or respond, concerned with task at hand. 11a. CONFUSION, NON-WORK-ORIENTED: More than one person at a time talking, so the interaction cannot be recorded. Students out-of-order, not behaving as the teacher wishes, not concerned with the task at hand.

12. LAUGHTER: Laughing, giggling by the class, individuals, and/or the teacher.

e. USES ENGLISH: Use of English (the native language) by the teacher or the students. This category is always combined with one of the 15 categories from 1 to 9.

n. NONVERBAL: Nonverbal gestures or facial expressions by the teacher or the student which communicate without the use of words. This category is always combined with one of the categories of teacher or pupil behavior.

(Moskowitz 1971:213)

H

Appendix C
Foci for Observing Communications Used in Settings (FOCUS)

FIve Characteristics of Communications in Settings

1. Who communicates?	2. What is the pedagogical purpose of the communication?*	3. What mediums are used to communicate content?	4. How are the mediums used to communicate areas of content?**	5. What areas of content are communicated?**
	to structure	linguistic	1 attend	language systems
teacher		aural		contextual
		visual	2 characterize	grammatical
				literary
			21 differentiate	
		ideogram		meaning
			22 evaluate	
		transcribed		mechanics of writing
		written	23 examine	
			24 illustrate	sound segmental supra-seg.
	to solicit	other	25 label	speech production
individual student		non-linguistic	3 present	unclassified
		aural	31 call words	life
		visual	32 change medium	
			33 question	
		real	34 state	formula
		representational	4 relate	imagination
		schematic	41 explain	personal
	to respond	symbolic	42 interpret	public
		other		skills

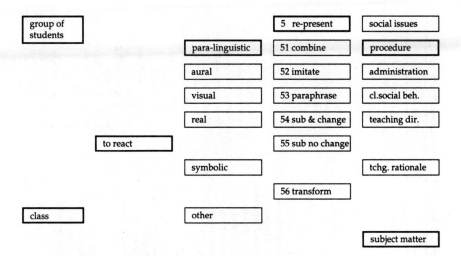

group of students				5 re-present	social issues
		para-linguistic		51 combine	procedure
		aural		52 imitate	administration
		visual		53 paraphrase	cl.social beh.
		real		54 sub & change	teaching dir.
	to react			55 sub no change	
		symbolic			tchg. rationale
				56 transform	
class		other			
					subject matter

* These four pedagogical purposes are from Bellack.
** The uses and areas of content are presented alphabetically.

[continues]

FIVE CHARACTERISTICS OF COMMUNICATIONS IN SETTINGS WITH EXAMPLES & DEFINITIONS

1 Source	2 Pedagogical Purpose*	3 Mediums	Messages** 4 Uses	5 Content
teacher t	structuring moves str prepare for the setting of tasks or other activities	linguistic aural fillers, individual letters, words, sentences, sounds, syllables, etc. (Add an s if the supra-segmentals are used to communicate a separate message as in the lengthening of vowels or rising intonation in repetitions, etc.)	attend not communicating content—listening, silent reading, tasting, feeling objects, etc. characterize communicating about content or things	language systems contextual: collocation, connotation, culture, detail and main idea, register, situation, etc. grammatical: function words, sentence forms, inflections, reduced forms, word, order, etc. literary: imagery, mood, style, etc. meaning: figurative, grammatical, historical, humorous, idiomatic, ironic, literal, etc. mechanics of writing: how to hold a pen, making capitals, punctuation, spelling, etc.
individual students s1 to sn			differentiate indicating that communications are the same or different evaluate	
assigned group of students g1 to gn	soliciting moves sol set tasks or ask questions	visual ideogram: $, #. etc. transcribed: phonetic writing of fillers, intonation, stress, words, sounds, etc. written: printed written individual letters, words, commas, periods, etc.	prescribing or indicating comms. are right or wrong or true or false; either/or questions ans. yes/no & examine counting or locating parts of words; emphasizing; diagramming sentences; infor. about size or shape	sound: segmental: consonant clusters, syllabification, sounds, etc. supra-segmental: intonation, rhythm, stress, etc. speech production: your tongue should be up; the voice box vibrates, etc. unclassified: many aspects of language
group of students ss1 to ssn	responding moves res perform tasks or answer	other	illustrate giving attributes of items, making judgments that are not explicitly good or bad	life formula: genuine greetings, leave-taking, etc.

imagination: what would happen if...?, etc.
personal: feelings, information, etc.
public: general knowledge about persons, places, things, aesthetics, religion, etc.
skills: cooking, studying, track, typing, etc.
social issues: population, prejudice, etc.

procedure
administration: calling roll; phoney greetings; checking questions—do you follow?; transition—OK, Uhm; query—repeating with rising intonation, etc.
classroom social behavior: discipline, etc.
teaching directions: setting tasks, communicating instructional information, etc.
teaching rationale: support for a method or procedure, etc.

subject matter
school subjects: biology, math, *not* language, etc.
survival skills: how to budget, understanding a lease, etc.

unspecified

[continues]

label
naming parts of speech or groups of items

present
communicating content itself
call words
change medium
question
state

relate
relating communications about content and content itself
explain
making generalizations, giving rules or reasons; explicitly relating, etc.
interpret
making inferences, generating new patterns, implicitly relating, etc.

re-present
communicating content another has just

Braille; drawing a letter or stress mark on one's hand, etc.

non-linguistic
aural
bell, clapping, humming, music, noise, tapping, etc.

visual
real: food, live things, objects, people, speech organs, voice box, working things, etc.
representational: cartoon, picture, puppet, sketch, etc.
schematic: diagram, erasing, line showing space, map, underlining, etc.
symbolic: rod representing a house, etc.

questions

class
c
reacting
moves rea reflexive communications that are not requested

informant
i

bearing
moves bea unconscious communications such as jiggling one's keys; the environment or situation one is in, etc.

textbook
b

209

visitor
v

other
clothing, furniture,
temperature, etc.

para-linguistic

aural
crying, laughing,
silence, tone of
voice, volume, etc.
visual
real: color,
faces, gazing, gesture,
movement, posture, etc.
symbolic: ges-
for summer, etc.
other
dance, distance,
touch, etc.

communicated in the
same medium with or
without change.
combining
imitating
paraphrasing
substituting with
changes
substituting with-
out changes
transforming

*from Bellack

**The term message refers to the combination of medium, use and content.

COMMUNICATIONS CODED WITH FOCUS[1]

Setting: An intermediate language classroom; students are seated in rows. Here are some excerpts from lessons:	Five Characteristics of Communication				
	Source	Pedagogical Purpose	Medium	Use	Content
1. Read this passage silently.	t	sol	la⁺ lv	pres:state	language+life
Was Truman from Texas?					
No, Missouri.					
What about Eisenhower?					
He was from Texas.					
(Student reads passage silently.)	s	res	lv	attend	language+life
2. What part of speech is from?	t	sol	la	pres:ques⁺	language:gram.
A preposition.	s	res	la	char:label	language:gram.
(Teacher shakes students's hand.)	t	rea	po	char:evaluate[2]	language:gram.
3. Is about a preposition too?	s	sol	la	pres:ques⁺	language:gram.
Yes.	t	res	la	char:label	language:gram.
Good question—glad you ask				char:evaluate[2]	
questions	t	rea	la	char:evaluate	procedure
4. Where was Johnson from?	s	sol	la	pres:ques	life
Texas.	t	res	la	pres:state	life
5. How many syllables in Eisen-	t	sol	la	pres:ques	language:sound
hower?	s	res	la	char:examine	language:sound
6. Does Truman have two?	s	sol	la	pres:ques⁺ char:examine	language:sound
Yes.	t	res	la	char:evaluate[3]	language:sound
7. We'll do some vocabulary work					
now.	t	str	la	pres:state	procedure⁺
8. Say something about this.	t	sol	la⁺ nvl	pres:state	language:mean.
(Holds up an old, torn plastic					
raincoat.)					
It's for the water.	s_1	res	la	char:illustrate	language:mean.
It's ugly.	s_2	res	la	char:illustrate	language:mean.
I like it.	s_3	res	la	char:evaluate	language:mean.
It is just like mine.	3_4	res	la	char:differentiate	life
Feel this. (Gives student a	t	sol	la⁺ nvl	pres:state	language:mean.
candle.)					
(Student feels candle.)	s	res	nvl	attend	language:mean.
Is it rough or smooth?	t	sol	la⁺ nvl	pres:state⁺ contrast	language:mean.
Smooth.	s	res	la	char:evaluate[3]	language:mean.
(Shakes head up and down.)	t	rea	pv	char-evaluate	language:mean.

[1]Practice coding of excerpts from lessons, texts, tests and conversations is needed to master FOCUS in much the same way that a great deal of transcription practice is needed before serious phonetic work can be done.

[2]Of course since there is a direction in the solicit the content of procedure is presented also. However, as a convention we do not code procedural content in solicits.

[3]An alternate way to code these responses, and all others, is to show what is given in the solicit on the response line. Here are three of the responses coded the alternate way.

    3 s res la evaluate language: grammar (la pres:ques+char:label)

    6 t res la evaluate language: sound (la pres:ques+char:examine)

    8 s res la evaluate language: meaning (la pres:state+contrast+nvl pres:state)

[continues]

Appendix C

Five Characteristics of Communication

Setting: An airport—first at the ticket counter, then at customs and finally on a plane

	Source	Pedago-gical Purpose	Me-dium	Use	Content
1. How much is a ticket to Chicago?	s[1]	sol	la	pres:ques	life
$120.00.	t[1]	res	la	pres:state	life
That's rather high.	s	rea	la	char:illustrate	life
It's gone up because of the price of fuel, the increased wages for pilots and higher fees at all the airports.	t	rea	la	relate:explain	life
Please book me on the next flight. (after checking)	s	sol	la	pres:ques	procedure
I've booked you on the 3 o'clock.	t	res	la	pres:state	procedure
Thank you. (and smiles in a friendly way)	s	rea	la⁺	pres:state	life:formula
			pv	char:evaluate	
2. How long have you been in Mon-treal?	t[1]	sol	la	pres:ques	procedure[2]
	s[1]	res	la	pres:state	procedure
For three days.	t	sol	la	pres:ques	procedure
Why were you here?	s	res	la	pres:state	procedure
To visit some friends.	t	sol	la	pres:ques	procedure
Please open your bags. (opens bags)	s	res	pv⁺	pres:state	procedure
			nvl		
(looks through the bags and checks with his hands the con-tents of some bags)	t	rea	pv⁺	attend	procedure
			nvl		
You have to pay duty on these shoes.	t	sol	la	char:evaluate	procedure
	s	rea	la⁺	char:evaluate	life
That's stupid!			pa		
Go over to the collection booth.	t	sol	la	pres:ques	procedure
It's to the left of Avis.			la	char:examine	procedure
(points to the collection booth)			pv	char:examine	procedure
(goes over to the collection booth)	s	res	pv	pres:state	procedure
3. Welcome aboard.	t[1]	rea	la	pres:state	life:formula
(passenger goes to seat)	s[1]	str	pv	pres:state	procedure
This is the captain speaking. We will be taking off soon—right on schedule. We will be flying at 35,000 feet. The weather is clear all the way and the ceiling in the Chicago area is high. Enjoy the flight.	t	str	la	pres:state	procedure⁺ life:formula
(one passenger to another)					
They all sound the same.	s	rea	la	char:differen-tiate	life
Would you like a cocktail or a soft drink?	t	sol	la⁺	pres:ques	life
			nvl	pres:state	
(pointing to both on the cart)					
A cocktail.	s	res	la	char:evaluate	life
(Steward begins to fill glass with ice)	s	str	nvl	pres:state	procedure
Light on the ice though.	t	rea	la	char:illustrate	life

(Here the roles are switched; the steward is serving the passenger and the passenger is coded as t.)

[1]We use the letter t for the knower or the one in charge and an s for the learner or the person being served or directed.

[2]The content of these same questions if asked over dinner by a friend would be coded *life*. But in the setting of the customs area the content is procedure. The official is only interested in whether you did or did not do something that was not allowed by the rules. Here is a good example of how crucial the setting is in determining the meaning of communications.

(Fanselow 1977a:35–9)

Appendix D
The Embryonic Category System

1. *Pedagogical Moves*
    P 1. Student initates discussion.
    P 2. Student focuses discussion.
    P 3. Student summarizes and completes a sequence/ends discussion or section of discussion.
    P 4. Student moves conversation on to a new topic.
    P 5. Student qualifies another person's contribution.
    P 6. Student implicitly accepts a qualification.
    P 7. Student extends a previous contribution of his own or of others.
    P 8. Student reformulates own or other's previous assertion.
    P 9. Student expresses understanding.
    P10. Student provides an example.
    P11. Student uses evidence to challenge an assertion.
    P12. Student asks for information.
    P13. Student asks for information about the target language.
    P14. Student gives information on request.
    P15. Student gives information about the target language.
    P16. Student asks for clarification.
    P17. Student clarifies.

2. *Social Skills.*
    S 1. Student competes for the floor.
    S 2. Student interrupts.
    S 3. Student completes other's unfinished utterance.
    S 4. Student contradicts.
    S 5. Student invites participation by other students.
    S 6. Student explicitly expresses agreement.
    S 7. Student makes explicit reference to other's contribution.
    S 8. Student encourages other.
    S 9. Student explicitly supports other's assertion with evidence.
    S10. Student jokes.
    S11. Student avoids discussion.
    S12. Student repeats.
    S13. Student confirms.

3. *Rhetorical Acts.*
    R 1. Student predicts.
    R 2. Student hypothesizes.
    R 3. Student makes an observation.
    R 4. Student deduces.
    R 5. Student induces.
    R 6. Student states generalization.
    R 7. Student defines.
    R 8. Student negates.
    R 9. Student expresses cause and effect relationship.
    R10. Student exemplifies.
    R11. Student identifies.
    R12. Student categorizes.
    R13. Student classifies.
    R14. Student concludes.
    •
    •
    •
    X Confusion/inaudible tape.

(Long, Adams, McLean, and Castaños 1976:144–5)

Appendix E
Summary of Sinclair and Coulthard's system of analysis

RANK II: Transaction

Elements of Structure	Structures	Classes of Exchange
Preliminary (P) Medial (M) Terminal (T)	PM (M^2 ... M^n) (T)	P. T: Boundary (II.1) M: Teaching (II.2)

This table identifies the rank as second from the top of the scale, i.e. transaction. It states that there are three elements of structure, called *Preliminary* (short symbol P), *Medial* (M), and *Terminal* (T). In the next column is given a composite statement of the possible structures of this transaction—PM (M^2 ...M^n) (T). Anything within brackets is optional, so this formula states:

a) there must be a preliminary move in each transaction.
b) there must be one medial move, but there may be any number of them.
c) there can be a terminal move, but not necessarily.

In the third column the elements of transaction structure are associated with the classes of the rank next below (exchange), because each element is realized by a class of exchange. Preliminary and terminal exchange, it is claimed, are selected from the same class of move called *Boundary* moves, and this is numbered for ease of reference. The element medial is realized by a class of exchange called *Teaching*. Later tables develop the structure of these exchanges at rank III.

RANK I: Lesson

Elements of Structure	Structures	Classes
	an unordered series of transactions	

RANK III: Exchange (Boundary)

Elements of Structure	Structures	Classes of Move
Frame (Fr) Focus (Fo)	(Fr)(Fo)	Fr:Framing (III.1) Fo:Focusing (III.2)

RANK III: Exchange (Teaching)

Elements of Structure	Structures	Classes of Move
Initiation (I) Response (R) Feedback (F)	I (R) (F)	I: Opening (III.3) R: Answering (III.4) F: Follow-up (III.5)

214

RANK IV: Move (Opening)

Elements of Structure	Structures	Classes of Act

signal (s)
pre-head (pre-h)
head (h)
post-head (post-h)
select (sel)
	(s) (pre-h) h (post-h)
	(sel)
	(sel) (pre-h) h
		s: marker (IV.1)
		pre-h: starter (IV.2)
		H: system operating at h;
		    choice of elicitation,
		    directive, informative,
		    check (IV.3)
		post-h: system operating
		      at post-h; choice
		      from prompt and
		      clue (IV.4)
		sel: ((cue) bid) nomination
		    (IV.5)

RANK IV: Move (Answering)

Elements of Structure	Structures	Classes of Act

pre-head (pre-h)
head (h)
post-head (post-h)
	(pre-h) h (post-h)	pre-h: acknowledge (IV.6)
		h: system operating at h;
		    choice of reply, react,
		    acknowledge (IV.7)
		post-h: comment (IV.8)

RANK IV: Move (Follow-up)

Elements of Structure	Structures	Classes of Act
pre-head (pre-h) head (h) post-head (post-h)	(pre-h) (h) (post-h)	pre-h; accept (IV.9) h: evaluate (IV.10) post-h: comment (IV.8)

RANK IV: Move (Framing)

Elements of Structure	Structures	Classes of Act
head (h) qualifier (q)	hq	H: marker (IV.1) q: silent stress (IV.11)

RANK IV: Move (Focusing)

Elements of Structure	Structures	Classes of Act

signal (s)
pre-head (pre-h)
head (h)
post-head (post-h)
	(s) (pre-h) h (post-h)	s: marker (IV.1)
		pre-h: starter (IV.2)
		h: system at h: choice
		    from metastatement or
		    conclusion (IV.12)
		post-h: comment (IV.8)

(Sinclair and Coulthard 1975:25–7)

Appendix F
COLT (Communicative Orientation of Lanaguge Teaching) category definitions

COLT Observation Scheme: Definition of Categories

The COLT observation scheme is divided into two parts. Part A describes classroom events at the level of episode and activity, while Part B analyzes the communicative features of verbal exchanges between teachers and students or among students themselves as they occur within each activity.

Part A: Classroom Events

I. Activity
   The first parameter is open-ended; no predetermined descriptors have to be checked off by the observer. Each activity and its constituent episodes are separately described: e.g., drill, translation, discussion, game, and so on (separate activities); alternatively, teacher introduces dialogue, teacher reads dialogue aloud, students repeat dialogue parts after teacher (three episodes of one activity).

II. Partcipant Organization
   This parameter describes three basic patterns of organization:
   A. Whole Class
      1. Teacher to student or class, and vice versa (One central activity led by the teacher is going on; the teacher interacts with the whole class and/or with individual students.)
      2. Student to student, or student(s) to class (Students talk to each other, either as part of the lesson or as informal socializing; one central activity led by a student may be going on, e.g., a group of students act out a skit with the rest of the class as the audience.)
      3. Choral work by students (The whole class or groups participate in the choral work, repeating a model provided by the textbook or teacher.)
   B. Group work
      1. All groups at work on the same task
      2. Groups at work on different tasks
   C. Individual seat work (Students work on their own, all on the same task or on different tasks.)
   D. Group/individual work (Some students are involved in group work; others work on their own.)

III. Content
   This parameter describes the subject matter of the activities, that is, what the teacher and the students are talking, reading, or writing about or what they are listening to. Three major content areas have been differentiated, along with the category Topic Control:
   A. Management
      1. Procedural directives
      2. Disciplinary statements
   B. Explicit focus on language
      1. Form (explicit focus on grammar, vocabulary, or pronunciation)
      2. Function (explicit focus on illocutionary acts such as requesting, apologizing, and explaining)
      3. Discourse (explicit focus on the way sentences combine into cohesive and coherent sequences)
      4. Sociolinguistics (explicit focus on the features which make utterances appropriate for particular contexts)
   C. Other topics (the subject matter of classroom discourse, apart from management and explicit focus on language)
      1. Narrow range of reference (This subcategory refers to the immediate classroom environment and to stereotyped exchanges such as "Good morning" or "How are you?" which have phatic value but little conceptual content. Included in this category are routine classroom references to the date, day of the week, weather, and so on.)
      2. Limited range of reference (Topics in this subcategory refer to information beyond the classroom but still conceptually limited: movies, holidays, school topics such as extracurricular activities, and topics which relate to the students' immediate personal and family affairs, e.g., place of residence, number of brothers and sisters, and so on.)

216

      3. Broad range of reference (Topics of broad range go well beyond the classroom and immediate environment and include reference to controversial public issues, world events, abstract ideas, reflective personal information, and other academic subject matter, such as math or geography.)

   D. Topic control (Who selects the topic that is being talked about—the teacher, the student, or both?)

IV.   Student modality
This section identifies the various skills involved in a classroom activity. The focus is on the students, and the purpose is to discover whether they are listening, speaking, reading, or writing, or whether these activities are occurring in combination. The category Other covers such activities as drawing, modeling, acting, or arranging classroom displays.

V.   Materials
This parameter describes the materials used in connection with classroom activities.

   A. Type of materials
      1. Text (written)
         a. Minimal (e.g., captions, isolated sentences, work lists)
         b. Extended (e.g., stories, dialogues, connected paragraphs)
      2. Audio
      3. Visual
   B. Source/purpose of materials
      1. Pedagogic (specifically designed for L2 teaching)
      2. Non-pedagogic (materials originally intended for nonschool purposes)
      3. Semi-pedagogic (utilizing real-life objects and texts but in a modified form)
   C. Use of materials
      1. Highly controlled (close adherence to materials)
      2. Semi-controlled (occasional extension beyond the restrictions imposed by the materials)
      3. Minimally controlled (materials as a starting point for ensuing conversation, which may cover a wide range of topics)

Part B: Communicative Features

I.   Use of target language
   A. Use of first language (L1)
   B. Use of second language (L2)

II.   Information gap
This feature refers to the extent to which the information requested and/or exchanged is unpredictable, i.e., not known in advance.

   A. Requesting information
      1. Pseudo (The speaker already possesses the information requested.)
      2. Genuine (The information requested is not known in advance.)
   B. Giving information
      1. Relatively predictable (The message is easily anticipated in that there is a very limited range of information that can be given. In the case of responses, only one answer is possible semantically, although there may be different correct grammatical realizations.)
      2. Relatively unpredictable (The message is not easily anticipated in that a wide range of information can be given. If a number of responses are possible, each can provide different information.)

III.   Sustained speech
This feature is intended to measure the extent to which speakers engage in extended discourse or restrict their utterances to a minimal length of one sentence, clause or word.

   A. Ultraminimal (utterances consisting of one word—coded for student speech only)
   B. Minimal (student utterances consisting of one clause or sentence, teacher utterances consisting of one word)
   C. Sustained speech (utterances longer than one sentence or consisting of at least two main clauses)

Appendix F

IV. Reaction to code or message
This feature refers to a correction or other explicit statement which draws attention to the linguistic form of an utterance.

V. Incorporation of preceding utterances
   A. No incorporation (no feedback or reaction given)
   B. Repetition (full or partial repetition of previous utterance/s)
   C. Paraphrase (completion and/or reformulation of previous utterance/s)
   D. Comment (positive or negative comment on, but not correction of, previous utterance/s)
   E. Expansion (extension of the content of preceding utterance/s through the addition of related information)
   F. Elaboration (requests for further information related to the subject matter of the preceding utterance/s)

VI. Discourse initiation
This feature measures the frequency of self-initiated turns (spontaneously initiated talk) by students.

VII. Relative restriction of linguistic form
   A. Restricted use (the production or manipulation of one specific form, as in a transformation or substitution drill)
   B. Limited restriction (a choice of more than one linguistic form but in a very narrow range, e.g., responses to *yes/no* questions, statements about the date, time of day, and so on)
   C. Unrestricted use (no expectation of any particular linguistic form, as in free conversation, oral reports, or personal diary writing)

(Fröhlich, Spada, and Allen (1985:53–6)

Communicative Orientation of Language Teaching (COLT): Part A

SCHOOL
TEACHER
SUBJECT

GRADE(S)
LESSON (Minutes)

DATE
OBSERVER

Col. 1

Column numbers: 2 3 4 5 6 7 8 9 10 11 12 13 14 15 16 17 18 19 20 21 22 23 24 25 26 27 28 29 30 31 32 33 34 35 36 37 38 39 40 41 42 43 44 45 46 47 48

TIME / ACTIVITIES

PARTIC. ORGANIZATION
- Class: T s/c, S s/c, Choral
- Same
- Different
- Individual
- Group: Gr/Ind.
- Comb.
- Man.: Procedure, Discipline

CONTENT

LANGUAGE:
- Form
- Function
- Discourse
- Socioling.

OTHER TOPICS:
- NARROW: Classroom, Stereotyp., Pers./Bio.
- Other
- Personal
- LIMITED: Rout./Soc., Fam./Com., School T.
- Other
- BROAD: Abstract, Pers./Ref., Imagination, World T.
- Other

TOPIC CONTROL:
- Teacher
- Teacher/Stud.
- Student

STUDENT MODALITY:
- Listening
- Speaking
- Reading
- Writing
- Other

MATERIALS:
- Text: Minimal, Extended
- Audio
- Visual
- Type: Pedagogic, Semi-Pedag., Non-Pedag.
- Use: High Control, Semi Control, Mini Control

Communicative Orientation of Language Teaching (COLT): Part B

TEACHER VERBAL INSTRUCTION

- COMMUNIC. FEATURES: No talk, Off-task
- TARGET LANG.: L_2, L_1
- INFORMATION GAP (Giving Request, Info. Info.): Predict., Unpred., Pseudo, Genuine
- SUST. SPEECH: Minimal, Sustained
- REACTION CO./MES.: Reaction, Explicity Code
- INCORPORATION of S. UTTERANCES: No Incorp., Reptition, Paraphrase, Comment, Expansion, Elaboration

STUDENT VERBAL INTERACTION

- TARGET LANG.: Choral, L_1, L_2, Disc-Initiation
- INFORMATION GAP (Giving Request, Info. Info.): Pred., Unpred., Pseudo, Genuine
- SUST. SPEECH: Ultraminimal, Minimal, Sustained
- FORM RESTR.: Restricted, Limited, Unrestricted
- REACTION CO./MES.: Reaction, Explicit Code
- INCORPORATION of S/T UTTERANCES: No Incorp., Repetition, Paraphrase, Comment, Expansion, Elaboration

(Allen, Fröhlich, and Spada 1984:251–2)

Appendix G Chaudron's Features and types of corrective reactions in the model of discourse

Feature or Type of "Act" (F and/or T)	Description	Example of Exponent of Expression
IGNORE (F)	Teacher (T) ignores Student's (S) ERROR, goes on to other topic, or shows ACCEPTANCE* of content.	Bon, oui, bien, d'accord
INTERRUPT (F)	T interrupts S utterance (ut) following ERROR, or before S has completed.	
DELAY (F)	T waits for S to complete ut. before correcting. (Usually not coded, for INTERRUPT is "marked")	
ACCEPTANCE (T)	Simple approving or accepting word (usually as sign of reception of ut.), but T may immediately correct a linguistic ERROR.	Euhh, regarde, attention, allez, mais.
ATTENTION (T-F)	Attention-getter; probably quickly learned by Ss.	Non, ne ... pas.
NEGATION (T-F)	T shows rejection of part or all of S ut.	S: Cinquante, uh ...
PROVIDE (T)	T provides the correct answer when S has been unable or when no response is offered.	T: Pour cent.
REDUCTION (F) (RED.)	T ut. employs only a segment of S ut.	S: Vee, eee ... (spelling) T: Vé ...
EXPANSION (F) (EXP.)	T adds more linguistic material to S ut., possibly making more complete.	S: Et c'est bien. T: Ils ont pensé que c'était bien?
EMPHASIS (F) (EMPH.)	T uses stress, iterative repetition, or question intonation, to mark area or fact of incorrectness.	S: Mille. T: Mille?
REPETITION with NO CHANGE (T) (optional EXP. & RED.)	T repeats S ut. with no change of ERROR, or omission of ERROR.	T: (les auto-routes) n'a pas de feux de circulation.
REPETITION with NO CHANGE and EMPH. (T) (F) (optional EXP. & RED.)	T repeats S ut. with no change of ERROR, but EMPH. locates or indicates fact of ERROR.	S: Mille. T: Mille?
REPETITION with CHANGE (T) (optional EXP. & RED.)	Usually T simply adds correction and continues to other topics. Normally only when EMPH. is added will correcting CHANGE become clear, or will T attempt to make it clear.	S: Le maison est jaune. T: La maison est jaune.
REPETITION with CHANGE and EMPHASIS (T) (F) (optional EXP. & RED.)	T adds EMPH. to stress location of ERROR and its correct fomulation.	S: Doo tout ... T: Du tout. (stress)

Term	Description	Example
EXPLANATION (T) (optional EXP. & RED.)	T provides information as to cause or type of ERROR.	
COMPLEX EXPLANATION (T)	Combination of NEGATION, REPETITIONs, and/or EXPLANATION.	
REPEAT (T)	T requests S to repeat ut., with intent to have S self-correct.	
REPEAT (implicit)	Procedures are understood that by pointing or otherwise signalling, T can have S repeat.	
LOOP (T)	T honestly needs a replay of S ut., due to lack of clarity or certainty of its form.	
PROMPT (T)	T uses a lead-in cue to get S to repeat ut., possibly at point of ERROR; possible slight rising intonation.	
CLUE (T)	T reaction provides S with isolation of type of ERROR or of the nature of its immediate correction, without providing correction.	S: Uh, E. (spelling 'grand') T: D. Non, il n'y a pas de E.
ORIGINAL QUESTION (T)	T repeats the original question that led to response.	
ALTERED QUESTION (T)	T alters original question syntactically, but not semantically.	
QUESTIONs (T) (optional RED., EXP., EMPH.)	Numerous ways of asking for new reponse, often with CLUEs, etc.	
TRANSFER (T)	T asks another S or several, or class to provide correction.	
ACCEPTANCE* (T)	T shows approval of S ut.	
REPETITIONs* (T)	Where T attempts reinforcement of correct response.	
EXPLANATION* (T)	T explains why response is correct.	
RETURN (T)	T returns to original error-maker for another attempt, after TRANSFER. A type of VERIFICATION.	S: Petit. Grande. T: Petit ... S: Les stations-services sont rares T: Sont rares? Au présent?
VERIFICATION (T-F)	T attempts to assure understanding of correction; a new elicitation is implicit or made more explicit.	
EXIT (F)	At any stage in the exchange T may drop correction of the ERROR, though usually not after explicit NEGATION, EMPH., etc.	

(Chaudron 1977:38–9)

J

Appendix H
Transcription conventions for classroom discourse

General layout

1 Leave generous margins, at least at first, to permit legible annotations as transcription gets refined.
2 Double space everything, for the same reason.
3 Number every fifth line in the left-hand margin, *but* do so only in pencil until transcription is complete, unless you are using wordprocessing with automatic line numbering.
4 Identify transcripts at the top of each page with some economical reference number.
5 Number all pages in the top right corner.
6 Identify participants, date and location on a separate sheet (separate in case participants' identities need to be kept confidential).
7 Decide whether to supply pseudonyms for participants' names, or to substitute numbers.
8 Enter participants' pseudonyms, where used, with gender, classroom layout, etc., also on a separate sheet (especially if using computer, since computer analysis must not include this page as data).
9 If using numbers, enter real name and associated numbers (with gender information) on a separate sheet.
10 On transcript pages, justify identifying material to the right, justify text to the left, as below.

Symbols to identify who is speaking:

T	teacher
A	aide
M1	identified male learner, using numbers (M1, M2, etc.)
F1	identified female learner, using numbers (F1, F2, etc.)
Su	use such two-letter abbreviations for pseudonyms, where used (note: gender information may be lost by this method)
M	unidentified male learner
F	unidentified female learner
MV	male voice from, for example, an audio or videotape
FV	female voice, as above
LL	unidentified subgroup of class
<u>LL</u>	unidentified subgroup speaking in chorus
LLL	whole class
<u>LLL</u>	whole class speaking in chorus

Symbols for relationships between lines of transcript

$\left\{ \begin{array}{l} M3 \\ F7 \end{array} \right.$ use curly brackets to indicate simultaneous speech

$\left[\begin{array}{l} M \\ T \\ M \end{array} \right.$ use to indicate same unidentified male speaker

$\left[\begin{array}{l} F \\ T \\ F \end{array} \right.$ use to indicate same unidentified female speaker

-T   use hyphen to indicate continuation of a turn without a pause, where overlapping speech intervenes.

Symbols to use in text

[	]	use for commentary of any kind (e.g. to indicate point in discourse where T writes on blackboard)
[=	]	use to introduce a gloss, or translation, of speech
/	/	use for phonemic transcription instead of standard orthography, where pronunciation deviant. Use with gloss if meaning also obscured.

( )	use for uncertain transcription
(/ /)	use for uncertain phonemic transcription
([ ])	use for uncertain gloss

X	incomprehensible item, probably one word only
XX	incomprehensible item of phrase length
XXX	incomprehensible item beyond phrase length
X——X	use optionally at early stages to indicate extent of incomprehensible item, as guide to future attempts to improve transcription

| . . . . . | use dots to indicate pauses, giving length in seconds in extreme cases, if potentially relevant to aims |
| " " | use to indicate anything read rather than spoken without direct text support |

Further notes

1 Use indentation to indicate overlap of turns, otherwise start all turns systematically at extreme left of text space.
2 Use hyphen in text to indicate an incomplete word (for example, Come here, plea-)
3 Omit the full stop (period) at the end of a turn, to indicate incompletion (for example, As I was going to)

OTHERWISE PUNCTUATE AS NORMALLY AS POSSIBLE, AS IF WRITING A PLAYSCRIPT

4 Use 'uh' for hesitation fillers, or give phonemic transcription if meaning differences are potentially important.
5 Use underlining for emphasis, if using typewriter, or **bold** if wordprocessing (for example, Come **here**!).

GENERAL PRINCIPLE: THE LAW OF LEAST EFFORT
AVOID REDUNDANCY. Use only the conventions that are necessary for your particular purposes, to record the information you are sure you will need. If you are wordprocessing it will always be possible to update the transcript later (though admittedly this will be much more laborious if only typewriting facilities are available).

Dick Allwright
Copacabana
September 1990

Bibliography

Adelman, C. 1981. 'On first hearing', in C. Adelman (ed.) *Uttering muttering: collecting, using, and reporting talk for social and educational research*:78–97. London: Grant McIntyre Ltd.

Allen, H. B. and R. N. Campbell (eds.) 1972. *Teaching English as a second language: a book of readings*. New York: McGraw Hill.

Allen, P., M. Fröhlich and N. Spada 1984. 'The communicative orientation of language teaching: An observation scheme', in Handscombe, Orem and Taylor:231–52.

Allwright, D. 1988a. *Observation in the language classroom*. London: Longman.

Allwright, D. 1988b. 'Autonomy and individualization in whole-class instruction', in A. Brookes and P. Grundy (eds.) *Individualization and autonomy in language learning*, ELT Documents 131:35–44. London: Modern English Publications, British Council.

Allwright, R. L. 1972. 'Prescription and description in the training of language teachers', in J. Qvistgaard, H. Schwartz and H. Spang-Hanssen (eds.) *Applied linguistics: problems and solutions*. AILA Proceedings, vol III:150–66, Copenhagen. Heidelburg: Julius Groos Verlag.

Allwright, R. L. 1975. 'Problems in the study of the language teacher's treatment of learner error', in M. K. Burt and H. C. Dulay (eds.) *On TESOL '75: new directions in second language learning, teaching and bilingual education*:96–109. Washington, D.C.: TESOL.

Allwright, R. L. 1980. 'Turns, topics and tasks: patterns of participation in language learning and teaching', in Larsen-Freeman 1980:165–87.

Allwright, R. L. 1981. 'What do we want teaching materials for?' *English Language Teaching Journal* 36:5–18.

Allwright, R. L. 1983. 'Classroom-centered research on language teaching and learning: a brief historical overview'. *TESOL Quarterly* 17:191–204.

Allwright, R. L. 1984. 'Why don't learners learn what teachers teach? – The interaction hypothesis', in D. M. Singleton and D. G. Little (eds.) *Language learning in formal and informal contexts*:3–18. Dublin: IRAAL.

Anthony, E. 1963. 'Approach, method and technique'. *English Language Teaching* 17: 63–7. Reprinted in Allen and Campbell: 4–8.

Asher, A. L. 1983. 'Language acquisition diaries: developing an awareness of personal learning strategies'. Unpublished Master's thesis, School for International Training, Brattleboro, Vermont.

Babble, E. R. 1975. 'Questionnaire construction', Chapter 5 of *The practice of social research*, pp. 104–33. Belmont, CA: Wadsworth.

Bailey, K. M. 1980. 'An introspective analysis of an individual's language learning experience', in Krashen and Scarcella:58–65.

Bailey, K. M. 1982. 'Teaching in a second language: the communicative competence of non-native speaking teaching assistants'. Unpublished doctoral dissertation, University of California, Los Angeles.

Bailey, K. M. 1983a. 'Competitiveness and anxiety in adult second language acquisition: looking *at* and *through* the diary studies', in Seliger and Long: 67–103.

Bailey, K. M. 1983b. 'Illustrations of Murphy's law abound in classroom research on language use'. *TESOL Newsletter* 17(4):1, 4–5, 22, 31.

Bailey, K. M. 1984. 'A typology of teaching assistants', in K. M. Bailey, F. Pialorsi, and J. Zukowski/Faust (eds.) *Foreign teaching assistants in U.S. universities*. Washington, D.C.: NAFSA.

Bailey, K. M. 1985. 'Classroom-centered research on language teaching and learning', in M. Celce-Murcia (ed.) *Beyond basics: issues and research in TESOL*: 96–121. Rowley, MA: Newbury House.

Bailey, K. M. 1986. 'Ethnographic observations in language teaching: a brief report of an observational study conducted at the Defense Language Institute Foreign Language Center'. *Conference report of the Bureau for International Language Coordination*, B.I.L.C. Secretariat, Bundessprachenamt D-5030, Hurth, F.D.R.

Bailey, K. M., M. L. Hulse, P. A. Shaw and D. Williams. 1990. 'A comparison of the DLI method and Suggestopedia for the teaching of Russian as a foreign language: Report of the Pedagogic Ethnographic Support Team'. Unpublished manuscript, Defense Language Institute, Monterey, CA.

Bailey, K. M., M. H. Long, and S. Peck (eds.) 1983. *Studies in second language acquisition: series on issues in second language research*. Rowley, MA: Newbury House.

Bailey, K. M. and R. Ochsner. 1983. 'A methodological review of the diary studies: windmill tilting or social science?' in Bailey, Long, and Peck:188–98.

Bailey, L. G. 1975. 'An observational method in the foreign language classroom: a closer look at Interaction Analysis'. *Foreign Language Annals* 8:335–44.

Bailey, N., C. Madden, and S. D. Krashen. 1974. 'Is there a "natural sequence" in adult second language learning?' *Language Learning* 24(2):235–43. Reprinted in Hatch 1978:362–70.

Beebe, L. M. 1983. 'Risk-taking and the language learner', in Seliger and Long:39–66.

Bellack, A. 1978. 'Competing ideologies in research on teaching', in Ahlstrom, Berglund, Dahllof, and Wallin (eds.), *Uppsala reports on education*, Department of Education, Uppsala University.

Bellack, A., H. Kliebard, R. T. Hyman, and F. L. Smith. 1966. *The language of the classroom*. New York: Teachers College Press.

Beretta, A. 1986. 'Program-fair language teaching evaluation'. *TESOL Quarterly* 20(3):431–44.

Beretta, A. 1989. 'Attention to form or meaning? Error treatment in the Bangalore Project'. *TESOL Quarterly* 23(2):283–303.

Bialystok, E. 1983. 'Inferencing: testing the "hypothesis-testing" hypothesis', in Seliger and Long:104–24.

Bibliography

Blair, R. W. (ed.) 1982. *Innovative approaches to language teaching*. Rowley, MA: Newbury House.

Bley-Vroman, R. (ed.) 1988. *University of Hawaii working papers in English as a second language* 7(2).

Bogdan, R. and S. J. Taylor. 1975. *Introduction to qualitative research methods*. New York: John Wiley.

Brock, C. 1986. 'The effects of referential questions on ESL classroom discourse'. *TESOL Quarterly* 20(1):47–59.

Brock, C., G. Crookes, R. R. Day, and M. H. Long. 1986. 'The differential effects of corrective feedback in native speaker–nonnative speaker conversation', in Day 1986:229–36.

Brown, C. 1983. 'The distinguishing characteristics of the older adult language learner'. Unpublished doctoral dissertation, Program in Applied Linguistics, University of California, Los Angeles.

Brown C. 1985a. 'Two windows on the classroom world: diary studies and participant observation differences', in P. Larson, E. Judd, and D. Messerschmitt (eds.) *On TESOL '84: a brave new world for TESOL*:121–34. Washington, D.C.: TESOL.

Brown, C. 1985b. 'Requests for specific language input: differences between older and younger adult language learners', in Gass and Madden (eds.): 272–81.

Brown, G. and G. Yule. 1983. *Discourse analysis*. Cambridge: Cambridge University Press.

Brown, H. D. 1987. *Principles of language learning and teaching* (second edition). Englewood Cliffs, N.J.: Prentice-Hall, Inc.

Brown, H. D. 1989. *The language learner's survival guide*. San Francisco: Random House.

Brown, H. D., C. A. Yorio, and R. H. Crymes (eds.) 1977. *On TESOL '77, teaching and learning English as a second language: trends in research and practice*. Washington D.C.: TESOL.

Brown, J. D. 1983. 'An exploration of morpheme-group interactions', in Bailey, Long, and Peck 1983:25–40.

Brown, J. D. 1988. *Understanding research in second language learning: a teacher's guide to statistics and research design*. Cambridge: Cambridge University Press.

Brown, R. 1973. *A first language: the early stages*. Cambridge, MA: Harvard University Press.

Brumfit, C. J. and K. Johnson. 1979. *The communicative approach to language teaching*. Oxford: Oxford University Press.

Bruton, A., and V. Samuda. 1980. 'Learner and teacher roles in the treatment of oral error in group work'. *RELC Journal* 11:49–63.

Burstall, C. A. 1970. *French in the primary school*. Slough, Bucks: National Foundation for Educational Research.

Burstall, C. A., M. Jamieson, S. Cohen, and M. Hargreaves. 1974. *Primary French in the balance*. Slough, Bucks: National Foundation for Educational Research.

Canale, M. and M. Swain. 1980. 'Theoretical bases of communicative approaches to second language teaching and testing'. *Applied Linguistics* 1:1–47.

Cancino, H., E. Rosansky, and J. Schumann. 1978. 'The acquisition of English negatives and interrogatives by native Spanish speakers', in Hatch 1978: 207–30.

Candlin, C. N. and D. F. Murphy. (eds.) 1987. *Language learning tasks.* Lancaster Practical Papers in English Language Education, Volume 7. Englewood Cliffs: Prentice Hall International.

Cardelle, M. and L. Corno. 1981. 'Effects on second language learning of variations in written feedback on homework assignments'. *TESOL Quarterly* 15(3):251–61.

Carr, W. and S. Kemmis. 1986. *Becoming critical: education, knowledge, and action research.* London: The Falmer Press.

Cathcart, R. L. 1986. 'Situational differences and the sampling of young children's school language', in Day 1986:118–40.

Cathcart, R. L. and J. W. B. Olsen. 1976. 'Teachers' and students' preferences for correction of classroom conversation errors', in Fanselow and Crymes: 41–53.

Chamot, A. U. 1984. 'Using learning strategies to develop skills in English as a second language'. *Focus: National Clearinghouse for Bilingual Education* 16:1–7.

Chaudron, C. 1977. 'A descriptive model of discourse in the corrective treatment of learners' errors'. *Language Learning* 27:29–46.

Chaudron, C. 1983. 'Foreigner talk in the classroom – an aid to language learning?' in Seliger and Long:127–45.

Chaudron, C. 1984a. 'The effects of feedback on students' composition revisions'. *RELC Journal* 15:1–14.

Chaudron, C. 1984b. 'Review of *Second language acquisition studies* (K. M. Bailey, M. H. Long, and S. Peck (eds.)'. *TESOL Quarterly* 18(1):129–32.

Chaudron, C. 1985. 'Intake: on models and methods for discovering learners' processing of input'. *Studies in Second Language Acquisition* 7(1):1–14.

Chaudron, C. 1986a. 'The interaction of quantitative and qualitative approaches to research: a view of the second language classroom'. *TESOL Quarterly* 20(4):109–17.

Chaudron, C. 1986b. 'Teachers' priorities in correcting learners' errors in French immersion classes', in Day 1986:64–84.

Chaudron, C. 1987. 'The role of error correction in second language teaching', in B. K. Das (ed.) *Patterns of classroom interaction in Southeast Asia*, RLC Anthology Series 17:17–50. Singapore: Regional Language Centre.

Chaudron, C. 1988a. *Second language classrooms: research on teaching and learning.* Cambridge: Cambridge University Press.

Chaudron, C. 1988b. 'Validation in second language classroom research: the role of observation', in Bley-Vroman:1–15.

Chenoweth, N. A., R. R. Day, A. E. Chun, and S. Luppescu. 1983. 'Attitudes and preferences of nonnative speakers to corrective feedback'. *Studies in Second Language Acquisition* 6:79–87.

Bibliography

Cherchalli, S. 1988. 'Learners' reactions to their textbooks (with special reference to the relation between differential perceptions and differential achievement): a case study of Algerian secondary school learners'. Unpublished doctoral dissertation, University of Lancaster.

Chesterfield, R. and K. B. Chesterfield. 1985. 'Natural order in children's use of second language learning strategies'. *Applied Linguistics* 6:45–59.

Chomsky, N. 1957. *Syntactic structures.* The Hague: Mouton and Company.

Chomsky, N. 1959. 'Review of B. F. Skinner, *Verbal Behavior* (1957)'. *Language* 35:26–58.

Chun, A. E., R. R. Day, N. A. Chenoweth, and S. Luppescu. 1982. 'Errors, interaction, and correction: a study of native–nonnative conversations'. *TESOL Quarterly* 16:537–47.

Clark, J. 1980. 'Lothian region's project on graded levels of achievement in foreign-language learning: from principles to practice'. *Modern Languages in Scotland* 19:61–74.

Clark, J. 1987. 'Classroom assessment in a communicative approach', in P. Green (ed.), *Communicative language testing: a resource handbook for teacher trainers*:53–77. Strasbourg: Council of Europe.

Clark, J. L. D. 1969. 'The Pennsylvania Project and the audiolingual vs. traditional question'. *Modern Language Journal* 53:388–96.

Clark, R. 1980. 'Errors in talking to learn'. *First Language* 1:7–32.

Cohen, A. 1985. 'What can we learn from the language learner?' School of Education, Hebrew University, Jerusalem.

Cohen, A. and C. Hosenfeld. 1981 'Some uses of mentalistic data in second language research'. *Language Learning* 31(2):285–313.

Cohen, L. 1976. *Educational research in classrooms and schools: a manual of materials and methods.* London: Harper and Row.

Corder, S. P. 1967. 'The significance of learners' errors'. *IRAL* 5:161–70. Reprinted in Richards 1974:19–27.

Corder, S. P. 1978. 'Language learner language', in J. C. Richards (ed.) *Understanding second and foreign language learning.* Rowley, MA: Newbury House.

Corder, S. P. 1981. *Error analysis and interlanguage.* Oxford: Oxford University Press.

Coulthard, M. 1977. *An introduction to discourse analysis.* London: Longman.

Courchêne, R. 1980. 'The error analysis hypothesis, the contrastive analysis hypothesis, and the correction of error in the second language classroom'. *TESL Talk* 11 (2):3–13, and 11 (3):10–29.

Crookes, G. 1988. 'Functional units of discourse for second language research', in Bley-Vroman:143–67.

Crookes, G., and K. A. Rulon. 1985. 'Incorporation of corrective feedback in native speaker/nonnative speaker conversation'. Center for Second Language Classroom Research, Social Science Research Institute, Technical Report No. 3. Honolulu: University of Hawaii.

Daly, J. A. and J. C. McCroskey. (eds.) 1984. *Avoiding communication: shyness, reticence and communication apprehension.* Beverly Hills: Sage Publications.

Day, R. R. 1984. 'Student participation in the ESL classroom or some imperfections in practice'. *Language Learning* 34:69–101.

Day, R. R. (ed.). 1986. *Talking to learn: conversation in second language acquisition.* Rowley, MA: Newbury House.

Day, R. R., N. A. Chenoweth, A. E. Chun, and S. Luppescu. 1984. 'Corrective feedback in native–nonnative discourse'. *Language Learning* 34(1):19–45.

Denzin, N. K. (ed.) 1970. *Sociological methods: a source book.* Chicago: Aldine.

Dickinson, L. 1987. *Self-instruction in language learning.* Cambridge: Cambridge University Press.

Doughty, C. and T. Pica. 1986. ' "Information gap" tasks: do they facilitate second language acquisition?' *TESOL Quarterly* 20:305–25.

Duff, P. A. 1986. 'Another look at interlanguage talk: taking task to task', in Day 1986:147–81.

Dulay, H. C. and M. K. Burt. 1974a. 'You can't learn without goofing', in Richards 1974:95–123.

Dulay, H. C. and M. K. Burt. 1974b. 'Natural sequences in child second language acquisition'. *Language Learning* 24(1):37–53. Reprinted in Hatch 1978:347–61.

Ehrman, M. and R. Oxford. 1989. 'Effects of sex differences, career choice and psychological type on adult language learning strategies'. *Modern Language Journal* 73(19):1–13.

Ellis, G. and B. Sinclair. 1989. *Learning to learn English.* Cambridge: Cambridge University Press.

Ellis, R. 1980. 'Classroom interaction and its relation to second language learning'. *RELC Journal* 11(2):29–47.

Ellis, R. 1984. *Classroom second language development.* Oxford: Pergamon.

Ellis, R. 1985. 'Teacher–pupil interaction in second language development', in Gass and Madden: 69–85.

Enright, D. S. 1984. 'The organization of interaction in elementary classrooms', in Handscombe, Orem, and Taylor:23–38.

Erickson, F. 1981. 'Some approaches to inquiry in school–community ethnography', in Trueba, Guthrie, and Au:17–35.

Faerch, C. and G. Kasper. (eds.) 1987. *Introspection in second language research.* Clevedon, Philadelphia: Multilingual Matters.

Fanselow, J. F. 1977a. 'Beyond Rashomon – conceptualizing and describing the teaching act'. *TESOL Quarterly* 11:17–39.

Fanselow, J. F. 1977b. 'The treatment of learner error in oral work'. *Foreign Language Annals* 10:583–93.

Fanselow, J. F. and R. Crymes (eds.) 1976. *On TESOL '76.* Washington, D.C.: TESOL.

Felix, S. W. 1981. 'The effect of formal instruction on second language acquisition'. *Language Learning* 31:87–112.

Flanders, N. A. 1960. 'Teacher influence, pupil attitudes and achievement'. US Office of Education Co-operative Research Project No 397. Minneapolis: University of Minnesota.

Bibliography

Flanders, N. A. 1970. *Analyzing teaching behavior*. Reading, MA: Addison-Wesley.

Florio, S. and M. Walsh. 1981. 'The teacher as colleague in classroom research', in Trueba, Guthrie, and Au:87–101.

Foss, K. A. and A. C. Reitzel. 1988. 'A relational model for managing second language anxiety. *TESOL Quarterly* 22(3):437–54.

Frick, T. and M. I. Semmel. 1978. 'Observer agreement and reliabilities of classroom observational measures'. *Review of Educational Research* 48(1):157–84.

Friedman, P. G. 1980. *Shyness and reticence*. Washington, D. C.: National Education Association.

Fröhlich, M., N. Spada and P. Allen. 1985. 'Differences in the communicative orientation of L2 classrooms'. *TESOL Quarterly* 19:27–56.

Gaies, S. J. 1977. 'The nature of linguistic input in formal second language learning: linguistic and communication strategies in ESL teachers' classroom language', in Brown, Yorio and Crymes:204–12.

Gaies, S. J. 1980. 'Classroom-centered research: some consumer guidelines'. Paper presented at the Second Annual TESOL Summer Meeting, Albuquerque, N.M.

Gaies, S. J. 1983a. 'The investigation of language classroom processes'. *TESOL Quarterly* 17:205–17.

Gaies, S. J. 1983b. 'Learner feedback: an exploratory study of its role in the second language classroom', in Seliger and Long:190–213.

Galvan, J. L., J. A. Pierce, and G. N. Underwood. 1976. 'The relevance of selected educational variables of teachers on their attitudes toward Mexican-American English'. *Journal of the Linguistic Association of the Southwest* 2:13–27.

Gardner, R. C. 1979. 'Attitudes and motivation: their role in second-language acquisition', in H. J. Trueba and C. Barnett-Mizrahi (eds.) *Bilingual multicultural education and the professional: from theory to practice*:319–27. Rowley, MA: Newbury House.

Gardner, R. C. and W. E. Lambert. 1972. *Attitudes and motivation in second language learning*. Rowley, MA: Newbury House.

Gardner, R. C., P. C. Smythe, R. Clement and L. Glicksman. 1976. 'Second language learning: a social-psychological perspective'. *Canadian Modern Language Journal* 32:198–213.

Garvey, C. 1977. 'Play with language and speech', in C. Mitchell-Kernan and S. Ervin-Tripp (eds.) *Child discourse*:27–47. New York: Academic Press.

Gaskill, W. 1980. 'Correction in native speaker–non-native speaker conversation', in Larsen-Freeman 1980:125–37.

Gass, S. M. and C. G. Madden. 1985. *Input in second language acquisition*. Rowley, MA: Newbury House.

Gass, S. M. and E. M. Varonis 1985. 'Task variation and nonnative/nonnative negotiation of meaning', in Gass and Madden:149–61.

Gathercole, V. C. 1988. 'Some myths you may have heard about first language acquisition'. *TESOL Quarterly* 22(3):407–35.

George, H. V. 1972. *Common errors in learning English*. Rowley, MA: Newbury House.

Giles, H. and R. N. St. Clair. 1979. *Language and social psychology*. Oxford: Basil Blackwell.

Glaser, B. and A. Strauss. 1967. *The discovery of grounded theory: strategies for qualitative research*. Chicago: Aldine.

Goldstein, L. M. 1987. 'Standard English: the only target for non-native speakers of English?' *TESOL Quarterly* 21(3):417–36.

Goswami, D. and P. R. Stillman. 1987. *Reclaiming the classroom: teacher research as an agency for change*. Upper Montclair, NJ: Boynton/Cook.

Grandcolas, B. and N. Soulé-Susbielles. 1986. 'The analysis of the foreign language classroom'. *Studies in Second Language Acquisition* 8:293–308.

Green, J. and C. Wallat. 1981. *Ethnography and language in educational settings*. Norwood, NJ: Ablex Publishing Corporation.

Green, P. S., and K. Hecht. 1985. 'Native and non-native evaluation of learners' errors in written discourse'. *System* 13:77–97.

Gregg, K. 1984. 'Krashen's Monitor and Occam's razor'. *Applied Linguistics* 5:79–100.

Grittner, F. M. 1968. 'Letter to the editor'. *Newsletter of the National Association of Language Laboratory Directors* 3:7.

Guba, E. G. 1978. 'Toward a methodology of naturalistic inquiry in educational evaluation'. CSE Monograph Series in Evaluation, No. 8. Los Angeles: Center for the Study of Evaluation, UCLA.

Hammersley, M. 1986. *Controversies in classroom research*. Milton Keynes: Open University Press.

Handscombe, J., R. A. Orem, and B. P. Taylor (eds.) 1984. *On TESOL '83: the question of control*. Washington, D.C.: TESOL.

Harris, T. A. 1967. *I'm OK – You're OK*. New York: Harper and Row.

Hatch, E. M. (ed.) 1978. *Second language acquisition: a book of readings*. Rowley, MA: Newbury House.

Hatch, E. M. 1983. *Psycholinguistics – a second language perspective*. Rowley, MA: Newbury House.

Hatch, E. M. and H. Farhady. 1982. *Research design and statistics for applied linguistics*. Rowley, MA: Newbury House.

Hatch, E. M. and M. H. Long. 1980. 'Discourse analysis – what's that?' in Larsen-Freeman 1980:1–40.

Hendrickson, J. M. 1978. 'Error correction in foreign language teaching: recent theory, research, and practice'. *Modern Language Journal* 62:387–98.

Heyde, A. W. 1977. 'The relationship between self-esteem and the oral production of a second language', in Brown, Yorio, and Crymes:226–40.

Heyde-Parsons, A. W. 1983. 'Self-esteem and the acquisition of French', in Bailey, Long, and Peck:175–87.

Hines, M. 1983. 'The relationship between teacher behavior and student learning in fourteen English as a second language lessons'. Unpublished Ed.D. dissertation, Teachers College, Columbia University, New York.

Holley, F. and J. K. King. 1974. 'Imitation and correction in foreign language learning', in J. H. Schumann and N. Stenson (eds.) *New frontiers in second language learning*:81–9. Rowley, MA: Newbury House.

Horwitz, E. K., M. B. Horwitz, and J. Cope. 1986. 'Foreign language classroom anxiety'. *Modern Language Journal* 70(1):125–32.

Bibliography

Hustler, D., T. Cassidy, and T. Duff. (eds.) 1986. *Action research in classrooms and schools*. London: Allen and Unwin.

Hymes, D. 1982. 'What is ethnography?' in P. Gilmore and A. A. Glatthorn (eds.) *Children in and out of school: ethnography and education*:21–32. Washington, D.C.: Center for Applied Linguistics.

Jaeger, R. M. 1983. *Statistics: a spectator sport*. Beverly Hills: Sage Publications.

James, C. 1980. *Contrastive analysis*. Harlow, Essex: Longman.

Jones, R. A. 1977. 'Psychological, social and personal factors in second language acquisition'. Unpublished MA thesis in Teaching English as a Second Language, University of California, Los Angeles.

Kasper, G. 1985. 'Repair in foreign language teaching'. *Studies in Second Language Acquisition* 7(2):200–15.

Kemmis, S. and Henry, J. A. 1989. 'Action research'. *IATEFL Newsletter* 102:2–3.

Kleifgen, J. 1985. 'Skilled variation in a kindergarten teacher's use of foreigner talk', in Gass and Madden:59–68.

Kleinmann, H. 1977. 'Avoidance behavior in adult second language learning'. *Language Learning* 27:93–107.

Krashen, S. D. 1977. 'Some issues relating to the monitor model', in Brown, Yorio, and Crymes:144–58.

Krashen, S. D. 1982. *Principles and practice in second language acquisition*. Oxford: Pergamon Press.

Krashen, S. D. 1985. *The input hypothesis: issues and implications*. London: Longman.

Krashen, S. D., N. Houck, P. Giunchi, S. Bode, R. Birnbaum, and G. Strei. 1977. 'Difficulty order for grammatical morphemes for adult second language performers using free speech'. *TESOL Quarterly* 11(3): 338–41.

Krashen, S. D. and Scarcella, R. (eds.) 1980. *Research in second language acquisition: Selected Papers of the Los Angeles Second Language Research Forum*. Rowley, MA: Newbury House.

Labov, W. 1972. 'Some principles of linguistic methodology'. *Language in Society* 1:97–120.

Lambert, W. E., M. Anisfeld, and G. Yeni-Komshian. 1965. 'Evaluational reactions of Jewish and Arab adolescents to dialect and language variation'. *Journal of Personality and Social Psychology* 2:84–90.

Lambert, W. E., R. Hodgson, R. C. Gardner, and S. Fillenbaum. 1960. 'Evaluational reactions to spoken language'. *Journal of Abnormal and Social Psychology* 60:44–51.

Larsen-Freeman, D. E. 1976. 'An explanation for the morpheme accuracy order of learners of English as a second language'. *Language Learning* 26(1):125–35. Reprinted in Hatch 1978:371–9.

Larsen-Freeman, D. E. (ed.) 1980. *Discourse analysis in second language research*. Rowley, MA: Newbury House.

Larsen-Freeman, D. 1986. *Techniques and principles in language teaching*. Oxford: Oxford University Press.

Leichman, H. 1977. 'A diary of one person's acquisition of Indonesian'.

Unpublished manuscript, English Department (ESL Section), University of California, Los Angeles.

van Lier, L. A. W. 1984. 'Discourse analysis and classroom research: a methodological perspective'. *International Journal of the Sociology of Language* 49:111–33.

van Lier, L. 1988. *The classroom and the language learner: ethnography and second language classroom research.* London: Longman.

Lightbown, P. M. 1983. 'Exploring relationships between developmental and instructional sequences in L2 acquisition', in Seliger and Long:217–45.

Lindblad, T. 1969. *Implicit and explicit – an experiment in applied psycholinguistics.* GUME-Projektet 1. Gothenburg: Pedagogiska Institutionen, Lärarhögskolan: Göteborg, Göteborgs Universitet, Engelska Institutionen.

Littlejohn, A. P. 1983. 'Increasing learner involvement in course management'. *TESOL Quarterly* 17(4):595–608.

Littlewood, W. 1981. *Communicative language teaching: an introduction.* Cambridge: Cambridge University Press.

Long, M. H. 1977. 'Teacher feedback on learner error: mapping cognitions', in Brown, Yorio, and Crymes:278–94.

Long, M. H. 1980a. 'Inside the "black box": methodological issues in research on language teaching and learning'. *Language Learning* 30:1–42. Reprinted in Seliger and Long 1983.

Long, M. H. 1980b. 'Input, interaction and second language acquisition'. Unpublished doctoral dissertation, University of California, Los Angeles.

Long, M. H. 1981. 'Input, interaction and second language acquisition', in H. Winitz (ed.) *Native and foreign language acquisition*:259–78. New York: New York Academy of Sciences.

Long, M. H. 1983a. 'Does second language instruction make a difference?' *TESOL Quarterly* 17(3):359–82.

Long, M. H. 1983b. 'Native speaker/non-native speaker conversation in the second language classroom', in M. A. Clarke and J. Handscombe (eds.) *On TESOL '82: Pacific perspectives on language learning and teaching*:207–25. Washington, D.C.: TESOL.

Long, M. H. 1983c. 'Linguistic and conversational adjustments to non-native speakers'. *Studies in Second Language Acquisition* 5:177–93.

Long, M. H. 1984. 'Process and product in ESL program evaluation'. *TESOL Quarterly* 18(3):409–25.

Long, M. H. 1985. 'Input and second language acquisition theory', in Gass and Madden:377–93.

Long, M. H., L. Adams, M. McLean, and F. Castaños. 1976. 'Doing things with words – verbal interaction in lockstep and small group classroom situations', in Fanselow and Crymes:137–53.

Long, M. H. and P. A. Porter. 1985. 'Group work, interlanguage talk, and second language acquisition'. *TESOL Quarterly* 19:207–28.

Long, M. H. and C. J. Sato. 1983. 'Classroom foreigner talk discourse: forms and functions of teachers' questions', in Seliger and Long:268–86.

Lucas, J. 1984. 'Communication apprehension in the ESL classroom: getting our students to talk'. *Foreign Language Annals* 17:593–8.

Ludwig, J. 1982. 'Native-speaker judgements of second language learners' efforts at communication: a review'. *Modern Language Journal* 66:274–83.

McCoy, I. R. 1979. 'Means to overcome the anxieties of second language learners'. *Foreign Language Annals* 12:185–9.

McCroskey, J. C. 1977. 'Oral communication apprehension: a summary of recent theory and research'. *Human Communication Research* 4:78–96.

McLaughlin, B. 1978. 'The Monitor Model: some methodological considerations'. *Language Learning* 28:309–32.

Malamah-Thomas, A. 1987. *Classroom interaction*. Oxford: Oxford University Press.

Maquet, J. J. 1964. 'Objectivity in anthropology'. *Current Anthropology* 5(1):47–55.

Matsumoto, K. 1987. 'Diary studies of second language acquisition: a critical overview'. *JALT Journal* 9(1):17–34.

Mitchell, R. 1985. 'Process research in second language classrooms'. *Language Teaching* 18:330–52.

Mitchell, S. K. 1979. 'Inter-observer agreement, reliability and generalizability of data collected in observational studies'. *Psychological Bulletin* 86(2):376–90.

Moskowitz, G. 1967. 'The FLint system: an observational tool for the foreign language classroom', in A. Simon and E. G. Boyer (eds.) *Mirrors for behavior: an anthology of classroom observation instruments*, Section 15:1–15. Philadelphia: Center for the Study of Teaching at Temple University.

Moskowitz, G. 1968. 'The effects of training foreign language teachers in Interaction Analysis'. *Foreign Language Annals* 1(3):218–35.

Moskowitz, G. 1971. 'Interaction analysis – a new modern language for supervisors'. *Foreign Language Annals* 5:211–21.

Moskowitz, G. 1976. 'The classroom interaction of outstanding foreign language teachers'. *Foreign Language Annals* 9:125–43 and 146–57.

Moss, W. A. and M. E. Corneli. 1983. 'Report on a study of turntaking and ethnicity in the ESL classroom'. Paper presented at the 1983 CATESOL Conference, Los Angeles.

Newmark, L. 1972. 'How not to interfere with language learning', in Allen and Campbell:37–42.

Nixon, J. (ed.) 1981. *A teacher's guide to action research*. London: Grant McIntyre.

Nunan, D. 1989. *Understanding language classrooms*. New York: Prentice Hall.

Nystrom, N. J. 1983. 'Teacher–student interaction in bilingual classrooms: four approaches to error feedback', in Seliger and Long:169–89.

Ochsner, R. 1979. 'A poetics of second language acquisition'. *Language Learning* 29:53–80.

Oller, J. W. 1979. *Language tests at school*. London: Longman.

Oller, J. W. 1981. 'Research on the measurement of affective variables', in R. W. Andersen (ed.) *New dimensions in second language acquisition research*:14–27. Rowley, MA: Newbury House.

Oller, J. W., and P. Richard-Amato (eds.) 1983. *Methods that work: a smorgasbord of ideas for language teachers*. Rowley, MA: Newbury House.

O'Malley, J. M., A. U. Chamot, G. Stewner-Manzanares, L. Kupper, and R. P. Russo. 1985a. 'Learning strategies used by beginning and intermediate ESL students'. *Language Learning* 35:21–46.

O'Malley, J. M., A. U. Chamot, G. Stewner-Manzanares, R. P. Russo, and L. Kupper. 1985b. 'Learning strategy applications with students of English as a second language'. *TESOL Quarterly* 19(3):557–84.

O'Neill, R. 1982. 'Why use textbooks?' *ELT Journal* 36:104–11.

Otto, F. M. 1969. 'The teacher in the Pennsylvania project'. *Modern Language Journal* 53:411–20.

Oxford-Carpenter, R. 1985. 'Second language learning strategies: what the research has to say'. *ERIC/CLL News Bulletin* 9(1):1, 3–5.

Page, B. 1985. 'Graded objectives in modern language learning', in V. Kinsella (ed.) *Cambridge language teaching surveys*. Cambridge: Cambridge University Press.

Pearson, C. R. 1983. 'Cross-cultural perceptions of ESL textbook illustrations'. Paper presented at the International TESOL Convention, Toronto.

Peck, S. 1980. 'Language play in second language acquisition', in Larsen-Freeman 1980:154–64.

Pica, T., and C. Doughty. 1985. 'Input and interaction in the communicative language classroom: a comparison of teacher-fronted and group activities', in Gass and Madden:115–32.

Pica, T. and M. H. Long. 1986. 'The linguistic and conversational performance of experienced and inexperienced teachers', in Day 1986:85–98.

Pienemann, M. 1984. 'Psychological constraints on the teachability of languages'. *Studies in Second Language Acquisition* 6(2):186–214.

Pike, K. 1982. *Linguistic concepts: an introduction to tagmemics*. Lincoln: University of Nebraska Press.

Plummer, D. 1976. 'A summary of a foreign language learning diary'. Unpublished manuscript, English Department (ESL Section), University of California, Los Angeles.

Politzer, R. L. 1970. 'Some reflections on "good" and "bad" language teaching behaviors'. *Language Learning* 20:31–43.

Porreca, K. L. 1984. 'Sexism in current ESL textbooks'. *TESOL Quarterly* 18(4):705–24.

Porter, P. A. 1986. 'How learners talk to each other: input and interaction in task-centered discussions', in Day 1986:200–22.

Progoff, I. 1975. *At a journal workshop*. New York: Dialogue House Library.

Reid, J. 1987. 'The learning style preferences of ESL students'. *TESOL Quarterly* 21(1):87–111.

Richard-Amato, P. A. 1988. *Making it happen: interaction in the second language classroom*. New York: Longman.

Richards, J. C. (ed.) 1974. *Error analysis: perspectives on second language acquisition*. London: Longman.

Richards, J. C. 1983. 'Listening comprehension: approach, design and procedure'. *TESOL Quarterly* 17(2):219–40.

Richards, J. C., J. Platt, and H. Weber. 1985. *Longman's Dictionary of Applied Linguistics*. London: Longman.

Richards, J. C. and T. S. Rodgers. 1986. *Approaches and methods in language teaching: a description and analysis.* Cambridge: Cambridge University Press.

Rist, R. 1980. 'Blitzkrieg ethnography: on the transformation of a method into a movement'. *Educational Researcher* 9(2):8–10.

Robb, T. N., S. Ross and I. Shortreed. 1986. 'Salience of feedback on error and its effect on EFL writing quality'. *TESOL Quarterly* 20:83–95.

Rowe, M. B. 1969. 'Science, silence and sanctions'. *Science and Children* 6(6):12–13.

Rubin, J. 1975. 'What the good language learner can teach us'. *TESOL Quarterly* 9(1):41–51.

Rubin, J. and I. Thompson. 1982. *How to be a more successful language learner.* Boston: Heinle and Heinle.

Rulon, K. A. and J. McCreary. 1986. 'Negotiation of content: teacher fronted and small-group interaction', in Day 1986:182–99.

Ryan, E. B. and H. Giles. 1982. *Attitudes towards language variation.* London: Edward Arnold.

Salica, C. 1981. 'Testing a model of corrective discourse'. Unpublished MA thesis in Teaching English as a Second Language, University of California, Los Angeles.

Sato, C. 1982. 'Ethnic styles in classroom discourse', in M. Hines and W. Rutherford (eds.) *On TESOL '81*:11–24. Washington D.C.: TESOL.

Sato, C. 1985. 'Task variation in interlanguage phonology', in Gass and Madden:181–96.

Schegloff, E. A., G. Jefferson, and H. Sacks. 1977. 'The preference for self-correction in the organization of repair in conversation'. *Language* 53: 361–82.

Scherer, G. A. C. and M. Wertheimer. 1964. *A psycholinguistic experiment in foreign language teaching.* New York: McGraw Hill.

Schinke-Llano, L. 1983. 'Foreigner talk in content classrooms', in Seliger and Long: 146–65.

Schinke-Llano, L. 1986. 'Foreigner talk in joint cognitive activities', in Day 1986:99–117.

Schmidt, R. W. and N. G. Frota. 1986. 'Developing basic conversational ability in a second language: a case study of an adult learner of Portuguese', in Day 1986:237–326.

Schumann, F. E. 1980. 'Diary of a language learner: a further analysis', in Krashen and Scarcella:51–7.

Schumann, F. E. and J. H. Schumann. 1977. 'Diary of a language learner: an introspective study of second language learning', in Brown, Yorio and Crymes:241–9.

Schumann, J. H. 1975. 'Affective factors and the problem of age in second language acquisition'. *Language Learning* 25(2): 209–35.

Schwartz, J. 1980. 'The negotiation for meaning: repair in conversations between second-language learners of English', in Larsen-Freeman 1980: 138–53.

Scovel, T. 1978. 'The effect of affect on foreign language learning: a review of the anxiety research'. *Language Learning* 28:129–42.

Seliger, H. W. 1977. 'Does practice make perfect? A study of interaction patterns and L2 competence'. *Language Learning* 27:263–78.

Seliger, H. W. 1983a. 'Learner interaction in the classroom and its effect on language acquisition', in Seliger and Long:246–67.

Seliger, H. W. 1983b. 'The language learner as a linguist: of metaphors and realities'. *Applied Linguistics* 4(3):179–91.

Seliger, H. W. and M. H. Long (eds.) 1983. *Classroom oriented research in second language acquisition.* Rowley, MA: Newbury House.

Selinker, L. 1972. 'Interlanguage'. *IRAL*, 10:201–31. Reprinted in Richards 1974:31–54.

Selinker, L., M. Swain, and G. Dumas. 1975. 'The interlanguage hypothesis extended to children'. *Language Learning* 25(1):139–91.

Sevigny, M. J. 1981. 'Triangulated inquiry – a methodology for the analysis of classroom interaction', in Green and Wallat:65–85.

Shavelson, R. J. 1981. *Statistical reasoning for the behavioral sciences.* Boston: Allyn and Bacon.

Shaw, P. A. 1983. 'The language of engineering professors: a discourse and registral analysis of a speech event'. Unpublished doctoral dissertation, Department of Linguistics, University of Southern California.

Sinclair, J. M. and M. Coulthard. 1975. *Towards an analysis of discourse.* London: Oxford University Press.

Skinner, B. F. 1957. *Verbal behavior.* New York: Appleton-Century-Crofts.

Slimani, A. 1987. 'The teaching/learning relationship: learning opportunities and the problems of uptake – an Algerian case study'. Unpublished doctoral dissertation, University of Lancaster.

Smith, P. D. 1970. *A comparison of the cognitive and audiolingual approaches to foreign language instruction: the Pennsylvania foreign language project.* Philadelphia: Center for Curriculum Development.

Spradley, J. P. 1979. *The ethnographic interview.* New York: Holt, Rinehart and Winston.

Spradley, J. P. 1980. *Participant observation.* New York: Holt, Rinehart and Winston.

Staton, J., R. W. Shuy, J. Kreeft-Payton, and L. Reed. 1988. *Dialogue journal communication: classroom, linguistic, social and cognitive views.* Norwood, NJ: Ablex.

Stern, H. H. 1975. 'What can we learn from the good language learner?' *Canadian Modern Language Review* 30:244–54.

Stevick, E. W. 1976. *Memory, meaning and method.* Rowley, MA: Newbury House.

Stevick, E. W. 1980. *Teaching languages: a way and ways.* Rowley, MA: Newbury House.

Stevick, E. W. 1982. *Teaching and learning languages.* London: Cambridge University Press.

Strickland, D. S. 1988. 'The teacher as researcher: toward the extended professional'. *Language Arts* 65:754–64.

Strong, M. 1986. 'Teachers' language to limited English speakers in bilingual and submersion classes', in Day 1986:53–63.

237

Swain, M. 1985. 'Communicative competence: some roles of comprehensible input and comprehensible output in its development', in Gass and Madden: 235–53.

Tarone, E. 1981. 'Some thoughts on the notion of communication strategy'. *TESOL Quarterly* 15:285–95.

Tollefson, J. W., B. Jacobs, and E. J. Selipsky. 1983. 'The Monitor Model and Neurofunctional Theory: an integrated view'. *Studies in Second Language Acquisition* 6(1):1–16.

Trudgill, P. 1974. *The social differentiation of English in Norwich*. Cambridge: Cambridge University Press.

Trueba, H., G. P. Guthrie, and K. H. P. Au (eds.) 1981. *Culture and the bilingual classroom: studies in classroom ethnography*. Rowley, MA: Newbury House.

Tuckman, B. W. 1978. *Conducting educational research* (second edition). New York: Harcourt Brace Jovanovich.

Vander Brook, S., K. Schlue, and C. Campbell. 1980. 'Discourse and second language acquisition of yes/no questions', in Larsen-Freeman 1980: 56–74.

VanPatten, B. 1987. 'On babies and bathwater: input in foreign language learning'. *Modern Language Journal* 71(2):156–64.

Vigil, N. A. and J. W. Oller. 1976. 'Rule fossilization: a tentative model'. *Language Learning* 26:281–95.

Von Elek, R. and M. Oskarsson. 1973. *A replication study in teaching foreign language grammar to adults*. The GUME/Adults Project. Gothenburg: Gothenburg School of Education, Department of Educational Research.

Walker, R. and C. Adelman. 1976. 'Strawberries', in M. Stubbs and S. Delamont (eds.) *Explorations in classroom observation*:133–50. Chichester: John Wiley.

Wallat, C., J. L. Green, S. M. Conlin, and M. Haramis. 1981. 'Issues related to action research in the classroom – the teacher and researcher as a team', in Green and Wallat:87–113.

Watson-Gegeo, K. A. 1988. 'Ethnography in ESL: defining the essentials'. *TESOL Quarterly* 22(4):575–92.

Watson-Gegeo, K. A. and P. Ulichny. 1988. 'Ethnographic inquiry into second language acquisition and instruction', in Bley-Vroman:75–92.

Wenden, A. L. 1985. 'Learner strategies'. *TESOL Newsletter* 19:1–17.

Wenden, A. L. and J. Rubin. (eds.) 1987. *Learner strategies*. Englewood Cliffs, NJ: Prentice Hall.

Wesche, M. B. and D. Ready. 1985. 'Foreigner talk in the university classroom', in Gass and Madden:89–114.

Williams, F. 1973a. 'Some recent studies of language attitudes', in R. W. Shuy (ed.) *Some new directions in linguistics*:121–49. Washington, D. C.: Georgetown University Press.

Williams, F. 1973b. 'Some research notes on dialect attitudes and stereotypes', in R. Shuy and R. W. Fasold (eds.) *Language attitudes: current trends and prospects*. Washington, D.C.: Georgetown University Press.

Wilson, S. 1977. 'The use of ethnographic techniques in educational research'. *Review of Educational Research* 47(1):245–65.

Wolfram, W. and R. W. Fasold. 1974. *The study of social dialects in American English*. Englewood Cliffs, NJ: Prentice Hall.

Wong-Fillmore, L. 1985. 'When does teacher talk work as input?' in Gass and Madden:17–50.

Woods, A., P. Fletcher, and A. Hughes. 1986. *Statistics in language studies*. Cambridge: Cambridge University Press.

Yoneyama, A. 1982. 'The treatment of learners' errors by novice EFL teachers'. *Bulletin of the College of Education, Human and Social Sciences Issue* 23:85–94. University of Niigata, Japan.

Young, D. J. and E. K. Horwitz (eds.) In press. *Anxiety in foreign and second language learning and performance*. Rowley, MA: Newbury House.

Index

Author index

240

Index

Index

Subject index

Index

Index

motivation *cont.*
  integrative 158, 182
  receptivity xviii, 161, 166, 172, 182–3,
    184
moves 12, 65, 98, 113, 139, 144, 147 *see*
  also discourse analysis

naturalistic enquiry 35, 40, 53, 54 *see also*
  experimental studies, self-reports,
  surveys
  autobiography 168
  combined approaches 45
  data collection 59
  error research 82
  generalisability 51–2
  interaction 126
  intervention 41–2
  objectivity/subjectivity 63
negotiated interaction 121–4, 126–7 *see also*
  interaction, management of interaction,
  turn distribution
  clarification checks/requests 123, 124,
    141, 142, 144, 148, 153
  confirmation checks 123, 141, 148, 153
  dyads 12, 62, 141, 147, 148
  lockstep condition 147
  two-way information exchange 148
'notice the gap' principle 92, 104, 113,
  115–16, 120

objectivity 62, 63–4, 65, 67, 75, 76 *see also*
  subjectivity
observation schedules 3, 4, 6, 10, 11, 12, 13,
  16, 54, 61, 64
  COLT, Communicative Orientation of
    Language Teaching 13, 16, 216–19
  Embryonic Category System 12, 147,
    213
  FOCUS, Foci for Observing
    Communications Used in Settings 11,
    16, 180, 206–12
  Interaction Analysis 10, 202–3
observations xiv, 3, 4, 5, 17, 68
  categories 3, 4, 6, 10, 11, 12, 13, 64, 80,
    115, 137–8, 153, 180
  'real time' 117, 118, 154
observer's paradox 70–1, 75, 97
output *see also* comprehensible output
  general 2
  participation 132

test results 130
treatment of error 99

'parent' role 180–1 *see also* Transactional
  Analysis
participation 5, 135 *see also* interaction,
  management of interaction, negotiated
  interaction, turn distribution
  achievement 130–3, 149–50, 195
  attention 169
  definition problem 67, 79–80, 127–9
  ethnicity 133–4, 135
  forced 119, 139, 144–7, 151, 152
  groupwork 147
  HIGs, high input generators 130–2, 135,
    152, 154, 155
  learning strategies 142
  LIGs, low input generators 130–2, 135,
    152, 154, 155
  management of learning 22
peer pressure 161, 166
Pennsylvania Project *see* experimental
  studies
practice opportunites *see also* learning
  opportunities
  as outcome of classroom interaction 22,
    23–4, 28, 31, 32, 149
presage variables 171
prescription 8, 10, 14, 15 *see also*
  description
present perfect 28, 59
'principle of economics' 9, 150
process–product studies 44–5, 48, 134
processes (classroom) 9, 14, 28; 34, 44, 130
profiles 68

qualitative research
  data analysis 52, 81
  discourse analysis 61
  ethnography 54, 78, 81
  naturalistic enquiry 42
  treatment of error 82
  versus quantitative 65–7, 68, 75, 76
quantitative research
  classroom interaction 130–4
  data analysis 52, 78–80
  discourse analysis 61
  naturalistic enquiry 42
  treatment of error 82
  versus qualitative 65–7, 68, 75, 76

Index